# SCANDINAVIA REFRACTED

Photo: Gunilla Blom Thomsen

Photo: Gunilla Blom Thomsen

# SCANDINAVIA REFRACTED
A Festschrift in Honour of
Bjarne Thorup Thomsen

Edited by Ian Giles

SCOTTISH
SOCIETY FOR
NORTHERN
STUDIES

Published in Scotland by
The Scottish Society for Northern Studies
c/o Scandinavian Studies, School of Literatures, Languages and Cultures,
University of Edinburgh
50 George Square, Edinburgh EH8 9LH
www.ssns.org.uk

© The Scottish Society for Northern Studies and individual contributors 2022

All rights reserved.
No part of this publication may be reproduced, stored in a retrieval system, or transmitted in any form, in any quantity, or by any means digital, electronic, mechanical, or otherwise without the prior written consent of the Society and appropriate contributors.

ISBN 978-1-3999-3524-1

Front Cover Image: Photo by FLY:D on Unsplash
Front Cover Design: Christian Cooijmans
Typesetting: Laura Kincaid (Ten Thousand)

The Scottish Society for Northern Studies is a registered charity (SC010647)

# Contents

| | | |
|---|---|---|
| Preface | | IX |
| Introduction | | XI |
| Ian Giles | | |

| | | |
|---|---|---|
| 1. | A Young Dane Named Bjarne<br>Gunilla Blom Thomsen | 1 |
| 2. | On a Bench in Edinburgh<br>Jakob Thorup Thomsen | 8 |

**Representations of Scandinavia**

| | | |
|---|---|---|
| 3. | Tradition and Innovation: The Function of Ambiguity in the Three Scandinavian Runic Conversion Monuments<br>Arne Kruse | 15 |
| 4. | The Zorns in St Ives<br>Helen Robinson | 45 |
| 5. | A Duel of Shine and Shadow<br>Eric Cain | 56 |
| 6. | *Bevægelsesdramatik*: The Railway Film and the Danish and British Documentary Movements<br>C. Claire Thomson | 60 |
| 7. | With Gratitude<br>Steinvör Pálsson | 87 |
| 8. | Winter Afternoons in Buccleuch Place<br>Dana Caspi | 88 |

## A Literary Lens on Scandinavia

9. Amalie Skram as a Travel Writer — 93
   Janet Garton

10. Flying Lessons with Bjarne — 116
    Anna Bohlin

11. Feminism, Interplay, and Cooperation: A Comparison of Selma Lagerlöf's 'Hem och stat' and Karen Blixen's 'En Baaltale med 14 Aars Forsinkelse' — 121
    Barbara Tesio-Ryan

12. Selma Lagerlöf's Transnational Terrains — 144
    Lisbeth Stenberg

13. Olof Högberg's Analogy for the Colonisation of the North of Sweden — 147
    Anders Öhman

## The Many Faces of Denmark

14. The Right Stuff: Gösta Winkler, *Akademisk Skytteforening*, and Churchill's 'Danish Demand' — 169
    John Gilmour

15. '*Jeg er ikke bange for dig*': Elements of the (Anti)Hero's Journey in Two Classics of 1970s Danish Children's Literature — 200
    Guy Puzey

16. On the Right Frequency — 220
    Charlotte Berry

17. Rewriting the Homeland – Danish Islands: Real, Imagined, and Between the Lines — 225
    Henk van der Liet

18. Our Nordic Neighbours: The Present State of the Danish Community in Scotland — 256
    Ruairidh Tarvet

## Understanding Scandinavia

19. Small Countries, Media, and Cosmopolitan Thinking   273
    Dominic Hinde

20. The Right Time for a Dane to Cross the North Sea   278
    Ian Giles

21. Bjarne's Quiet Wisdom   315
    Julie Larsen

22. Anger and Hypocrisy in Vigdis Hjorth's *Et norsk hus* – Is Alma Complicit?   317
    Anja Tröger

23. What Have the ~~Romans~~ Vikings Ever Done For Us?: A 'Postcard' on How Studying Literature and Mythology Equips You for a Career in Politics   342
    Fiona Twycross

## A Life in Print

24. Moving Currents: A Note of Appreciation   349
    Laura Alice Chapot

Bibliography of Bjarne Thorup Thomsen   353

Notes on Contributors   361

# Preface

It seems incredible that Bjarne Thorup Thomsen has been in Edinburgh for thirty-five years. In 1987, we were moving our Scandinavian Studies department from Aberdeen down to Edinburgh, and for the first time it became possible to appoint a full-time lecturer in Danish, followed by Norwegian in 1989. It was important to select the right candidates, and Bjarne and Arne Kruse, respectively, proved to be excellent choices and valued colleagues. Working together, we were able to build from the ground up a reputable Scandinavian centre of note in Edinburgh. It was particularly gratifying that both men have played important roles in the fortunes of the Scottish Society for Northern Studies in the years since, and it is little wonder that the society's journal continues to go from strength to strength following their stringent and expert rejuvenation of the organ.

We are delighted by developments in and around the University of Edinburgh Scandinavian Studies department over the years since its inception, and note that it has not only produced many hundreds of alumni through its rich and varied undergraduate teaching, but that it also remains consistently one of the most well-liked language and area studies degrees offered. Upon our arrival from Aberdeen, we inherited just one PhD student, and it has been most gratifying to see the nurturing of researchers blossom over the years.

The solid work in this centre of research is not confined to the graduate students: it was apparent to us both from our very first encounter with him that Bjarne was a young man of considerable intellect and eloquence, and we were quite certain that a career of insightful research outputs lay ahead of him. We were not wrong.

Given Bjarne's modesty and kindness, as well as his attentiveness and skill as a supervisor, we have found him to be a first-rate friend, colleague, and mentor. We are not surprised to see that this sentiment is one shared by many others featured as contributors to this splendid volume.

We greatly appreciate all Bjarne has done since our paths first crossed thirty-five years ago, and wish him a long and happy retirement.

**Irene Scobbie**                                                                  **Peter Graves**
*Corbridge, July 2022*                                      *Edinburgh, July 2022*

---

Irene Scobbie was editor of Northern Studies from 1989 until 1992. Until her retirement in 1991, she was Reader in Swedish and Head of Scandinavian Studies at the University of Edinburgh. She was appointed a Commander of the Royal Swedish Order of the Polar Star in 1986.

Peter Graves gave the fourth Hermann Pálsson Lecture in 2008. Until his retirement in the same year, he was Senior Lecturer in Swedish and Head of the School of Literatures, Languages, and Cultures at the University of Edinburgh. He was appointed Knight (First Class) of the Royal Swedish Order of the Polar Star in 2009.

# Introduction

## Ian Giles

> The wild geese were not flying very high because their new companion was not used to breathing in the thinnest air. And for his sake, they were also flying a little slower than usual.
>
> Finally the boy forced himself to turn his eyes down to the earth beneath. What he saw looked like a huge cloth spread out below him, a cloth that was divided into an unbelievable number of large and small checks.
>
> 'Where in heaven's name am I?' he wondered.
>
> Selma Lagerlöf, *Nils Holgersson's Wonderful Journey through Sweden*[1]

This festschrift honours the highly esteemed Dr Bjarne Thorup Thomsen, who retired from his role as Reader in Danish at the University of Edinburgh in 2021, following almost three and a half decades of inspirational teaching, mentorship, and research.

Given his personal and professional disposition towards the literature of travel and movement, his own origins in

---

1. Lagerlöf 2013: 28.

*udkantsdanmark*, and his love of hillwalking, it might seem obvious to the casual bystander that Bjarne was always destined to end up in Scotland, but Edinburgh was no foregone conclusion.

Born in North Jutland in 1955 to Gerda and Hugo, rumour has it that, in his early years, Bjarne was quite the footballing talent and the decision to focus on his studies was much to the chagrin of his coach. Bjarne's wanderlust had already manifested itself in 1974 when he set out for Copenhagen to pursue his university studies rather than remaining in his native tract. After completing his cand.philol. in Scandinavian Literature at the University of Copenhagen, he was drawn back to Jutland and teacher training in Aalborg, where he was first student and later teacher. The limits of the Danish job market – and indeed, young Bjarne's yearning for adventure – saw him cast his net wider.

It is rare that a book of celebration such as this volume begins by identifying axe wielding by the University Grants Commission as a good thing, but in this particular case it does. The Department of Swedish at the University of Aberdeen came into being shortly after the Second World War, and by the early 1970s, it was a veritable hive of teaching and research activity spanning all manner of Swedish and Scandinavian interests.[2] Nonetheless, the Commission reached the decision in 1986 that there was a surfeit of small language departments and in its view there was only one possible solution: closure. In the case of Aberdeen's Scandinavian department, the 1986/87 academic year was its last.

At a meeting of the Scottish Society for Northern Studies (SSNS) late in 1986, Irene Scobbie met the University of Edinburgh's Professor Peter Brand, who offered the closing department an opportunity to rise from the ashes as Edinburgh's

---

2. Scobbie 1973: 13–15.

new Department of Scandinavian Studies. With its new lease of life, the department was able to appoint its first ever full-time lecturer in Danish.

In its 'wisdom', the Commission had also precipitated the closure of Newcastle's Scandinavian Studies department,[3] where one Bjarne Thorup Thomsen had arrived in the autumn of 1986 to take up the post of Lecturer in Danish. This unhappy decision by the Commission was in fact the cause of the refraction that brought Bjarne to Edinburgh in 1987, to the rejuvenated department of Scandinavian Studies.

Bjarne flourished in Edinburgh. His teaching over more than thirty years has not only delivered hundreds of new Danish speakers, but also expanded horizons and given rise to new young researchers. While there are many highlights to focus on, various courses on Scandinavian children's literature convened by Bjarne are often fondly mentioned by former students, and this editor would note that Bjarne's course exploring the cinema of Ingmar Bergman made a lasting impression on him.

As a mentor and supervisor, calm composure has characterised his approach to some fifteen doctoral candidates, many more master's students, and countless undergraduate dissertation writers under his charge. He has always offered a little balm to the soul, plenty of wisdom, and a dash of humour in his meticulous-yet-dense handwriting and in supervision meetings looked forward to by many.

On a personal level, living in Edinburgh introduced Bjarne to many important people in his life. The arrival of Arne Kruse in 1989 as the department's Lecturer in Norwegian marked

---

3. Another significant Scandinavian Studies department of yesteryear, cf. Mennie 1973: 10–12. Duncan Mennie was responsible for almost single-handedly building Newcastle's department during the 1940s and 1950s at what was then Durham's King's College, and his impact on both SSNS and Scandinavian Studies was significant, cf. Scobbie 1998: 7–10.

the beginning of an enduring friendship,[4] and their colleague Peter Graves went on to become a next-door neighbour, while love blossomed with the department's Swedish teaching fellow Gunilla Blom, and they married in 1993. When not at their Edinburgh base, Bjarne and Gunilla are to be found in northern Denmark, northern Sweden, or sometimes – as a *lagom* compromise – in their small flat in Gothenburg.

Yet it was surely as a writer, editor, and well-rounded researcher that Bjarne really came into his own in Edinburgh. A perusal of Bjarne's publications reveals an output that was measured and thoughtful, yet always impactful.[5] As one might expect over a career as long and fruitful as his, Bjarne's interests developed over time, but there is – to literally translate a Danish phrase – a red thread to be found binding them together.

A nascent interest in the proletarian literature of Denmark, especially first-person narratives and works focused on minorities, began to morph into explorations of modernity, place, and topography in the literature of the late nineteenth and early twentieth centuries. The remit of this work also assumed an increasingly broader view, encompassing all of Scandinavia. While a rich sideline in considerations of the interplay between Danish and Scottish literature is also in evidence, Bjarne's scholarship came to focus on many of the aforementioned themes in the works of seminal Swedish writers such as Selma Lagerlöf and Eyvind Johnson.

To fully grasp the impact and robust variety in Bjarne's work, 2007 serves as an excellent illustration. That year marked the

---

4. Arne and Bjarne (or Arnie and Barney, as they were fondly known to several Edinburgh University servitors) would argue this friendship was based on mutual passions for hillwalking and the rich literary traditions of Scandinavia, but many external observers also noted an inclination towards amused playfulness never better illustrated than by their focus on the preparation of mulled wine for the annual departmental Lucia procession in December.
5. For a full overview of Bjarne's publications, see the bibliography on p.353.

publication of an edited volume on new approaches to H.C. Andersen; another on peripheral literature in the Nordic region and Scotland; also his monograph exploring nation, mobility, and modernity in Lagerlöf's *Nils Holgersson*.[6] This editor notes that on more than one occasion, the latter work has been described by multiple experts in the field as the definitive and final volume on the matter. It would be no surprise were Bjarne's ongoing work examining the legacy of Nobel Prize laureate Eyvind Johnson to assume a corresponding position in future.

Bjarne's impact on published scholarship elsewhere has also been significant. He served as editor of *Northern Studies* from 1996 until 2004, latterly working alongside his good friend Arne Kruse, and has been a frequent contributor to the journal over the years. His past editorial board appointments have included the *European Journal of Scandinavian Studies*, while many of his former students and doctoral candidates have gone on to serve not only SSNS but also sister organisations and periodicals such as the Viking Society and *Scandinavica*. All the while, he continued to deliver his own stellar research and teaching. Writing in 2017, Janet Garton noted that 'UCL and Edinburgh are now holding the fort as the only two institutions left in the UK to offer a full provision of modern Scandinavian languages at honours level. They are doing so splendidly, with active teaching and research departments and a team of energetic researchers'.[7] Edinburgh has much to thank Bjarne Thorup Thomsen for in this respect.

The breadth of research, notes, and insights offered in this volume are a tribute to Bjarne's own wide-ranging interests on both a personal and research level, serving very much as refractions of Scandinavia. The twenty-four contributors explore

---

6. 'Thorup Thomsen 2007a; 2007b; Thorup Thomsen et al. 2007.
7. Garton 2017: 98.

literary themes and trends, concepts of identity, travel, exchanges across the North Sea, visual representations, history, and much more. While the editor has endeavoured to bring order to this smörgåsbord of tributes, the reader is encouraged to dip in and out at their leisure. They will not be disappointed. In addition to a number of shorter, more personal notes, there are twelve chapters in this volume which have been peer-reviewed,[8] and the editor wishes to acknowledge the input of the anonymous reviewers who were so generous with their time and expertise.

The volume begins with two portraits of Bjarne: his wife, Gunilla, explores Bjarne's early years and traces his trajectory into the world of literary scholarship, while his brother, Jakob, reflects on how the adventures of two young Danes armed with Britrail passes sowed the seeds of a future Scottish life. The volume then turns its attention to representations of Scandinavia, beginning with a touching and personal survey of three Scandinavian runic conversion monuments by Bjarne's long-term Edinburgh colleague, Arne Kruse. Leaping forward more than a millennium, Helen Robinson gives a succinct account of the renowned Swedish painter Anders Zorn's sojourn in Cornwall, while Eric Cain contemplates the significance of light and dark in Carl Theodor Dreyer's 1932 classic *Vampyr*. Next, C. Claire Thomson considers the interplay between the British and Danish documentary film movements in the late 1940s, and the section draws to a close with brief postcards from Steinvör Pálsson and Dana Caspi.

The following section offers a literary lens on Scandinavia as it revisits and re-examines some of Bjarne's favourite strands of research: travel, place, and literature of the late nineteenth and early twentieth century. This begins with an account of the Norwegian feminist author Amalie Skram as a travel writer

---

8. Chapters 3, 4, 6, 9, 11, 13, 14, 15, 17, 18, 20, and 22.

by Janet Garton. Anna Bohlin then provides a delightful interlude that details Bjarne's aptitude as a research mentor, before Barbara Tesio-Ryan compares works by Karen Blixen and Selma Lagerlöf. A further postcard from Lisbeth Stenberg interrogating Lagerlöf's transnationalism is the prelude for a chapter by Anders Öhman that examines Swedish novelist Olof Högberg's attempt to analogously novelise the colonisation of northern Sweden.

Moving on to a section exploring the many faces of Denmark during Bjarne's lifetime and the formation of modern Denmark in reality and the popular imagination, John Gilmour begins with a chapter reflecting on Danish resistance hero Gösta Winkler and his experiences in 1945. Guy Puzey then investigates the emergence of the anti-hero in Danish children's literature of the 1970s, drawing on two key works. Charlotte Berry's postcard describes Bjarne as a recruiter to all things Danish, while Henk van det Liet's chapter on island writing within the broader multidisciplinary context of islands as a whole is rich in detail and Danish examples. Ruairidh Tarvet closes the section with a survey of the Danish community in twenty-first century Scotland.

The last section presents understandings of Scandinavia from a variety of perspectives. Dominic Hinde begins with a whistlestop tour of the way that Britain has viewed Scandinavia through its journalistic reporting, while Ian Giles explores the modern-day British focus on Scandinavian literature through the lens of Danish author Peter Høeg. Bjarne's Edinburgh colleagues Julie Larsen and Anja Tröger then follow. The former provides insight into the quiet wisdom of Bjarne, while the latter digs deep into the themes of anger and hypocrisy in the contemporary work of Norwegian author Vigdis Hjorth. Finally, Fiona Twycross provides a light-hearted account of exactly what the Vikings – and their Scandinavian successors

– have done for us, and how learnings from them can be applied elsewhere. The volume concludes with a comprehensive bibliography of Bjarne's work, preceded by a meticulously crafted note of appreciation from Laura Alice Chapot, who gives close attention to the language of Bjarne Thorup Thomsen the writer.

It will not surprise the reader that in the preparation of this manuscript, the responses from all individuals approached (regardless of eventual participation) has been one of tremendous positivity. This editor has long held that Bjarne is one of the most well-liked academics of recent decades, and it has been gratifying to find that others hold him in similarly high esteem. On a personal note, I must also offer my heartfelt thanks to Bjarne. While memories of our early meetings have been blurred by time, a chance encounter with Bjarne in Uppsala where we firmly agreed that the best cafés were those offering unlimited coffee refills left me with the firm impression that he was a man of taste. His input since then as a teacher and mentor has inspired me in my own journey as a researcher and translator, while the sangfroid and grace with which advice and feedback has *always* been provided has instilled much-needed calm and served as an example to live by. I know with certainty that a great many of us feel this way.

## Bibliography

Garton, Janet. 2017. 'Scandinavian Studies in 1977: A Retrospective'. *Scandinavica* 56:2, 94–100.

Lagerlöf, Selma. 2013. *Nils Holgersson's Wonderful Journey through Sweden*, Vol. 1. Peter Graves (trans.). London: Norvik Press.

Mennie, D.M. 1973. 'Scandinavian Studies, Newcastle upon Tyne'. *Northern Studies* 1, 10–12.

Scobbie, Irene. 1973. 'Scandinavian Studies at Aberdeen University'. *Northern Studies* 1, 13–15.

——. 1998. 'Professor Emeritus Duncan M. Mennie (1909–1998)'. *Northern Studies* 33, 7–10.

Thorup Thomsen, Bjarne. 2007a. *Lagerlöfs litterære landvinding: Nation, mobilitet og modernitet i Nils Holgersson og tilgrænsende tekster*. Amsterdam: Amsterdam Contributions to Scandinavian Studies.

—— (ed.). 2007b. *Centring on the Peripheries: Studies in Scandinavian, Scottish, Gaelic and Greenlandic Literature*. Norwich: Norvik Press.

Thorup Thomsen, Bjarne and Andersen, Hans-Christian (eds). 2007. *Hans Christian Andersen – New Approaches*. Norwich: Norvik Press.

## · 1 ·

## A Young Dane Named Bjarne

### Gunilla Blom Thomsen

> There was once a sculptor named Alfred, who having won the gold medal and obtained a travelling scholarship, went to Italy, and then came back to his native land. He was young at that time – indeed, he is young still, although he is ten years older than he was then.
>
> H.C. Andersen, *Beauty of Form and Beauty of Mind*, in translation

There was a young Dane named Bjarne, who having won the golden post of lecturer at the University of Edinburgh, settled in the city's New Town and moved into an office at 18 Buccleuch Place. He was a young man at that time – indeed, he is young still, although he is thirty-four years older than he was then. Glimpses of what went before these decisive steps in Bjarne's life, and where everything started, will be related below.

September was an unusually mild month in 1955, the year when Bjarne, the second child of Gerda and Hugo, was born in North Jutland. Although described by his mother as 'a happy child', as a young boy he occasionally suffered setbacks. For example, when he was learning to speak, Bjarne for a while struggled to pronounce the 'r' sound. He and his sister used to visit a local seamstress who made new clothes for them – her first name being Sørine – and she used to challenge him to pronounce her name, with the promise of an ice cream for them both if he got it right. Luckily, we learn from his sister that Sørine was a very forbearing lady.

Bjarne spent his formative years in the environment of the family grocery shop. With its large expanse of exciting names and slogans printed on the product ranges on the shelves, this was a world of wonder for a boy with an early fascination for letters. 'Valo' was the brand name of a Danish washing powder which promised to give 'a new brightness to your clothes', being in sharp competition with the brand 'Snevit' (or snow white) which promised to make your laundry 'white enough to be hung out to dry in the town square of Copenhagen'.

On a warm day in August 1961 and holding his mother's hand, Bjarne set off for his first day of school in the small town to the east of Aalborg where his family had moved. A brand-new satchel in his other hand, he was too impatient to stay by his mother's side and skipped along well ahead of her.

Bjarne loved school. He stayed at the first one for seven years, before taking his warm feelings on to another school for the next two. However, as his change of school required him to travel there by bus, another misfortune befell the young boy: he was obliged to get up extremely early in the morning, an activity which has never been Bjarne's cup of tea! All the same, it was a challenge he met with composure – as indeed he still does. On the way home from school, one of his fellow students was playing around with a ball in the school bus, when it happened to hit the back of the driver's head. As the young culprit would not admit the offence and his classmates would not tell on him, every single one of the youngsters had to leave the bus and cover the remaining eight miles on foot.

In his leisure time as a child, apart from reading books, Bjarne loved playing football and frequently played around the family house with his friend Ove. Not infrequently one or other of the window panes was smashed in the process. Bjarne later joined the Romdrup-Klarup Gymnastikforening, where he was considered quite a football talent. Rumour has it that a coach of his back then very much regretted seeing him stop playing. Bjarne still enjoys using his dribbling skills whenever an opportunity comes his way, despite having been injured and having to visit A&E after a match with students at a summer course in Denmark. As we all know, Bjarne has not lost his love for the beautiful game, and his disappointment is discernible whenever 'his' team loses a match.

When they came home from school, Bjarne and his elder sister used to assist in the family business, for instance by delivering shopping that had been ordered by local customers. The goods were usually placed in a basket on the back of their bicycles. One of the children's favourite regular customers was a certain Mrs Luther, who used to tip the youngsters twenty-five øre for their service. Deliveries to another customer were held not in favour by the siblings – in fact, they were slightly afraid, as an aggressive Alsatian dog tended to 'welcome' them at this address. The most popular activity in the shop occurred in the run-up to Christmas, when they were asked to assist by transferring particularly yummy sweets from large glass jars into small cellophane parcels, which they then sealed using an electric device which to their eyes seemed positively magical. It is rumoured that a not inconsiderable quantity of the Christmas sweets ended up in small 'containers' other than the fancy cellophane parcels.

For his upper secondary education Bjarne headed to a respected school in the city of Aalborg. This was a famous and very traditional seat of learning; on the very first day of term, during assembly, the staff made their ambitions plain to the students by urging each one of them to bring a suitcase to school the next day to accommodate all the books needed for the upcoming year's studies. One tradition in Denmark is for students leaving secondary school to mark the end of this period of intense learning by wearing a formal type of hat. However, at the time of Bjarne's graduation in the 1970s, there was a wave of protests among young people against this tradition, with many of them, as was the case with Bjarne, refusing to don this head gear.

Photo: Jakob Thorup Thomsen

Bjarne was keen to get his driver's licence at the age of eighteen, something which served him well in the summer following graduation, when he and three of his friends planned to spend several weeks travelling across Europe, taking turns to drive. They set off in a VW camper van, a popular vehicle of the time – known in Denmark as 'rye bread' – owned by the father of one of his friends. On approaching Paris, the three brave boys headed straight for the main attraction of the city, the Champs-Élysées, where, unsurprisingly, they were soon caught in a mire of traffic and ended up being escorted to a safer place by French police.

When the time came for him to apply to university, Bjarne had the choice of going either to the university of Aarhus or that of Copenhagen. His parents would probably have preferred the former, which was closer to home, but on the advice of one of his teachers, he decided on the latter, leaving for the capital in 1974 in the company of two of his friends. After that, his parents contented themselves with receiving frequent calls from Bjarne's new base courtesy of one or other of Copenhagen's phone boxes, and regularly welcoming him home at weekends. A new member of the family at this time, one that everybody adored, was Kasper, a Labrador. Rumour has it, Bjarne spent so long saying goodbye to the dog before leaving for Copenhagen that he more often than not risked missing his return flight.

After completing his cand.philol. in Scandinavian Literature at the University of Copenhagen, Bjarne bought a flat in Reberbanegade in Aalborg and returned home with a view to spending a semester honing his pedagogic skills at the local Danish Teachers' Training College. Later on, his younger brother joined Bjarne in the flat upon his own graduation, chipping in to cover the household bills. They were both serious about physical exercise, their main choice of sports being running, which they practised together. When taking part in amateur running competitions, Bjarne wasn't too happy to see his brother sometimes overtake him in the sprint.

Photo: Jakob Thorup Thomsen

Academic posts in Bjarne's field were few and far between in his native country at this time, but on widening his perspective, Bjarne soon spotted a position of interest to him in the UK – not in Scotland yet but very close by. This led to him moving to the North of England in autumn 1986 to take up a post at the University of Newcastle. Although he struggled to keep his rented room in the Gateshead area of the city warm enough during the winter, Bjarne thoroughly enjoyed his new life in Newcastle and might very well have stayed on, had the university not suddenly decided to close down its Scandinavian Department, just one year after his arrival.

As luck would have it, a crucial decision was made at the University of Edinburgh, leading to a new Department of Scandinavian Studies being set up less than two hours' drive north of Hadrian's Wall. Bjarne was invited to join the new department together with two colleagues from the University of Aberdeen, where Scandinavian Studies had also closed down that year.

This is how Bjarne came to settle in Scotland's capital, where he moved into an office at 18 Buccleuch Place in the autumn of 1987. Which just so happened to be where the writer of these lines would meet him for the first time upon moving into the office next door some two years later.

Photo: Jakob Thorup Thomsen

## · 2 ·

# On a Bench in Edinburgh

## Jakob Thorup Thomsen

Photo: Jakob Thorup Thomsen

An old photograph shows Bjarne sitting on a bench in Edinburgh's Charlotte Square, wearing a pair of shorts and bare-chested in the sunshine. He's examining a map of the city and smiling up at the photographer.

This was Bjarne's first visit to Edinburgh. His accommodation was the relatively pleasant youth hostel in the New Town, not far from where that photograph was taken. At this moment in time, young Bjarne had no inkling that he was visiting the city where he would spend most of his working life.

Just a few years later, Bjarne took a big leap and moved to the UK for work. To begin with, this was just for a single year in Newcastle. Later, he moved to Edinburgh, and, as I'm sure readers know, he remained in Scotland until retirement – albeit while retaining strong ties to Scandinavia.

The author of the piece you are reading just so happens to be Bjarne's slightly younger brother. I may not have been there when Bjarne began his British career, but I was most certainly present when Bjarne met the Brits for the first time. Over the course of two summers in the early 1980s, we headed off to the UK on our holidays and it was on one of these tours up and down the country that Bjarne and I happened upon verdant Charlotte Square.

Armed with Britrail passes, we and our big rucksacks had unlimited access to the full extent of British Rail's network. While we were at liberty to travel anywhere we liked, our journeys tended to draw us away from the traditional centres and towards the peripheries – with a particular emphasis on Scotland. Admittedly, I believe we may have spent a day or two in London as well… This trajectory allowed us to observe that not only is John O'Groats the northernmost point in the mainland British Isles, but it is also one of the most boring places we could ever conceive of. We were rather more excited about our trips along the West Highland Line to Mallaig and Oban. It was fantastic to walk along the harbour front in Oban and experience the incredible atmosphere amongst the retired holidaymakers in the town's hotels. Every evening, there was the distant sound of bagpipes, and it seemed as if the place hadn't changed in decades.

Our travels took us to the Hebrides and to places that were most definitely not tourist hotspots. Lochmaddy on North Uist might not be the kind of place that would land a spot on the front page of the tourist guidebooks, but as I mentioned, we were drawn to the peripheries of these islands. An amazing highlight was the Isle of Raasay. The island youth hostel, long since closed down, was located up a narrow lane a couple of miles from the pier and had incredible views across the water to Skye. The men's dormitory was housed in a former sheepfold behind the main building, and one day we climbed to the highest point on Raasay – the summit of Dun Caan. Hardly a mountain peak of international renown, but shaped by a volcano and most definitely exotic for two lads from flat Denmark.

Photo by Jakob Thorup Thomsen

I am in no doubt whatsoever that the British made a very positive impression on both Bjarne and me. From a Scandinavian point of view, they were more open, welcoming, and talkative than we were used to back home. That positive impression must have played its part when Bjarne chose to work so far from home. It was a big decision to work in the UK – don't forget that at the time, the cities of Edinburgh and Newcastle seemed much further away from Denmark than they do nowadays. This was before globalisation. There was no internet or email, so staying in touch with family and friends back home was confined to letters – phone calls were generally too expensive. The same was true of plane tickets, so the preferred route to Britain was by boat on the Esbjerg–Harwich sailing, which took twenty hours.

Britain was truly fascinating to two young Danes. It was at once modern and old-fashioned. The country was more densely populated, meaning there were far more people in the streets of the towns and cities than we would ever see in Denmark. It was also more multicultural than Denmark, and the trains ran faster – at least on the main lines. The selection of beers (not to mention crisps) was greater, but in contrast we were baffled by the existence of just two types of bread in the shops – white and brown – and the fact that filter coffee was a posh new concept for the British. Milk in glass bottles with a thick layer of cream on top was something we had said goodbye to in Denmark a couple of decades earlier, but the fatty British milk tasted incredible on a bowl of muesli. Many of the homes, and most definitely the youth hostels we visited, were cold and draughty (at least to Scandinavians). Indeed, they still are.

Nevertheless, the British made a highly positive impression on the two of us. This certainly played a role when Bjarne accepted the offer to teach Scandinavian languages and literature in the UK. To begin with, he could hardly have planned to spend his entire career doing so, but I am convinced that it was a good decision, and it has given him an exciting and stimulating working life in an environment in which he thrived. It was also where he met Gunilla – in Scandinavian Studies – leading to another good decision when he married her.

Now Bjarne has departed from his role in Scandinavian Studies and has more flexibility to visit Denmark and Sweden and spend time with his family and friends. Of course, Bjarne and Gunilla are eager to keep in touch with their Scottish friends while pursuing their passion for walking in the nation's great outdoors. To my knowledge, Bjarne has never set foot on the Isle of Raasay since our visit there in the 1980s, but perhaps there may yet be an opportunity to climb Dun Caan again.

Representations of Scandinavia

· 3 ·

# Tradition and Innovation: the Function of Ambiguity in the Three Scandinavian Runic Conversion Monuments

## Arne Kruse

*Det ruller i Horizontens Himmel*
*og sagtelig skielver Hav og Jord.*
*De gamle Guders brogede Vrimmel*
*forsvinder, og kommer ej meer til Nord.*
*Istedet for Lundens ærværdige Minder*
*man idel Kirker og Klostere finder.*
*Kun hist og her*
*man fiern og nær*
*en Höi og en opreist Kampesteen skuer,*
*som minder om Oldtidens slukte Luer.*

From 'Hakon Jarls Död, Eller Christendommens Indförsel i Norge' by Adam Oehlenschläger (1803)[1]

In the following, we will observe not only one *opreist Kampesteen* but as many as three stone monuments from Scandinavian

---
1. From: Adam Oehlenschläger: *Digte*, Fr. Brummers Forlag, Kbh. 1803: 16–22.

antiquity: Harald's stone at Jelling, Denmark (DR 42)[2]; the Frösö stone in Jämtland, Northern Sweden (J 66); and the stone on the island of Kuli, Norway (N 449). What justifies a grouping and discussion of these three runic stones is not only the happenstance that the locations of these runic monuments are not far from where respectively the recipient, the wife of the recipient, and the contributor to this volume come from, but also the content of the inscriptions on the monuments. All three refer to an official act of conversion to Christianity – and with it the religious, cultural, and legal inclusion of Scandinavia into a common-European civilisation. Both the missionary stage that led up to the conversion and the practical implementation of the legal decision were of course lengthy processes, but a formal act of conversion that the three stones refer to will have been momentous in the progression towards a religious shift. In addition to being the only contemporary Scandinavian written evidence for acts of conversion, the three runic stones are also the first Scandinavian sources of the names of the young nations 'Denmark'[3] and 'Norway', and the region 'Jämtland' in today's Sweden.

The attention in this piece, however, will for once not be on linguistic aspects of the inscriptions, and neither will it be on the historical implications of the inscriptions. The following will rather home in on how the three monuments functioned as a medium of communication in their respective milieus, and how the message conveyed can be regarded as ambiguous in relation to tradition and to the new world view they announce. After a brief demonstration of how the transition to a new belief system could be experienced at an individual level, the

---

2. Signum in *Scandinavian Runic-text Database* 2020.
3. 'Denmark' is first mentioned on Jelling 1, the stone erected by Gorm c. AD 958, before the name is repeated on Jelling 2, the stone raised by his son Haraldr.

focus will be on how religious syncretism and cultural blending and ambiguity can be observed in the inscriptions and artistic expressions of the three monuments.

## The personal dilemma

According to Widukind's account[4] the cleric Poppo, who AD 963–65 baptised King Haraldr, did not deny the existence of the heathen gods that the Danes believed in, but they existed in his opinion in the form of demons. Syncretistic ideas of this kind, where elements of two competing belief systems are present, are witnessed also in individuals other than Poppo. Even royals who had been baptised sometimes struggled to follow the straight and narrow path, and some even abandoned their new religious belief and went apostate. King Hákon Aðalsteinsfóstri, who was brought up a Christian in the English court before he claimed the Norwegian crown and began missioning c. AD 930, seems to have at least partly lapsed from his Christian faith and was buried in a half-heathen and half-Christian manner.

A window to how the individual may have experienced the belief change is passed on to us in an unusually personal account by the contemporary skald Hallfreðr vandræðaskáld. The Icelandic poet first serves the pagan Earl Hákon of Hlaðir, and then the Christian King Óláfr Tryggvason, and he converts to Christianity at the behest of Óláfr. The switch of religious allegiance is the theme of his so-called 'Conversion Verses'.[5] The religious oscillation in these verses is commonly seen as showing a progression from paganism through to gradual acceptance of Christianity,[6] but they can just as well be read as

---

4. Widukind, Book 3: 65.
5. *Hallfreðar saga*: 46–50.
6. See for example Whaley 2003: 237.

much more unstructured and almost desperate utterances from a man in religious agony; a man who is in a liminal position between two spiritual camps.[7] The last of the 'Conversion Verses' may illustrate how Hallfreðr negotiates the pagan and the Christian worlds:

*Sás með Sygna ræsi*
*siðr, at blót eru kviðjuð;*
*verðum flest at forðask*
*fornhaldin skǫp norna;*
*láta allir ýtar*
*Óðins blót fyr róða;*
*verðk ok neyddr frá Njarðar*
*niðjum Krist at biðja.*

That is the custom of the chief of the people of Sogn, that sacrifices are forbidden; we must shun most of the long-held decrees of the norns. All men throw Óðinn's sacrifices to the winds, and I am forced away from Njǫrðr's kinsmen to pray to Christ.[8]

The verse portrays a man who reluctantly feels he must follow what he sees as inevitable. There is no religious conviction behind his choice to give up the old gods, just a resigned capitulation to the changing times, to what everyone else does, and to the shifting politics of power.

Hallfreðr's personal account gives us an insight into the mental quandary at least some will have felt during the conversion. What about those who raised the conversion stones? We know that King Haraldr was baptised just before he raised the

---

7. Goeres 2011.
8. The translation is from Goeres 2011: 58.

stone in honour of his heathen father and (probably) Christian mother. We will never know his inner feelings, but we may be permitted to see Haraldr behind some of the choices made concerning the monument in honour of his parents. What we will see of Haraldr in the following is not someone in inner torment but rather someone proud of who he is and where he comes from, and someone willing to take on anything new only if what is new can be expressed within a context he recognises. His choice to raise the monument at Jelling is significant, and we will see that the choice of sites for his own monument, as well as the other two conversion stones, may indicate concession or adaptation between two cultures and belief systems.

Let us now present the three monuments and the locations they are placed in before we focus on some particular aspects of the inscriptions and the ornamentation in our hunt for ambivalence or compromise. The general impression of the three places – Jelling, Kuli, and Frösö – is that they are all locations associated with pagan cultic activities. All of them show an exceptional concentration of archaeological remains of pre-Christian burials or ritual constructions.

## Jelling

The earliest, and in all respects most impressive, is the Jelling monument. Located in central, north-east Jutland, the two runestones at Jelling are part of a tenth-century royal monument from the reigns of King Gormr ('Gorm the Old') and his son, Haraldr ('Harald Bluetooth'). The complex – the origin of which is likely to pre-date this era – consists of two large mounds: the smaller runic stone created c. AD 958 under King Gormr (Jelling 1) and the large runic stone dating to the reign of his son, Haraldr (Jelling 2), raised AD 963–65. A stone church now stands on the site of earlier wooden churches. Recent excavations have established evidence of a c. 360-metre-long ship setting and a palisade surrounding the whole monument. The sheer scale of the complex is striking even today, and the ambitious royal power behind the monument is evident.

Excavations in the 1970s established the likelihood that Gormr was first interred in the northern of the large mounds at Jelling and that he was later reburied by the altar of the first wooden church built next to the mound.[9] It is further likely that this *translatio* was done by his newly baptised son, Haraldr, but we take note that Haraldr did not attempt to eliminate the mounds. The mounds may have been left in respect as part of a memorial site, but now with a church at the centre of the complex.

In addition to the runes that run over the three faces of Jelling 2 (A, B, C), the large boulder is decorated with elaborate ornamentations. In transliteration, the inscription runs as follows (with letters in parenthesis indicating runes where the reading is uncertain):[10]

A : haraltr : kunukʀ : baþ : kaurua ¶ kubl : þausi : aft : kurm faþur sin ¶ auk aft : þourui : muþur : sina : sa ¶ haraltr (:) ias : soʀ · uan · tanmaurk

B ala · auk · nuruiak

C (·) auk t(a)ni (k)(a)(r)(þ)(i) kristno

The text reads as follows in English:

---

9. Pedersen 2017: 7–8.
10. The transliterations and translations of the three inscriptions are from *Scandinavian Runic-text Database* 2020.

**A** King Haraldr ordered these monuments made in memory of Gormr, his father, and in memory of Þyrvé, his mother; that Haraldr who won for himself all of Denmark

**B** and Norway

**C** and made the Danes Christian.

## Kuli

The runic stone on the island of Kuli is humbler in all respects. The monument consists of a single stone, erected on the island of Kuli, Smøla in Nordmøre. The almost-two-metre-tall, slender, and four-sided slab carries a hollowed-in cross on one of the broad sides and a runic inscription in two vertical lines on one of the narrow sides. Each line begins with a small cross, and the text is read from the bottom up. Both lines go all the way up to the top edge of the stone. The stone was shortened in modern time, leaving the possibility that the text may have been longer. On linguistic grounds, the stone is dated to the very beginning of the millennium, and it is likely to refer to a formal acceptance of the Christian faith during the reign of King Óláfr Tryggvason (AD 995–1000).[11] In transliteration, the established reading of the inscription (which we will return to) runs as follows:

**þurir : auk : hal(u)arþr : rai(s)(t)(u) · stain : þins(i) · aft u(l)f(l)iu(t) […] ¶
tualf · uintr · ha(f)(þ)i : (k)r(i)(s)(t)(i)(n)·(t)umr : (u)iri(t) · (i) n(u)riki […]**

---

11. Kruse 2021a: 26–28.

Figure 1: The author showing the cross on the broad side of a replica
of the original runic stone at Kuli.
Photo: Svein Olav Kruse.

Figure 2: The middle part of the Kuli stone.
Photo: Åge Hojem/NTNU Vitenskapsmuseet.

In English this will read as follows:

Þórir and Hallvarðr raised this stone in memory of Ulfljótr [...]

Christianity had been twelve winters in Norway [...] There is a large number of burial mounds and cairns on the island of Kuli, most of them dating to the older Iron Age. The likelihood of ritual activity is suggested by a stone setting with a central, white, phallus-shaped stone.[12] Not far from Kuli is *Nerdvika*, in 1559 written 'Neruigh', from *\*Njarðarvík*, containing the name of the god *Njǫrðr*, associated with seafaring and with fertility. Bergljot Solberg[13] has suggested a pattern where there is a link between stone phalluses and the cult around *Njǫrðr*.

The neighbouring island of Edøy must be seen in connection with Kuli through both proximity and ownership. Edøy also has unusually many Iron Age finds, including a star-shaped stone setting, which has been associated with cultic activities, possibly around Yggdrasill.[14] There are relatively fewer mounds dating to the Viking Age, but they are larger and would have been more dominant in the landscape. In 2019, a ship of c. 17 m and preliminarily dated to the Viking Age was found on Edøy, close to one of the earliest churches in the region. The important location of Kuli and Edøy – at the beginning of the protected sailing course to the north and a dangerous stretch of open sea to the south – will have been of significant motivation behind the many finds on the islands, and probably also for the raising of the runic stone.[15]

---

12. Ellingsen 2021.
13. Solberg 2001.
14. Orten Lie 2014.
15. Kruse 2020.

## Frösö

The stone from Frösö is the only runic stone in Sweden that mentions the christening of an area, in this case Jämtland. The stone is dated from around AD 1050. In transliteration the text can be read as follows:

> **austmoþ[(r)] kuþfastaʀ sun ' lit ra(i)[(s)]... ...(-)[(n)] (þ)(i) no auk| |kirua bru þisa| |auk h[on] [li](t) kristno eo(t)alont (o)sbiurn kirþi bru (t)riun rai(s)t auk (t)sain runoʀ þisaʀ**

And in English:

> Austmaðr, Guðfastr's son, had this stone raised and this bridge made and he had Jamtaland Christianized. Ásbjǫrn made the bridge, Trjónn and Steinn carved these runes.

The inscription is on the broad face of the stone and runs inside a zoomorphic band made up of a stylised serpent biting its own tail. Some of the text spills over outside the serpent. There is a cross in the middle of the upper part of the stone. The design of the stone is typical for Central Swedish runestones of the eleventh century. This is significant because Jämtland was a Norwegian province in the Viking Age, while the layout of the inscription and the cross point to a Christian influence from Sweden and not from Norway, as one would have expected.[16]

---

16. Some have argued that the name of the commissioner of the monument, *Austmaðr* ('the man from the east') can also be seen as a Swedish indication, but this is a personal name, given by birth, and not a byname, given in his lifetime, and can therefore hardly be carried by a man who has come from Sweden to Jämtland.

The onomastic surroundings to the stone are noteworthy. The name *Frösö*, in 1263 written 'Fræseyiar', means 'the island of *Frö/Frey*', the god of fertility. To the south-west is another large island called *Norderön*, in 1438 written 'Nærdrø', containing the name of the god *Njǫrðr*,[17] and there is a small island in the middle of the lake, Åsö, with the likely meaning 'god's island'. The place-name element *hov* appears five times around the lake, out of thirty-five such named locations in the whole of Sweden. Place-names with *hov* are usually associated with cultic locations, and possibly large halls with religious functions.[18] Additional cultic names appear in the vicinity: *Vi* ('sacred place'), *Ullvi* (with the name of the god *Ullr*), and *Odensala* (with the god's name *Oðinn*). This exceptional concentration of cultic names complements the archaeological findings on Frösö, as we will see later.

Figure 3: The Frösö stone.

---

17. *Svenskt ortnamnslexikon* 2003: 223.
18. Ibid.: 242–243.

## Runes announcing Christianity

The three stone monuments proclaim the arrival of Christianity in the medium of runes. It is not an obvious choice. It is conceivable to imagine that this could have been the moment in Scandinavian history where Latin scripture started to be used in such contexts, for the Christian culture was closely linked to the Latin writing system, and Latin scripture was already used by some in the Scandinavian elite at the time. The first coins made for Northumbrian Viking chieftains around AD 900 made use of Latin script. One name is Latinised: 'Siefredus' (*Sigfriðr*), and the coins are equipped with Latin phrases like 'Dominus Deus Rex'. They have clearly been issued in a Christian milieu, following an Anglo-Saxon pattern, and the first coins issued in Scandinavia were also based on English coinage. Around AD 995 the two kings Óláfr Tryggvason and Sweyn Haraldsson (Forkbeard) both made use of the same Anglo-Saxon moneyer, Godwine, to issue the first Norwegian and Danish coins.

The use of Latin script on coins was as unquestioned as the use of Latin script on parchment, which, in the form of minuscules had been successfully standardised and utilised under the Carolingian revival, while on the British Isles, the insular variant of Latin scripture was still preferred in the tenth century for manuscripts in the vernacular. The choice of runes for the stone monuments, however, will have been based on a long-standing Scandinavian tradition where runes had been used on raised stones. In this sense, the format of the medium of the raised stone will have been more important than the message: the announcement of the arrival of Christianity.

Pragmatically, the choice of runes gives away the intended audience of the message. While the exact rate of literacy is up for debate, runes will of course have been the most familiar writing system in Scandinavia at the time. While the runemasters themselves may have had contact with a learned Christian milieu (as argued below), their intentional readers were not from such circles but rather from the local population. The seminal choice to make use of the traditional Scandinavian writing system introduces a chapter in the history of western European Christianity where runes, and not only Latin scripture, could be used in sacral contexts; a chapter that culminates in the eleventh century with hundreds of Swedish runestones with a Christian content.

## The inscriptions

The runic inscriptions on Jelling 2, Kuli, and Frösö are traditional in so far as they are commemorative stones, containing the expected raiser formula 'NN raised this stone after MM'.[19] We will have known about King Haraldr from other sources than his runestone, but on the Kuli stone, three named individuals, otherwise surely forgotten, step forward: *Þórir*, *Hallvarðr*, and *Ulfljót*,[20] and on the Frösö stone we meet an unusually long list of personal names: *Austmaðr*, *Guðfast*, *Ásbjǫrn*, *Trjónn*, and *Steinn*, providing us with an invaluable impression of naming habits at the time. In this context, we take note of the fact that pagan names, even names that directly refer to heathen cult, such as *Guðfast* ('firm believer of (heathen) god') and Ásbjǫrn

---

19. An unusual aspect of Jelling 2 is the commemoration of both parents, and the Frösö stone exceptionally does not commemorate a deceased person.
20. The last name, *Ulfljót*, is carved at the end of the line and is very worn and difficult to read. After Liestøl first proposed the reading *Ulfljót* (Liestøl 1957), many who have written about the inscription have avoided transliterating the name because they have found the reading too unreliable. A new reading of the inscription with the use of new visualisation techniques has confirmed Liestøl's reading to be the most probable and relatively secure (Kleivane 2021: 156).

('(heathen) god + bear'), seem not to be regarded as a problem worth playing down in a Christian context. It shall in fact take hundreds of years yet before Christian personal names dominate over the traditional Scandinavian names.

The Frösö stone is one of relatively few that is not raised in memory of a deceased person. The inscription does, however, contain the expected phrase with the name of the person who raised the stone. What is unusual with our three stones is that they in addition to the raiser formula provide extra information. In the case of the Jelling stone, the addition comes in the form of a long relative clause, supplying exactitude about Haraldr: 'that Haraldr who won for himself all of Denmark and Norway and made the Danes Christian'. It is the only Danish runic inscription to contain self-praise of the monument's commissioner,[21] a self-confident young king listing his hitherto achievements.

Instead of incorporating the relative sentence immediately after the name *Haraldr*, the clause comes at the end, almost as an afterthought. We can of course excuse the grammatically slightly awkward syntax by the lack of any precedents for this kind of solipsistic formulation,[22] but there is clearly planning behind the phrasing, for the inscription looks to be arranged to follow the layout of the decorations of the three faces of the monument. We notice that the phrase *Danmork* is on the main face of the stone, while *(alla) ok Norwæg* comes on a separate side, making it possible for Haraldr to claim that he had won the whole of Denmark but not necessarily all of Norway.[23] As already pointed to, the final phrase 'and made the Danes Christian' is cleverly arranged

---

21. Nielsen 1974: 164.
22. Jesch 2013: 13.
23. This reflects the reality that certainly Vík (the area around the Oslo Fjord) was under Harald's control at the time. The inscription probably counts Harald's formal overlordship over Earl Hákon Sigurðsson, who was the *de facto* ruler over Norway (Kruse 2021b).

on the third face of the stone under the victorious Christ figure, completing the innovative and successful cooperation between the runemaster and the decorative artist – and perhaps with the involvement of the commissioner himself, Haraldr.

The text on most runestones from Denmark before Jelling 2 is arranged vertically, like Jelling 1, and commonly the lines run *boustrophedon*, i.e. 'as the ox turns in ploughing'.[24] The inscription on Jelling 2 runs horizontally, and each line starts from the left. This, and the unusually long text on the first face of the stone have understandably made scholars[25] suggest manuscripts or books as the inspiration for the arrangement and the length of the text. An evident part of the argument is that the ornamentation on the stone reflects the medieval book illuminations, as already mentioned.

The text on the Kuli stone is much shorter, and a book or manuscript inspiration behind the inscription is far from evident. Recently, however, it has been argued that the inscription's provision of a precise number of years since the introduction of Christianity is so unique and unexpected in the runic corpus that the inspiration may come from Christian manuscripts. Elise Kleivane[26] makes the point that the runemaster at Kuli is likely to have had a foot in the learned literary tradition using Latin script on parchment that came to Norway with English missionaries in the tenth century. One may add that it would not be surprising if the runemaster[27] had also come into contact with annals or chronicles, where it was customary to first state a point of reference according to the death of a bishop or a king. If this is a correct assumption, it can have a consequence for how the inscription should be read.

---

24. Although this is not the case on Jelling 1.
25. E.g. Roesdahl 1999.
26. Kleivane 2021: 161–165.
27. Certain features in the runemaster's Old Norse may be seen as interference from Old English (Kleivane 2021: 166).

The reading of the inscription was established by Aslak Liestøl.[28] He set up the following line arrangement:

A line: *Þórir ok Hallvarðr reistu stein þenna ept Ulfljót* [...]

B line: *Tolf vetr hafði kristindómr verit í Nóregi...*

Liestøl arranged the two lines in the inscription into A and B in a manner that has since become the 'official' reading, where line A – meant to be read first, according to Liestøl – actually comes *under* line B in the actual inscription when read horizontally. Following Liestøl, the reader first identifies those who raised the stone and the person in whose memory the stone is raised before we are told when the monument was created.

Liestøl could lean on a solid tradition within runic inscriptions for this arrangement of the lines. The memorial aspect in the raiser formula, which typically runs 'NN raised this stone after MM', is a common feature in all areas where Viking Age runestones are found,[29] while an indication of time is highly unusual. From this reasoning it is fair to assume that Liestøl found that the important message in the Kuli inscription intentionally will have been the raiser formula in what he called line A, and that the additional information in line B was a tangential extra that should be read at the end. If, however, it is correct that the idea to inform about the time of the event originates in a learned or annalistic practice, it is of importance to notice that in this tradition, the custom is to *first* inform about the time. Following this argument, the reading of the Kuli inscription should first state the time and then who did what. This reading will respect the writing practice that may be the inspiration

---

28. Liestøl 1957: 283.
29. Barnes 2012: 68.

behind the formulation both when it comes to the arrangement of information and the established reading of manuscripts where the scripture is always read from the top down and from left to right. Consequently, the reading should run (in translation):

Christianity had been twelve winters in Norway [...]

Þórir and Hallvarðr raised this stone in memory of Ulfljótr [...]

In sum, when analysing the Kuli inscription, we ought to give concession to the possibility that a writing tradition other than the runic lies behind the unusual information about time, and if so, we should allow for a reading of the inscription that pays respect to the reading practice in this tradition.

The Frösö stone is the most northerly runestone in Sweden and the only one found in Jämtland. The inscription informs us that in addition to letting the stone be raised and converting Jämtland, *Austmaðr* also let a bridge be built, and that *Ásbjǫrn* built the bridge. From this we read that while the latter was behind the actual building of the bridge, *Austmaðr* – clearly a chieftain with the contacts and power to convert a whole district, if we are to believe his own words – was initiating and probably financing the building of the bridge.[30]

This is not the place to discuss the likelihood of a bridge actually having been built from where the stone was placed, across the sound from the island over to the mainland – a distance close to 300 metres. More relevant here, it is worth noting that the

---

30. A wooden construction found close to the Kuli monument was long interpreted as a bridge but is now categorised as an unspecified structure. The bridge at Ravning Enge is presumably built by Harald Bluetooth but is not mentioned on the Jelling 2 inscription. Neither structures are considered in this article.

inscription mentions the completion of the bridge twice, thus giving it more prominence than the christening of Jämtland. In this way too, the Frösö stone links up with Central Swedish stones where bridgebuilding is a major topic in the commemorative inscriptions. A high percentage of runestones are located close to a bridge or a crossing, and of the seventy-six stones in Uppland and Södermanland with the word 'bridge', more than half have a cross.[31] The point has been made that on quite a few of these stones there is even a link between the cross and certain words in the inscription, where the arms of the cross point either to the name of the deceased or to the word 'bridge', and in that way link the person or the bridge to Christianity.[32] In the case of the Frösö stone, the left arm of the cross points to one of the two times 'bridge' is mentioned.

In both Norse pagan belief and in Christian cosmology, the bridge takes on the symbolic role as the liminal place between the living and the dead, and also the stage the traveller is in between departure and arrival. Both are dangerous stages, and bridges can help the transition. Many Scandinavian deposits of valuables and weapons by locations involving crossings confirm the importance given to such locations,[33] as do medieval Old Norse texts where we hear about *Gjallarbrú*, the bridge over to the world of the dead, and *Bifrost*, the bridge to the world of the gods, and in medieval Christian iconography, the bridge to Paradise becomes a frequent motif. In a situation where the bridge was a familiar symbol with a similar meaning in both pagan and Christian belief systems, it could be implied as a useful image that could help the transformation from the old to the new cosmology.

---

31. Lund 2005: 121.
32. Ibid.: 122.
33. Ibid.: 109–117.

## The Kuli stone: a recycled *bautastein*?

A monument can have had changing functions over time, and the Kuli stone may help to illustrate this point, for there is good reason to believe that the runestone on Kuli is a recycled raised stone.

Raised stones without inscriptions are in Norwegian referred to as *bautastein*. They are notoriously difficult to date, but the practice is likely to pre-date raised stones with runic inscriptions, and they may run as a parallel practice. A stone with a similar shape and geology to the stone on Kuli was discovered in the graveyard by the early medieval church on the neighbouring island Edøy,[34] and in the walls of the church are smaller pieces – possibly broken-up larger stones – with the same geological signature; a type of stone which is not local and is likely to have been transported over to the island.[35] There is a good chance that the runestone on Kuli will once have been a *bautastein*, and possibly one of several on the islands of Edøy and Kuli.

The prominent placement of many such scripture-less stones as part of grave structures and on top of burial mounds gives reason to believe that at least some will have had a commemorative function after a person or an event. A raised stone, however, is all that is left of a process of communication where, in most cases, we will never know the sender, the meaning of the message, and the intended receiver. As long as there is no inscription to communicate the purpose of the erected stone, its function will vanish with the memory of the person or event it was meant to pay tribute to. If a commemorative inscription is added to a standing stone, it secures at least the intention of the stone, although we are of course still left to interpret the complexity of the message.

---

34. This stone is now put up by the entrance of Edøen Mekaniske Verksted.
35. Heldal 2021: 129–132.

A monument can synchronically carry diverse messages to different but overlapping social layers. In the socially top-down type of conversion that took place in Scandinavia – as everywhere else – the newly Christened aristocracy will have seen the three monuments as externalised visual markers of their religious adherence, while locals – maybe still in a hiatus between beliefs – may have associated both the use of a standing stone and the use of runes with tradition and stability; a fact that will have lessened the impact of the message proclaiming a break with tradition.

During the tenth century, there was a tendency that many large burial mounds in the central Vestland region were no longer adorned with a bautastein but rather with a high stone cross, presumably with the intention to transform the pagan burial place of ancestors into a Christian site. In a wider social context, it is reasonable to interpret the action as dual communication. While signalling to the local population the upkeep of practice and ritual around the mound and the stone, the aristocracy could at the same time announce to their peers their novel faith by introducing the new symbol of the cross within the old routines.

## Jelling 2 and the missing cross

The grand layout of the Jelling complex itself may be inspired from Frankish and German rulers' demonstration of authority through monumental architecture,[36] and the immediate idea behind the big beast on face B may have been specific works by German goldsmiths.[37] In the main, however, the decoration on Jelling 2 shows inspiration from illuminated manuscripts from the ninth and tenth centuries. This is far from surprising

---

36. Pedersen 2012: 76–78.
37. Wamers 2000: 135–142.

in the light of Harald's own conversion, which came as a result of political pressure and missioning from the German Empire.

Two broadsides of Jelling 2 are dominated by skilful decorations. The main motives on the two faces are framed with connecting bands – an indication that the intention is to view the two pictures in connection with each other. Following the inscription that runs over the three sides of the stone and dominate Face A, we then on Face B see the figure of a lion-like beast: scary, with open mouth, fighting a zoomorphic snake-like creation, and on the subsequent Face C is a character with a halo, as a type familiar on icons of holy persons and arranged in the traditional Christ-on-the-cross position with arms stretched out. Naturally, the figure is assumed to be a depiction of Christ, and if so the oldest in Scandinavia.

Figure 4: Drawing of face B and C of Jelling 2 by Ida Schouw Andreasen, Benni Schouw Andreasen, Municipality of Vejle.
CC 2. The colours are speculative.

The reading of the two illustrations makes most sense if we follow the progression from the scary beast, which can represent the old beliefs, to the image of the victorious Christ; the triumphant king with raised head and open eyes. As such it is a characteristically early depiction of Christ, far from the suffering Christ with lowered head and closed eyes which become usual later in the medieval crucifix tradition. The fact that the figure is depicted over the runes that read 'and made the Danes Christian' strengthens the interpretation that this is a portrayal of Christ.

Following the assumption that there is a close connection between the runic text and the ornamentation, it may be more than a coincidence that the scary beast is placed over the name 'Norway' on Face B. When the runic text declares that Harald has won all of Denmark and Norway but has Christened Denmark only, it is fair to assume that Norway is left pagan and, consequently, that the illustration above the name 'Norway' attempts to illustrate exactly the fact that Norway is still left in pagan horror.

Remarkable, however, is the missing cross on Face C. Substituting the cross are intertwined vines around the figure's body and arms. This may illustrate Christ in the tree of life (in the Garden of Eden, Genesis 2:9), but also that there may be an allusion to Óðinn's sacrifice by hanging himself in the branches of Yggdrasill to attain knowledge about the world beyond our own.[38] Yet another possibility is that we see Christ but that he is hanging, not on a cross but in a tree, and not necessarily the biblical tree of life.

One of the motives discernible on the ornamental tapestries from the ninth-century ship-burial at Oseberg, Norway, is several people hanging from the branches of a tree.[39] The German

---

38. *Hávamál*, verses 138–141; Kure 2007: 69–70.
39. The branches end in heads of animals, possibly horses, and could be meant to illustrate *Yggdrasill*, which means '*Óðinn's horse*', where *Yggr* ('horror') is another name for *Óðinn*. The name *Yggdrasill* may then be a

bishop Thietmar of Merseburg[40] writes around AD 1015 about the christening of the Danes, but he also talks about the heathen practice at Lejre, Zealand, where every nine years they sacrifice ninety-nine humans along with an equal number of horses, dogs, and cocks. A similar practice is described by Adam of Bremen[41] at Old Uppsala in Sweden, adding the detail that the killed male humans and animals were strung up in trees. Archaeological excavations at Hov on Frösö have documented tenth-century human and animal bones around a large tree which had been cut down and had a church placed over it, with the altar placed on top of the stub of the tree. It has been suggested that the site can be associated with the ritual depicted by Thietmar and Adam.[42]

Figure 5: Section of the Oseberg tapestry. Reconstruction by Stig Saxegaard of Storm Studios as commissioned by the Museum of Cultural History. Reproduced with kind permission as first published in Vedeler 2019.

The practice above is described by Christian scholars with an agenda to portray the heathens in a negative light and who did not themselves observe the rituals first-hand. Further, the

---

kenning for 'gallow' (Heggstad 1975: 509).
40. Thietmar of Merseburg, Book I: chapter 17.
41. Adam of Bremen, Book IV: chapter 27.
42. Sandberg 2016: 20.

archaeological evidence is too scarce to claim a widespread practice, and we do not know if the ritual was familiar to people who saw the stone at Jelling. There is still a chance that the audience to the artist behind the Christ-like figure on Jelling 2 may have been more familiar with the branches of a tree as a place for sacrifice rather than a cross, and consequently, it can be claimed that even the Jelling depiction of Christ is a compromise between a traditional pagan and a new Christian iconography.

## Frösö and the Swedish rune cross

Both the Kuli and the Frösö stones are not free-standing high crosses but rather cross-stones where a cross is carved on the broad face of the slab, and as such they are probably less of a Christian statement and possible provocation than a free-standing cross will have been.

Found in 58% of the Swedish runestones,[43] the cross forms a visual, non-verbal expression to communicate a Christian concept. The frequency in Sweden of eleventh-century runestones with crosses forms a striking contrast to the resistance to Christianity among the Uppland royals and the fact that Sweden was not formally converted before the end of the eleventh century. It has been suggested[44] that the many runestones with a Christian content are raised at a time of religious and political tension by an aristocracy that – as a result of active English and German missioning – had converted and wished to express their new belief visually, while the Uppland royalty were fearful of losing their status as cultic leaders of the old faith.

---

43. Lager 2002: 73–75.
44. Brink 1990: 47.

The layout of the Frösö stone follows a well-established design from central Sweden. Typically, the cross is placed in the centre of the upper part of the monument where it forms a separate visual entity without any connection to the inscription or the rest of the ornamentation.[45] While the inspiration behind the crosses may be British,[46] the runestone crosses are unmistakably Swedish in shape and ornamentation, and the original designs are integrated into a unique context and a Scandinavian visual language.

## The cross on the Kuli stone

A single cross is the only decoration on the Kuli stone. The simple cross that ornates the broad face of the stone, without the complexity of sacrifice, is the type of Christian symbol that people from further south on the west coast of Norway will have been accustomed to seeing by the time the Kuli stone was erected. Many will have seen crosses during Viking expeditions to the British Isles, where crosses of various shapes and sizes furnished the landscape and buildings, and especially the Irish and Pictish Christians had perfected the carving of elaborate free-standing stone high crosses as well as cross-stones with elaborate ornamentations. Also, in the tenth century, stone crosses became a familiar sight along the Vestland region in Norway itself, and although much simpler than the insular crosses, an inspiration from the Irish and British practice

---

45. Another usual design, featuring on the runestone from Lilla Ramsjö, Heby, which is now prominently placed outside the School of Literatures, Languages and Cultures at the University of Edinburgh, has the cross in the centre of the stone, framed by the serpent and the runic inscription and is more integrated into the overall design on the stone.
46. Lager 2002: 193–195.

appears evident behind the Norwegian crosses and cross-stones.[47] Remarkably, many of the largest crosses are from the same quarry at Hyllestad, Sogn, and it has been suggested they should be associated with the tenth-century royal missioning attempts.[48]

The monument on Kuli is likely to have had a function as a domain marker for the current extent of the Christian faith. Kuli forms part of the portal of Trondheimsleia, the coastal entrance to Trøndelag, which in the second half of the tenth century was a region notoriously opposed to the advancement of Christianity along Vestlandet. Up till 995, it was ruled by Hákon, Earl of Lade, who aggressively burned churches and was praised by his court poets as a defender of the old beliefs, probably with the same fear as the rulers in Uppsala of losing his status as cultic leader. As *de facto* ruler of Norway, Hákon had first been under Danish overlordship but around AD 975 he broke his alliances with King Haraldr and blocked Danish attempts at regaining control of the Norwegian west coast. It is likely that Hákon's insistent opposition to Christian expansion was linked to his attempts to stem Danish political influence. The sons of Eiríkr Haraldsson (Bloodaxe) had ruled over Norway under Danish overlordship. These were Christians, brought up in Denmark and England, they had actively tried to destroy temples and symbols of the old faith, and most certainly will have had Danish support not only to win Norway politically but also to promote the Christian faith.

It makes sense on linguistic grounds[49] but also politically to date the Kuli stone to the very beginning of the millennium. The stone can in such a scenario be regarded as a demarcation for the west-Norwegian Christian domain, illustrated by the

---

47. Crouwers 2019.
48. Birkeli 1973; Crouwers 2019.
49. Schulte 2018: 154–155.

fact that the monument is the most northerly of the stone crosses and the cross-stones, and – prominently placed at the entrance to Trøndelag – it proudly announces to travellers that this is Christian land and that it has been so for twelve winters. If it is correct that the event that the inscription refers to took place under the early years of Óláfr Tryggvason's reign,[50] the runes would have been carved around the year 1007.

## Conclusion

Harald's stone at Jelling, the Kuli stone, and the Frösö stone are from an early and intensely transitional phase of the conversion. This article has hopefully demonstrated how the personal and social upheaval involved in this transformation found artistic expressions. However, none of Hallfreðr vandræðaskáld's personal religious torment is discernible in the three stone monuments. Instead, we notice the assured self-confidence of the aristocracy to whom Hallfreðr was a servant, a class that embraced the new religion in the knowledge it would sanction and secure their social position, but only if they could cleverly convince their people to take to the new faith without upsetting the social order. In this perspective there was a measured motive behind the compromise to promote the new faith in a recognisable framework, and the cultural luggage that came with the new faith was adapted to an indigenous familiar setting in order to minimise cultural provocation. And still, despite the possible tactical considerations, one can without difficulty admire the cultural confidence, even pride, behind the three monuments that first announce the new religion in Scandinavia.

---

50. Kruse 2021a: 26–28

## Bibliography

Adam of Bremen, *Gesta Hammabirgemsos ecclesiae Pontificum*; here referred after Lund, A. 2000. *Adam af Bremens Krønike*. Wormanium, 220–224.

Barnes, Michael P. 2012. *Runes: A Handbook*. Woodbridge: Boydell Press.

Birkeli, F. 1973. *Norske steinkors i tidlig middelalder. Et bidrag til belysning av overgangen fra norrøn religion til kristendom*. Oslo: Skrifter utgitt av Det Norske Videnskaps-Akademi i Oslo II. Hist.-Filos. Klasse. Ny Serie 10.

Brink, S. 1990. *Sockenbildning och sockennamn. Studier i äldre territoriell indelning i Norden*. Uppsala: Acta Academiae Regiae Gustavi Adolphi LVII.

Crouwers, I. 2019. *Late Viking-age and medieval stone crosses and cross-decorated stones in Western Norway. Forms, uses and perceptions in a Northwest-European context and long-term perspective*. PhD thesis. University of Bergen.

Einarsson, Bjarni (ed.) 1977. *Hallfreðar saga*. Reykjavík: Stofnun Árna Magnússonar.

Ellingsen, E.G. 2021. 'Arkeologien på Kuli'. In M. Stige and O. Risbøl (eds), *Kulisteinen – grensemerke i tid og rom*. Kristiansund: Nordmøre museum, 85–104.

Goeres, E.M. 2011. 'The Many Conversions of Hallfreðr vandræðaskáld'. In *Viking and Medieval Scandinavia* 7, 45–62.

Heggstad, L. 1975. *Norrøn ordbok*. Oslo: Det norske samlaget.

Heldal, T. 2021. 'Kulisteinens geologi og utforming'. In M. Stige and O. Risbøl (eds), *Kulisteinen – grensemerke i tid og rom*. Kristiansund: Nordmøre museum, 129–139.

Jesch, J. 2013. 'Reading the Jelling Inscription'. In P. Gammeltoft (ed.), *Beretning fra enogtredivte tværfaglige vikingesymposium*. Worminanum: Højbjerg, 7–18.

Kleivane, E. 2021. 'Kulisteinen og kommunikasjonen'. In M. Stige and O. Risbøl (eds), *Kulisteinen – grensemerke i tid og rom*. Kristiansund: Nordmøre museum, 151–170.

Kruse, A. 2020. 'On Harbours and Havens: Maritime Strategies in Norway during the Viking Age'. In A. Pedersen and S.M. Sindbæk (eds), *Viking Encounters. Proceedings of the Eighteenth Viking Congress, Denmark, August 6–12, 2017.* Aarhus University Press: Aarhus, 170–185.

———. 2021a. 'På grensa: Kulisteinen som geografisk og kulturell grensemarkør'. In M. Stige and O. Risbøl (eds) *Kulisteinen – grensemerke i tid og rom.* Kristiansund: Nordmøre museum, 13–33.

———. 2021b. 'Landsnamnet'. In M. Stige and O. Risbøl (eds), *Kulisteinen – grensemerke i tid og rom.* Kristiansund: Nordmøre museum, 106–112.

Kure, H. 2007. 'Hanging on the World Tree: Man and Cosmos in Old Norse Mythic Poetry'. In A. Andrén et al. (eds), *Old Norse Religion in Long-Term Perspectives: Origins, Changes and Interactions.* Nordic Academic Press: Lund, 68–73.

Lager, L. 2002. *Den synliga tron: runstenskors som en spegling av kristnandet i Sverige.* Occasional Papers in Archaeology 31. Institutionen för arkeologi och antik historia, Uppsala University.

Liestøl, A. 1957. '449. Kuli'. In M. Olsen (ed.), *Norges innskrifter med de yngre runer* 4. Oslo: Bokcentralen, 280–286.

Lund, J. 2005. 'Thresholds and Passages: The Meanings of Bridges and Crossings in the Viking Age and Early Middle Ages'. *Viking and Medieval Scandinavia* 1, 109–135.

Nielsen, K.M. 1974. 'Jelling problems: a discussion'. In *Mediaeval Scandinavia* 7, 156–179.

Orten Lie, R. 2014. 'Stjerneforma gravanlegg på Edøya'. Digitalt Museum. Kulturavdelinga, Møre & Romsdal fylke. https://digitaltmuseum.no/011085440404/stjerneforma-gravanlegg-pa-edoya Accessed 20 December 2021.

Pedersen, A. 2012. 'Nabo, fjende og forbillede – Danernes forhold til Tyskland i det arkæologiske fundbillede'. In P. Gammeltoft and N. Lund (eds), *Beretning fra tredivte tværfaglige vikingesymposium.* Worminanum: Højbjerg, 55–82.

———. 2017. 'Monumenterne i Jelling. Fornyet tradition på tærsklen til en ny tid'. In M. Manoe Bjerregaard and M. Runge (eds), *At være i centrum. Magt og minde – højstatusbegravelser i udvalgte centre 950–1450.* Odense, 44–61.

Roesdahl, E. 1999. 'Jellingstenen – en bog af sten'. O. Høiris et. al. (eds), *Menneskelivets mangfoldighed. Arkæologisk og antropologisk forskning på Moesgård.* Århus, 235–244.

Scandinavian Runic-text Database 2020, Department of Scandinavian Languages, Uppsala University. https://app.raa.se/open/runor/search. Accessed 15 April 2022.

Sandberg, N. 2016. 'Offerträdet. Spår av offer, blot och kult under vikingatiden på Frösön, Jämtland'. Kandidatuppsats i arkeologi. University of Stockholm.

Schulte, M. 2018. 'Vikingtiden (700–1050)'. In *Tidslinjer. Norsk språkhistorie* IV. Chapter 3. Novus. Oslo, 119–196.

Thietmar of Merseburg, here quoted from *Ottonian Germany. The Chronicon of Thietmar of Merseburg.* 2001. Translated and annotated by David A. Warner. Manchester University Press, 80.

Vedeler, Marianne. 2019. *The Oseberg Tapestries.* Oslo: Scandinavian Academic Press.

Wahlberg, M. (ed.). 2003. *Svenskt ortnamnslexikon.* Uppsala: Språk och folkminnesinstitutet.

Wamers, E. 2000. '… ok Dani gærði kristna […] Der große Jellingstein im Spiegel ottonischer Kunst'. In *Frühmittelalterliche Studien* 34. Taf. X–XVI, 132–158.

Whaley, D. 2003. 'The "Conversion Verses" in Hallfreðar saga: Authentic Voice of a Reluctant Christian?'. In Margaret Clunies Ross (ed.), *Old Norse Myths, Literature and Society*, Viking Collection 14. Odense: Odense University Press, 234–235.

Widukind: *Die Sachsengeschichte des Widukind from Korvei.* 1935 (repr. 1989). Paul Hirsch and H.-E. Lohmann (eds), Monumenta Germaniae Historica, Scriptores rerum Germanicarum in usum scholarum, Book I–III. Hannover: Hahn.

· 4 ·

# The Zorns in St Ives

## Helen Robinson

*Bjarne supervised my undergraduate dissertation in 2012–13 on the Swedish artist Anders Zorn with kindness and firmness that recognised my enthusiasm for Zorn's work. I first met Bjarne when I came to the Scandinavian Department in Buccleuch Place as a non-graduating student in 1987. His calm and patient teaching opened up the world of Scandinavian literature especially of H.C. Andersen and C.L. Almqvist and in my final year as a graduating student 2013 a love of Ingmar Bergman's films.*

Anders Zorn and his wife Emma were both only twenty-seven when they decided to spend some time in St Ives. Zorn was already a renowned watercolour painter and a great traveller. He and Emma had returned from France, Spain, and Algiers and had already had a trip back to Sweden in the summer. Zorn had been based in London since 1883 and had married Emma in October 1885. They were on their way to Spain via Plymouth when they visited St Ives and decided to linger there for a while. After the time in St Ives, they settled in Paris for eight years but continued to travel. It was during these few months at St Ives that Zorn started to paint in oils. This essay aims to investigate further the Zorns' sojourn in St Ives by considering the place, the people, and the point in time in Zorn's career. Three of Zorn's works painted in St Ives will be discussed in detail; *Emma läsande, Fiskare i St Ives* and *Fiskmarknad i St Ives*.

In 1887, St Ives was a small fishing town which had been discovered by a few artists. As Hermione Lee says in her biography of Virginia Woolf, 'from the early 1880s – long before the town had been made famous by its associations with Alfred Wallis, Bernard Leach, Barbara Hepworth or Patrick Heron – painters were arriving, drawn by the soft Mediterranean light and the seascapes and the picturesque fishing community'.[1] At that time there were artists' colonies in north-west France, particularly in Brittany. It has been suggested that some artists moved to Cornwall to escape an epidemic in Brittany.

St Ives is on the north coast of Cornwall. The main industry was fishing, especially for pilchards. The number of shoals of pilchards coming to St Ives declined drastically in the late 1880s. The coming of the railways made St Ives more accessible to visitors. St Ives station opened in 1877, as a branch line from St Erith on the main GWR line, a year later than Penzance station.

Artists came to both Newlyn from 1882 on the south coast of Cornwall, just beside Penzance, and then St Ives in 1885 to paint and establish new artists' colonies.[2] It has been said the St Ives was more international. The artists in both Newlyn and St Ives painted scenes of the sea and the fishing community. Joseph Mallord William Turner (1775–1851) had visited Cornwall and Devon as early as 1811. There are four sketches of St Ives in the British Museum.[3] It may be that Zorn saw these when he was in London as he is known to have visited the British Museum. He had an entry ticket to the print collection there.[4]

---

1. Lee 1997: 27.
2. Brown 1985: 1.
3. Ibid.
4. 'Anders Zorn Konstnären & samlaren'. http://www.alsing.com/zorn_sv/zorn.html. Accessed 25 August 2021.

Whistler was also a visitor to St Ives, though it is not certain that his visit coincided with the Zorns' stay. They did meet later in 1895, as Zorn noted in his autobiographical notes.[5]

Anders and Emma Zorn travelled to St Ives with Alice Miller, an English artist, at the beginning of December 1887.[6] Zorn described St Ives as a little international artists' colony.[7] They decided to stay and spend Christmas in St Ives. Emma and Alice, who shared lodgings, decorated them so that it was as much like a Swedish Christmas as possible. They had a pine tree and a Christmas tree and exchanged Christmas presents. It was the Zorns' third Christmas as a married couple and the third one spent away from Sweden.[8] There are a number of artists that we know were in St Ives at the same time as the Zorns thanks to autobiographical notes by Anders Zorn himself and by Henry Harewood Robinson in his article 'St Ives as an Art Centre'.[9] There are also several accounts of the early days of the St Ives artists' colony.[10]

Those most often mentioned are the Finnish artist Helene Schjerfbeck (1862–1946); the English artist Adrian Stokes (1854–1935) and his Austrian wife Marianne née Preindlesberger (1855–1927), who had previously been in Skagen artists' colony; Emma Löwstädt Chadwick and Frank Chadwick; Edward Simmons, an American artist; and the Norwegian artist Bernt Grönwold and his wife. W.H.Y. Titcomb, an English artist, was also resident in St Ives in 1887. Marianne Stokes was at Pont-Aven, in Brittany, with Helene Schjerfbeck.

The two years after their marriage had been very busy for

---

5. Brummer 1994: 298.
6. Anders Zorn Konstnären & samlaren'. http://www.alsing.com/zorn_sv/zorn.html. Accessed 25 August 2021.
7. Zorn 1982: 57.
8. Sandström 2010: 60.
9. Robinson in Whybrow 1994: 21.
10. Whybrow 1994: 21.

Zorn and Emma. They had travelled extensively although based in England. Their honeymoon in Istanbul had been complicated by Zorn becoming seriously ill with typhoid fever. He took three months to recover.[11] They then spent summer in Sweden, both in Dalarö in the Stockholm archipelago and in Mora in Dalarna. The winter and spring of 1887 were spent in north Africa and Spain. In autumn they returned to England, and in December came to St Ives. This was a time for relaxation according to Zorn.

The combination of place, people, and a period of 'free time' may have led to Anders Zorn experimenting with oil paint and changing the trajectory of his career. Up to 1887, Zorn had made his reputation as a renowned watercolourist who painted portraits and landscapes and genre paintings. He had of course had experience of painting with oils when a student at the Konstakademien in Stockholm and had produced the occasional oil painting such as *The artist's studio, Brook Street* in 1882. He worked equally happily with watercolours and oil painting according to the author of Mollbrinks booklet.[12]

It has been pointed out that Zorn was already good at oils, though Zorn himself thought that the move to oils was a breakthrough. Emma regarded it with more practical criticism, complaining about the smell and the difficulty of cleaning the brushes. Brigitta Sandström says that St Ives was where Zorn painted his first more important oil paintings.[13]

*Emma läsande* (*Emma reading*) was painted in 1887. It is Zorn's first serious oil painting. It measures 40.2 cm by 60 cm and shows Emma reading a newspaper in a domestic setting. Emma is in the foreground and is wearing a high-necked grey blouse or dress. Only her head and shoulders are seen. She has a

---

11. Den svenska mästaren Anders Zorn', https://www.barnebys.se/blogg/den-svenska-mastaren-anders-zorn. Accessed 25 August 2021.
12. Mollbrinks: 1.
13. Sandström 2005: 71.

brooch at her neck which Zorn has made sparkle. Her face is in three-quarter view, and her left hand is in the foreground. This shows her rings and may underline the fact that the Zorns are relatively recently married. She is engrossed in what she is reading and appears to be short-sighted. The newspaper itself has no writing on it. The columns of print are implied by the different tones of white. This may be an artistic device or an attempt 'to rub out the extremely stormy times he lived through' (author's translation) as the journalist and poet, Göran Greider says.[14]

Emma's face is well lit from the left of the picture and is its focal point, even though the newspaper takes up more space. The background shows a corner of a room with a mantel shelf behind her, wallpapered walls, and a picture on the back wall. The mantelpiece has a shiny metal bowl on it with flowers and a mirror behind it. There is a cloth hanging from the mantelpiece which is patterned and looks modern, like part of an Elizabeth Blackadder painting. There is some writing in Latin along the top left – 'AETATIS SUAE 27' (her age 27). This is a device more often used in Renaissance paintings as Brigitta Sandström pointed out.[15]

The style of the painting is impressionistic, and the colours in the palette are muted. The American artist Edward Simmons helped Zorn to choose the range of colours of his oil paints. According to Sandström's research, the colours which dominated were cinnabar (red) and light ochre. Both zinc white and lead white, ivory black, cadmium yellow, emerald green, and cobalt blue are also used.[16] The brushstrokes are visible, particularly in the bottom left. Zorn has signed the painting and dated it 1887. Beneath that he has written St Yves.[17]

---

14. Greider 2010.
15. Sandström 2010: 60.
16. Ibid. 2005: 34.
17. *Emma läsande* is now in the Zorn Museum art gallery in Mora. The

Figure 1: *Emma läsande* (Zorn Museum).

The next oil painting Zorn produced was *Fiskare i St Ives* (*Fisherman in St Ives*). This is considered to be a more technically accomplished work. It is dated 1888 and is now in the Musée des Beaux Arts in Pau in south-west France. It was shown in the Paris Salon in spring of 1888 and bought by the French State for 1,000 Francs. This was a great honour for Zorn.[18] It was then on view in the Luxembourg Gallery in Paris. Zorn made an etching of *Fiskare i St Ives* in 1891 and this is in Mora, Sweden, in Zornmuseet. This is the image more often shown in books on Zorn. The etching measures 27.8 cm by 20 cm.

The oil painting shows two figures, a man and a woman, leaning over a wall. They are looking out over the harbour. The two figures are in the middle ground of the painting with their backs turned towards the viewer. The woman is standing next to a lamp post which is at the right side of the painting.

---

author and editor gratefully acknowledge the museum and the Zorn Collections' extensive work in preserving the works of Zorn, and thank them for their permission to reproduce the picture here.
18. Sandström 2010: 60.

The lamp post is remarkable because it makes the picture look asymmetrical and was itself a fairly recent invention. There is a road between the viewer and the figures. The woman is wearing a pink dress with an apron. In the background is the harbour and part of the town of St Ives. The colours, as seen in reproductions, are muted. Both figures are in workaday clothes and are presumed to represent local fishing people.

Figure 2: *Fiskare i St Ives.*

Whilst he was in St Ives, Zorn painted a large watercolour of a woman selling fish on the beach, *Fiskmarknad i St Ives* (*Fish Market in St Ives*). This is a large painting, which is a very jolly picture and measures 100 cm by 76.5 cm. The main figure is in the middle ground to the right of centre and is looking over her shoulder at a group of fishermen who are standing near the edge of the sea to the left of the picture. There are several boats near the shore on the top left. One of the fishermen is looking directly at the fishwife. She is a strongly built woman who is holding a large fish in her left hand and wearing a straw hat which covers her eyes. She is said to be a woman Zorn saw in St Ives and wanted to paint.

Figure 3: *Fiskmarknad i St Ives*.

In the foreground there is part of a boat which appears to be full of seaweed. The three fish in the foreground on the left appear to be looking at the viewer. They may be gurnards. In the absence of the shoals of pilchards St Ives was originally famous for, the fishermen caught other fish, including gurnards, and which were sold on the beach and then transported to London. The coming of the railways would have made this easier.

The water is portrayed with Zorn's usual mastery. The reflections of the boats make the sea look dark and make a contrast with the figures of the fishermen. This picture was on show at Börjeson art collection at the Green Hotel in Tällberg, Sweden, but was sold at auction in 2018. Its present whereabouts are unknown. There is a good reproduction online.[19]

The Newlyn painter, Stanhope Forbes (1857–1947) painted *A Fish Sale on a Cornish Beach* in oils in 1884–85 which was shown at the Royal Academy in London. It is possible that Zorn may have seen it when he was in London and been influenced by it. It is a much busier picture than *Fiskmarknad i St Ives*, but the arrangement of the fish in the foreground and the people between the viewer and the sea is familiar. Perhaps Zorn's decision to come to Cornwall was influenced in part by Forbes' painting and those like it.

Zorn also painted a portrait of Alice Miller, *Målarinnan Alice* (*The Painter Alice*) in oils at St Ives in 1887. It shows a serious woman looking out of the picture at the viewer. She may be sitting at a table as there is a dining chair to her left. There is a pot plant and a wall with two pictures behind her. The portrait lacks the feeling of tenderness and affection engendered in *Emma läsande*. This painting may have been an

---

19. 'Den svenska mästaren Anders Zorn', https://www.barnebys.se/blogg/den-svenska-mastaren-anders-zorn. Accessed 25 August 2021.

'exercise' for Zorn, as Alice was one of the main people in St Ives who helped and encouraged him in his oil painting.

The Zorn couple's three months in St Ives is remembered mostly as the springboard for Zorn's career as a successful oil painter. Most of the portraits Zorn painted after his time in St Ives were in oil. This part of his career flourished in the following eight years that Anders and Emma spent based in Paris (1888–96). They did not stop travelling in those years. The partnership between Anders and Emma Zorn continued for the whole of Anders' life. Emma was often his model and his muse. The newly regained mastery of oil paint was added to Zorn's mastery of watercolour painting, etching, and sculpture. There is no denying Zorn's technical skill, which Göran Greider said *'känns som trolleri'* ('feels like enchantment').[20]

## Bibliography

'Anders Zorn Konstnären & samlaren'. http://www.alsing.com/zorn_sv/zorn.html. Accessed 25 August 2021.

Brown, David. 1985. *'Introduction' in Cornwall 1925–1975 'a sense of place… a sense of light'*. London: The Ranelagh Press.

Brummer, Hans Henrik. 1994. *Till ögats fröjd nationens förgyllning – Anders Zorn*. Stockholm: Norstedts.

Cederlund, Johan et al. 2013. *Anders Zorn Sweden's Master Painter*. New York: Fine Arts Museums of San Francisco and Skira Rizzoli Publications Inc.

'Den svenska mästaren Anders Zorn'. https://www.barnebys.se/blogg/den-svenska-masteren-anders-zorn. Accessed 25 August 2021.

Greider, Göran. 2010. '"Zorns mästerverk" på Zornmuseet'. *Dagens Nyheter*. 19 May.

Lee, Hermione. 1997. *Virginia Woolf*. London: Vintage.

Mollbrinks Konst. *Zorn*. Uppsala: Mollbrinks Konst AB.

---

20. Greider 2010.

Sandström, Birgitta. 2005. *Anders Zorn*. Stockholm: Natur och Kultur.

———. 2010. In Johan Cederlund (ed.), *Zorn Mästerverk*. Mora: Zornmuseet.

Siden, Karin and Meister, Anna (eds). 2016. *Ljusets magi. Friluftsmåleri från sent 1800-talet*. Stockholm: Prins Eugens Waldemarsudde.

Whybrow, Marion. 1994. *St Ives 1883–1993 Portrait of an Art Colony*. Woodbridge, Suffolk: the Antique Collector's Club Ltd.

Zorn, Anders. 1982. *Självbiografiska anteckningar* (autobiographical notes) with commentary by Hans Henrik Brummer. Stockholm: Bonniers.

## Works Cited

Forbes, Stanhope. 1884–85. *A Fish Sale on a Cornish Beach*. [Oil on canvas].

Zorn, Anders. 1882. *The artist's studio, Brook Street*. [Oil on canvas].

———. 1887a. *Emma läsande*. [Oil on canvas].

———. 1887b. *Målarinnan Alice*. [Oil on canvas].

———. 1888a. *Fiskare i St Ives*. [Oil on canvas].

———. 1888b. *Fiskmarknad i St Ives*. [Watercolour].

· 5 ·

# A Duel of Shine and Shadow

## Eric Cain

*I spent a year studying under Bjarne earning a MScR degree focusing on narrative and genre in crime fiction and fantasy horror fiction works, both literature and film. Excited by the rich history of fable and folklore in Danish and other Nordic cultures, I keyed in on classic and modern works alike, spanning Benjamin Christensen and Victor Sjöström to contemporaries such as Lars von Trier and Tomas Alfredsson. Among the innovative early films,* Vampyr, *stands out in particular due to a combination of visual and story cues via light and shadow that arouses our suspicion of fantasy while we look in on the travels of the young male protagonist. Bjarne's enthusiasm for this film and many others encouraged me to partake on later study specifically discussing narration qualities in a few early, Nordic horror films.*

Light and dark, objective and subjective. Either/or, but with a space between? Like the gauze pulled over his camera lens to set the visual atmosphere, Carl Theodor Dreyer, in his 1932 film, *Vampyr*, casts a haze over our clear impression of the mysterious events of Allan Gray's nocturnal encounters and their meaning in the sense of an orderly, concrete understanding of life experiences.

A studious and enthusiastic traveller himself, our guide soon encounters an unknown visitor, an unintelligible warning, and an unopened parcel. Gray senses a plea for assistance and ventures out, only to find himself drawn into a vampire's cruel seduction and capture of two young sisters with the aid of an enabling doctor. We move along with Gray, investigating the activities of a cohort of witches, ghosts, shadows, and a vampire through the contours of a countryside village and its residents. But beyond the explicit narrative of Dreyer's supernatural story, the optic vicissitudes of shine and shadow slowly dance before us in this tale of investigation and discovery, evoking brooding questions and challenging settled notions about things known and unknown.

As we follow Gray and others in their attempts to ward off the vampire, we are as much looking at their soft-focus shadows as themselves in each frame. Although it is a black-and-white film, in nearly every shot, light shining upon each actor generates a shadow on the background set, used both in the fabulaic sense, such as to depict Gray's engagement with the supernatural when he witnesses dancing shadows on the wall of an uninhabited house interior, and in the metaphorical sense, such as to denote the constant accompaniment of mystery and unease to our concrete and objective notions of space and time. Dreyer's film exploits this visual motif to impose an anxiety about unnatural, unreal, or otherwise indeterminate experiences, not only of Gray and others within his narrative but also inclusive of our own, human experiences, beyond those which are easily explained. Shadows partake in activities such as playing music and dancing, performing manual labour like digging, opening and closing doors, and even shooting a rifle. While we do not see the character from which the shadow emanates in the frame, the visuals imply a disembodiment of the shadow from its antecedent.

For maximum effect, a late sequence depicts Gray's shadow rising from a park bench while its host slumbers, shortly after giving blood to save an ailing young woman's life. We follow Gray's shadow in an out-of-body experience through a dreamy, future scenario foretelling the vampire asserting its grip over Gray's soul and the interment of his body in a coffin. While Gray looks at himself in a prospective future, the shadow's experience offers himself, and thus the viewers ourselves, as a metaphorical extension, a moment of hesitation, or a suggestion to think outside of our collective sense of objectivity.

This moment instigates the twitch when our head tilts slightly, or when a crack appears in the door left slightly ajar, and something from outside our understood, definitive experience creeps in, by invitation or not. Dreyer's use of light and dark directs us to follow the diegetic assertions of objectivity and subjectivity, such as through Gray's experiences in normal state and in dream state, but it is the shadows throughout that mar the obvious distinction between these dimensions. In turn, the visual foxtrot of shine and shadow fill the film and its viewers with an ever more blurred sense of real and unreal amid the ensemble of grey hues. Even though Gray arrives at the village by boat in the darkness of night and he leaves the village walking into the glow of the day, it is the sequence, in terms of both plot and metaphor, between these checkpoints that really evokes the ponderance and wonder central to the film.

Dreyer's film is thus suggestive of an existing space between the obvious comfort of black or white, and the simple, precise nature of objectivity. A cast shadow exhibits a liminality in that its body is not tangible like wood or animal flesh, but the form appearing from blocked light rays is easily recognised by human senses. This quality lends credence to our human perception of fantastic experiences, which are not easily understood or acknowledged, and fall somewhere between fully objective or subjective. The fantastic begs us to evaluate the far reaches of our 'safe haven' notions of what is and is not.

The power of the film is to invite us to revisit our own frameworks of experiential sentiment, just like Bjarne's supervision regularly forced me to critically examine my own approaches to literature and film and then test out new ones, which more often than not bore the fruit of novel strands of discourse in my thinking. Watching the film, we are invited to articulate the existence of something beyond our typical wisdom but meanwhile not altogether an abstract conception. The shine and shadow employed extensively throughout the work pose a visual interpretation of broad and complex human experiences which ask more questions than provide corresponding answers.

## Filmography

*Vampyr*. 1932. Film. Directed by Carl Theodor Dreyer. Germany: Carl Theodor Dreyer-Filmproduktion Tobis-Filmkunst.

· 6 ·

# *Bevægelsesdramatik*: The Railway Film and the Danish and British Documentary Movements

## C. Claire Thomson

In August 1948, a group of four young Danish filmmakers piled into a Ford Anglia and set off from Copenhagen. Festooned with a yellow pennant reading 'DANISH DOCUMENTARY', the car's destination was Edinburgh, where the International Festival of Documentary Films[1] was about to take place for the second time. Their road trip took them across the Netherlands and through London, where they stopped for a few days to visit Film Centre on Soho Square. There, they met with two of the leading lights of the British Documentary Movement, Arthur Elton (later Sir Arthur) and Alberto Cavalcanti.[2] Waiting for the Danes in Edinburgh were their more senior compatriots Ebbe Neergaard, head of the national film distribution centre Statens Filmcentral, and two leading documentarists, Theodor Christensen and Søren Melson, not to mention international grandees such as Robert Flaherty. In the guestbook of the film

---

1. The festival was established under this title in 1947, later changing its name and remit to the Edinburgh International Film Festival for its fourth iteration in 1950. A year-by-year record of opening galas, programmes, and memories can be found at the EIFF Memories web resource: http://www.edfilmfestmemories.org.uk/timeline/home.html.
2. Sevel 2006: 46–47.

festival that August, the signatures of all seven of the Danish contingent can be seen.³

At the festival, they would have seen the world premiere of Flaherty's *Louisiana Story* (1948) and Roberto Rossellini's *Germania anno zero* ('Germany Year Zero', 1948). They would have been able to 'meet and mingle with their colleagues and discuss their common problems', and listen to lectures and discussions that aimed to 'create an opportunity for the reconsideration and reassessment of the principles and methods of the documentary movement'.⁴ The festival was explicitly designed as an event that would showcase international documentary productions and provide a milieu where filmmakers could exchange ideas and push the field forward.

The Edinburgh International Festival of Documentary Films was Britain's first film festival, and it seemed natural to the organisers that it would specialise in 'the factual film', the sphere in which 'Scotland can claim to have made a distinctively national contribution to the cinema'.⁵ From the festival's first iterations, the organisers recognised Denmark as a nation whose 'documentary film movement is quite out of proportion to the size of the country'⁶; as 'a spirited documentary movement, serving its country's needs with resource and imagination' and whose principles and practice were very much in line with 'the British example'.⁷ The admiration was mutual, and inspiration flowed in both directions. Evidence for the bilateral influence of Danish and British documentary movements is more than circumstantial and is predicated on movement: the travels of filmmakers, film reels, equipment, books, papers, sounds, and images.

3. EFDF guestbook 1948, Edinburgh Film Guild Archive.
4. Hardy 1950: 35.
5. Ibid.: 34.
6. Hardy 1948: 18.
7. Hardy 1949: 18.

This essay considers a sub-genre of the mid-century documentary or informational film in which the cross-currents of influence across the North Sea are easy to discern: the railway film. This enables us to consider how the representation of movement, in a medium predicated on movement, was indeed dependent on the movements of films and filmmakers between festivals, screening rooms, and cities – in a range of vehicles.

## Planes, trains, and automobiles

These cross-currents between the Danish and British documentary scenes were nothing new. The director and theorist Theodor Christensen (1914–67), often referred to as the 'grand old man' of Danish documentary, had travelled to London with colleagues in 1939. He was to screen his new documentary for Minerva Film about the trans-Iranian railway, built by the Danish firm Kampsax. Christensen had been able to gather Cavalcanti, Basil Wright, Harry Watt, Paul Rotha, and the legendary Scottish film pioneer John Grierson to watch *Iran – Det nye Persien* ('Iran – The New Persia', 1939).[8]

This forty-six-minute film documents the feat of Danish engineering in great detail, as well as the changing culture of Iran and its varied terrain, which had necessitated the building of 250 bridges and 250 tunnels. But the final two minutes of the film descend into a fast-paced choreography of steam, pistons, wheels, and criss-crossing rails, overlaid with a Danish-language voiceover reciting a poetic text about the thrill of train travel and the marvels of Scandinavian engineering. The flagrant borrowings from Watt and Wright's 1936 classic documentary about the postal train from London to Edinburgh, *Night Mail*,

---

8. *Iran – Det nye Persien*.

were impossible to miss, even if the British filmmakers in the room could not understand the film's Danish voiceover. As the credits rolled, Grierson drily remarked: 'In Scotland we kill people for less than that.'[9]

Nonetheless, it was probably on this trip that another filmmaker from the Minerva stable and a co-director of the Iran film, Ingolf Boisen (1904–90), bought a camera from the London documentarists. It was a Newman-Sinclair, a lightweight workhorse of a camera, and had been used to film *Night Mail*. Boisen would later use it on the set of his film about the new transatlantic aviation route from Scandinavia to New York pioneered by SAS, *They Guide You Across* (1949).

In April 1948, cameraman Nic Lichtenberg was positioned towards the end of the runway at Copenhagen Kastrup airport, primed to film the take-off of a transatlantic DC4. The plane's captain, 'Yankee' Hedall-Hansen, had been asked to try to lift wheels as close to the camera as possible. In the event, he overshot, hitting the Newman-Sinclair with the front wheel of the aircraft. Lichtenberg jumped clear, and lived to make the road trip to Edinburgh with Ove Sevel a few months later. But the camera was smashed to smithereens; sixty metres of precious footage and hundreds of shards of glass and metal lay strewn across the runway. From Prestwick in Scotland, where the plane had to stop to refuel, came a telegram: 'SORRY OLD BOY COULD NOT SEE THE BOX – HEDALL'.[10]

These anecdotes illustrate not only the professional and personal links between Danish and British documentarists before and after the Second World War but also the extent to which modes of transportation served as subject matter for documentary and informational filmmaking at the time. There is nothing

---

9. Roos 1968: 150; Boisen 1977: 151.
10. Boisen 1977: 227–228; Thomson 2018: 88–89.

mysterious about this: such films tend to be commissioned to document or explain novelties and achievements, to reassure the public about safety, or to inculcate particular behaviours, and to enlighten domestic and international audiences about national heritage, landscape, culture, or infrastructure. Films about railways can fulfil all these criteria. But filming rail travel also affords many exciting possibilities for the filmmaker: fast and slow sonic and visual rhythms; the geometry of the tracks and the machinery; the motion of the train against static landscape, cityscape, or sky; the intersecting stories and paths of passengers and railway workers; the connective tissue of rail routes across nations and national borders. We might even say that such films enact a kind of *landvinding*, to use the term that Bjarne Thorup Thomsen adopts in his monograph on Selma Lagerlöf's literary 'land acquisition'. But they do so in ways that are medium-specific and peculiar to the political, cultural, and technological context of mid-twentieth-century informational filmmaking.

## The Danish and British documentary scenes

The road trip with which this essay opened is recounted in a biography by Ove Sevel (1922–2006), who later rose to be CEO of Nordisk Film, the Danish film company founded in 1906 and still dominant to this day. With him in the little car were Jørgen Roos (1922–98), later a renowned director of documentaries, talented film editor, and Academy Award nominee for his short *A City Called Copenhagen* (1960). Two men from the smaller company Minerva Film came along too: Erik Witte (1919—), who had worked at Ministeriernes Filmudvalg, the Danish Government Film Committee, and Nicolai (Nic) Lichtenberg (1915–78), at that point a cinematographer, who would go on to be a prolific writer and director of documentary and educational films.[11] In the car, then, was a microcosm of the Danish documentary scene at the time.

In 1947, the Scottish film pioneer Forsyth Hardy had written that Denmark's documentary production 'would not shame a country six times its size'[12]; indeed, the inaugural Edinburgh festival had featured no fewer than half a dozen Danish shorts that had been produced in the immediate post-war period.[13]

This new 'golden age' for Danish documentary had its roots during the German occupation of Denmark (April 1940–May 1945). The invasion had triggered counter-measures on the part of the Danish government to bolster the somewhat anaemic state-sponsored film institutions: In 1941, Beskæftigelsesfilmudvalget (the Committee for Employment Films) was established to coordinate funding and production of short informational films designed to promote the Danish war effort and wartime industries – as well as to keep German National Socialist films out of the cinemas. This committee soon acquired a remit to coordinate filmmaking across government, morphing into Ministeriernes Filmudvalg, which would grace the opening titles of many an informational film across the world in the decades to come as The Danish Government Film Committee.[14] This committee worked in tandem with Dansk Kulturfilm, a semi-governmental agency established in 1932 and tasked with making films for '*uddannelse, oplysning og almen propaganda*' ('education, enlightenment and general propaganda') in support of Denmark's many civil associations, tourist boards, charities, and so on.[15] Taking charge of the

---

11. 'Filmdatabasen'.
12. Hardy 1947: n.p.
13. Thomson 2018: 64.
14. Nørrested and Alsted 1987: 175–187; Sørensen 2014: 105–108, 340–356.
15. Thomson 2018: 48–49.

distribution of the film output of these organisations was Statens Filmcentral, the State Film Centre, established in 1938, and later a production house in its own right.

These agencies provided funding and infrastructure for a generation of Danish filmmakers to consolidate their skills in the service of the war effort, making films that informed the public about the needs of the wartime economy – encouraging the collection of scrap metal, documenting housing improvement projects, promoting Danish agricultural produce, directing unmarried mothers to sources of aid. But they also indirectly facilitated an environment in which the Danish documentary scene forged links with the emerging Resistance movements.

The manoeuvres and actions of the latter were often captured on film; it was possible, by 1944, for Major Ole Lippmann (pseudonym Lund) to travel to London to be groomed for leadership of the SOE (Special Operations Executive). With him he carried a batch of illegal footage of Resistance activities provided by Theodor Christensen that made its way to the US; the footage was edited into the English-language film *Denmark Fights for Freedom* and distributed to twenty-four countries by the US Office of War Information while the war was still raging.[16]

Ministeriernes Filmudvalg was acutely aware of the potential of film to promote Denmark as a small, modern, peaceful, progressive nation on the side of the Allies, and even before the Liberation in May 1945 had laid plans for after the expected defeat of Hitler: they would invite English documentarist Arthur Elton (1906–73) to oversee the production of one or more short films about Denmark to be distributed in the UK. The resulting series of five films, under the rubric *Social Denmark*, was completed by 1947 – and several of them

---

16. 'Denmark Fights for Freedom'.

were screened at the first Edinburgh International Festival of Documentary Film.[17]

That the British Documentary Movement was such an inspiration for the Danes was not just because of the historical and cultural ties between the two countries. As we have seen, Danish filmmakers were excited, both before and after the war, to visit London and Edinburgh as centres of documentary film culture. The aforementioned John Grierson (1898–1972) was a dour and canny Scot who had tested out his wealth of ideas about the purpose of filmmaking with the documentary *Drifters* (1929), before pouring his energies into creating an infrastructure to support informational filmmaking in Britain and worldwide. Recognised as a 'producer, organiser, facilitator, recruiter and propagandist'[18] for his movement, he was a key figure in British film organisations including the Empire Marketing Board Film Unit, the GPO (General Post Office) Film Unit, the Central Office of Information, Film Centre, and the Films of Scotland Committee.

The influence of Grierson and the British Documentary Movement was felt worldwide – Grierson moved to Canada in 1938 to establish the National Film Board there, and the British Colonial Office established film units and training in Malaya, Ghana, India, and elsewhere with a 'missionary zeal'.[19] Denmark, too, played a leading role in the worldwide dissemination of the documentary idea and its necessary infrastructure: the head of Ministeriernes Filmudvalg, Mogens Skot-Hansen (1908–84), moved to Paris as early as 1947 to work at the United Nations Film Board, and Theodor Christensen was instrumental in developing filmmaker training in Cuba at the pioneering Instituto Cubano del Arte

---

17. Thomson 2018: 64–85.
18. Richards 2011: 1.
19. Grierson 1979: 206–207.

e Industria Cinematográficos (ICAIC, Cuban Institute of Cinematographic Art and Industry).[20]

Grierson had defined the term 'documentary' in a review of Robert Flaherty's *Moana* (US, 1926), and his turn of phrase, 'the creative treatment of actuality', is well known as encapsulating the central power and paradox of documentary. As an instinctive social democrat, he regarded the task of documentary to be a 'socially purposive cinema which would bestow recognition and dignity on the working man [...] and would at the same time inform and educate the newly enfranchised mass electorate to function in a participatory democracy'.[21] To achieve this, films did not need to be dull and didactic, but could adopt a number of aesthetic strategies:

> The documentary idea demands no more than that the affairs of our time shall be brought to the screen in a fashion which strikes the imagination and makes observation a little richer than it was. At one level, the vision may be journalistic, at another, it may rise to poetry and drama. At another level again, its aesthetic quality may lie in the mere lucidity of its expression.[22]

The Danish documentarists found such ideas *simpatico*, engaged as they were in mediating the burgeoning welfare state to their fellow citizens and to admiring international audiences. But their practice was also directly informed to an extent by the advice received from Arthur Elton in his post-Liberation report commissioned by Ministeriernes Filmudvalg. For Elton, the Danes were a little too good at poetry and drama: in his 1945 report, he described the qualities of the Danish films he had been shown as including 'fresh, lively and human direction'; 'a gay and

---

20. Roos 1968: 151.
21. Richards 2011: 2.
22. Cited in Hardy 1979: 13.

imaginative touch in a number of propaganda films'; 'imaginative and clever editing'; and 'fine and luminous photography' but warned that 'any preoccupation with film technique for its own sake' would hinder their ability to communicate their message.[23] These, then, are the sometimes conflicting priorities that we can glimpse in the films at which we now turn to look more closely.

## Choreographies of the tracks

*Night Mail* (1936) needs no introduction, such is its place in the British film canon. But for the same reason, it is easy to forget that for much of its twenty-four minutes, the film is essentially a process film, detailing how the mail is sorted and distributed on the route from London to Edinburgh Waverley. Much attention is paid to the laborious sorting of mail into pigeonholes, and especially to the correct techniques for securing postal sacks so that they are caught by spring-loaded hooks beside the track as the train whistles past.

Equally, the film is concerned with mapping the geography of mainland Britain; as the train forges northwards, letters destined for east and west are discussed, and workers' accents evolve as new staff are taken on board. Not until the last five minutes does the famous poem by W.H. Auden emerge in the voiceover (partly in Grierson's voice), intoning over the clickety-clack of the train: 'This is the night mail crossing the border, bringing the cheque and the postal order…' For many viewers today, the preceding twenty minutes with muddy sound and interminable sorting processes are something of a trial, though contemporary audiences were enthusiastic.[24]

---

23. Elton 1945: 2.
24. Sargeant 2011: 56.

For the Danish filmmakers of the time, however, *Night Mail* seems to have functioned as a cultural lodestone. In his memoir, Ingolf Boisen relates how he and his colleagues at Minerva Film ordered copies of GPO Film Unit productions: Basil Wright's *Song of Ceylon* (1934), Paul Rotha's *Shipyard* (1935) – and of course, a copy of *Night Mail*:

*Gang på gang sad vi i Minervas lille biograf og fulgte natposttogets ekspresfart fra London til Aberdeen i Skotland, betaget af filmens intense billedvirkning og fascinerende lydside – den perfekte balance mellem de hårde reallyde fra toget, arbejdet med postsækkene, de korte replikker og mod slutningen af filmen Benjamin Brittens musik og W.H. Audens digt [...] strofer, der som en syntese af billed og lyd blev hængende i erindringen.*[25]

Again and again we sat in Minerva's little screening room and followed the journey of the night mail express from London to Aberdeen [sic] in Scotland, enchanted by the film's intense visual effects and fascinating soundtrack – the perfect balance between the harsh recorded sounds from the train, the hard work with the postal sacks, the short lines of dialogue and towards the end of the film, Benjamin Britten's music and W.H. Auden's poem [...] stanzas that lingered in the memory as a synthesis of image and sound.

These viewings took place before Boisen, Christensen, and their colleagues Axel Lerche and Tove Hebo set off to film Kampsax's work in Iran. Thus, the influence of *Night Mail* on *Iran – Det nye Persien*, to which Grierson responded with teasing Scots menace, is more than circumstantial. More interesting is Boisen's emphasis on how *Night Mail* inspired the Danes to

---

25. Boisen 1977: 148.

develop their mastery of sound. This was no more than a decade after the advent of sound films, and for documentarists shooting out in the open, the challenges of sound were enormous. As Boisen explains, there was no such thing as a tape recorder in the 1930s, nor was it possible to record satisfactory sound on the narrow-gauge film that documentarists typically used. A soundtrack had to be recorded in the studio or in the field on 35 mm film, developed, and then scaled down to 16 mm and printed onto the 16 mm image track. However, Minerva Film decided to set an engineer by the name of P.F. Beer at the Copenhagen company Fonofilm the challenge of developing a portable 16 mm camera that could also record high-quality sound – which he did, in 1938. The Danish company Minerva was thus the first in the world to boast such a camera, and the creative possibilities that it opened up for capturing and mediating the sounds of the railway in Iran were considerable.[26]

In practice, however, much of the film's soundtrack relies on the original musical score, composed by the renowned Kai Rosenberg[27], and a dramatic voiceover whose echoing, booming tone emphasises the diktat to perform the impossible and build the railway in just six years. There are, though, sequences in the film when environmental sound features. The baa-ing of a flock of sheep, for example, is captured on a mountain road, and contrasts with the hum of the crew's car engines. One sequence records the clack of typewriter keys and the Morse code of telegram signals, as instructions are transmitted from Kampsax in Copenhagen to its engineers in Iran. But the new sound technology is primarily employed to capture the sound of the trains: the steam, whistles, pistons, the rhythm of wheels

---

26. Boisen 1977: 148–150.
27. Rosenberg's contribution to Danish documentary was immense. Over a quarter of a century from the late 1930s, he composed the scores for some eighty films. 'Kai Rosenberg'.

on tracks. The final few minutes descend into a whirlwind of fast cutting between tracks, wheels, pistons, viaducts, tunnels, and scenery – and then, suddenly, there is a whistle, the train enters a tunnel, and the film fades to black.

Boisen claims that the impact of *Iran – Det nye Persien* was considerable. It was a popular choice for the film evenings with lectures (and often snacks) that were a popular pastime in mid-century Denmark, and the film also played in theatres, including a dozen sold-out screenings at the large Copenhagen cinema Odd Fellow Palæet. It was also instrumental in persuading other Danish companies that commissioning informational films about their business could be a good investment.[28] Certainly, if one compares the Iran film to the first handful of films produced for the government agency Dansk Kulturfilm in the mid-1930s – silent, plodding process films with muddy images that expound the process of brick-making and meat-processing[29] – *Iran – Det nye Persien* throws down the gauntlet for Danish documentary. As an industrial film, showcasing Danish know-how against the exotic backdrop of the Middle East, it was also able to experiment with sound and images while escaping the fate of another outstanding documentary of the mid-1930s: Poul Henningsen's *Danmark* (1935). This was an experimental documentary mapping the nation and its traditions against a jazz soundtrack, and deemed far too modern and cultural-radical for a state-sponsored film by contemporary critics.[30] The railways, on the other hand, were a safe space for audio-visual experimentation.

---

28. Boisen 1977: 152.
29. Thomson 2018: 49–50.
30. Ibid.: 51–52.

## 'Don't you make proper films?'

Of course, sound was not the only dimension of filmmaking whose influence echoed back and forth across the North Sea. Christensen returned to the Iran film a few years later, when writing a speech about the nature of documentary in particular and film in general. The precise date and purpose of the speech are uncertain, but his handwritten notes and typescript are filed amongst papers from 1945–46 in his archive, and in it he refers to projects from 1941 and 1942; he is thus looking back at *Iran – det nye Persien* (and by extension *Night Mail*) at around seven or eight years' remove, yet he still draws on the film as the quintessential example of his practice. In these papers, the potential of the railway to express filmic movement in its purest form is laid out.

The typescript starts with a question that Christensen is sometimes asked: *'Laver De ikke rigtige Film?'* ('Don't you make proper films?') This gives him occasion to start by outlining the nature of documentary. Documentary film, he writes, has its own ways of handling reality:

> *Den nøjes ikke med at give et Billedreportage af et eller andet Stof eller Miliø – den forsøger at faa det Drama frem, som findes overalt i Virkeligheden – men det skal være et virkeligt Drama med virkelige Mennesker. Dets Konflikt skal springes ud af Hverdagen, maa ikke være en eller anden opfundet Hændelse.*[31]

It is not satisfied with giving a pictorial report of some or other material or milieu – it tries to draw out the drama which is everywhere to be found in reality – but it must be a

---

31. 'Laver De ikke rigtige Film?': 1.

real drama with real people. Its conflict must arise from the everyday, must not be some invented incident or other.

Christensen goes on to explain to his audience that the fundamental quality of the documentary drama is movement. Film, he writes, is a mechanically produced illusion of movement, through the projection of twenty-four frames per second. That films are referred to in Danish as *levende billeder* ('living pictures') stems from the movement of the film strip itself, the movement of the camera, and the movement of things on screen.[32] The rhythms, directions, and tempo of these movements creates the film's drama: '*Kombinationen af forskellige Bevægelser, Montagen giver Udtryksmuligheder og giver Grunden for Filmens Opbygning, Drama*' ('The combination of different movements, the montage, provides expressive possibilities and is the basis of the construction of the film, its drama').[33] The closing sequence of the Iran film, discussed above, is the example he plans to use in his talk to illustrate the maxim that we as viewers become one with the movement of the camera.

It can be seen, then, that Christensen had developed – and articulated in public – a fully formed philosophy of documentary, rooted in his practice as screenwriter, cinematographer, editor, and director. He also uses examples from his many industrial films in the speech to illustrate how the elements of film create movement and rhythm from the machinery and are thus suggestive of more abstract ideas such as threat, triumph, freedom, slavery, riches.[34] But he returns again to the train to insist that '*det er hele Tiden Bevægelse, der er Bærer af disse Betydninger*' ('at all times, it is movement that carries these meanings').[35]

---

32. 'Laver De ikke rigtige Film?': 2.
33. Handwritten notes on film as movement, n.d.: E.
34. Handwritten notes on film as movement: D.
35. Handwritten notes on film as movement: E., emphasis original.

Around the time he was writing the speech, Christensen briefly returned to the trope of the railway again, for a three-minute public health film to be shown in cinemas encouraging Danes to take part in the national mass screening programme for tuberculosis.

Produced for Ministeriernes Filmudvalg and the health authorities of the Copenhagen region, *1337 Mennesker* ('1337 People', 1946) opens and closes with trackside shots of a passing train. Indeed, the opening shot is of a train bearing down on a camera that had obviously been left on the rails to capture the dramatic image – and the cinemagoers' attention. One thousand three hundred and thirty-seven, the voiceover claims, is the number of passengers on the train, and also the number of people in Copenhagen who had died of tuberculosis the previous year.

The film injects some theatrical urgency into the standard-issue elements of the many public information films used in the post-war campaigns against tuberculosis,[36] but can hardly be said to push Christensen's art further. It is, however, an elegant example of how the movement of the train can, in a small number of shots, serve as a vehicle for a range of implications in the way that Christensen suggests in his writing: the threat of disease bearing down, the community of Copenhageners in transit, the white heat of modern medicine carrying them into the future.

## 'Speed through the landscape of duty'

Christensen would soon have the opportunity to apply these ideas to another film about railway travel. The centenary of the

---

36. Thomson 2019.

Danish railways was looming, and the national rail company, Danske Statsbaner (DSB), commissioned a film with Dansk Kulturfilm to celebrate not the past but the future of the network.[37] Christensen was appointed to start work on a film that was initially conceived as lasting ten to fifteen minutes (the upper limit for a film to be screened pre-feature in cinemas) and entitled *Vi er Banerne* ('We are the Railways'). What became a much longer and thus more expensive film at twenty-six minutes – the expansion attesting to Christensen's influence at the time – would have the title *Her er Banerne* ('*Here are the Railways*')[38] and had its first public screening together with three other informational shorts in February 1948.[39]

For this film, Christensen decided to tone down what he referred to as the *bevægelsesdramatik* (drama of movement) that concluded *Iran – Det nye Persien*, and make this new film more psychologically and narratively satisfying.[40] But *Her er Banerne* is still obviously influenced by *Night Mail*, to the extent that filmmaker Jon Bang Carlsen, when viewing the latter for the first time in film school, was struck by the notion that '[*l*]*ighederne mellem de to film var så markante, at det var som delte de to instruktører hjerne og øjne*' ('the similarities between the two films were so marked, it was as though the two directors shared minds and eyes').[41]

The underlying conceit of *Her er Banerne* is that Fredericia station – located at the western end of the bridge over Lillebæltet (the Little Belt) between the island of Funen and Jutland – is a nodal point in the national network, with trains, as the voice-over intones, running in all directions from the town. While

---

37. For a more extensive discussion of this film, see Thomson 2018: 120–123.
38. Christensen 1947a.
39. Dansk Kulturfilm & Ministeriernes Filmudvalg. 1948.
40. Christensen 1947b.
41. Carlsen 2014.

narratively, there is emphasis on the directions of travel and origins and destinations of the trains, the film is shaped by the clock – or rather, the railway timetable. The confluence of time and space is visualised in cutting-edge style on a control panel in the signal room which lights up to indicate trains' progress in and out of the station. Down on the ground, Christensen had allegedly memorised the station timetable so that he and the crew could maximise time filming on the tracks.[42] As Forsyth Hardy commented when the film screened at the Edinburgh Festival in 1949, Christensen was 'working from the inside' to reveal Fredericia as 'the nerve-centre of the country's railway system'.[43]

Structuring the film around the railway timetable, however, enables another quality of time to emerge. An echo of the film's working title – *We are the Railways* – is to be heard in the cacophony produced by passengers and workers as they flow through and around the station. Repeated aerial shots show the station concourse filling and emptying as commuters ebb and flow throughout the day.

After the last of the mid-afternoon express trains leave, there is a sudden lull in footfall. A different rhythm of movement is sustained by the station workers. The early morning and mid-afternoon witness an intensification of activity, with cleaning teams jumping on and off trains, tray tables being set with tea cups, and, most exhilaratingly, railwaymen (and the cameraman!) in the sidings throwing brake blocks at the rails and jumping nimbly between tracks as wagons screech and lumber all around.

It is in the choreography of these workers that Christensen's principles of cinema as movement come into their own: from his synthesis of the things and people moving in the frame, the

---

42. Roos 1968: 150.
43. Hardy 1949: 18.

camera movement (often hand-held, by Jørgen Roos amongst others), and the montage, emerges a palpable sense of the lived spacetime of labour. *'Arbejdet kan aldrig gøres færdigt'* ('the work can never be finished') declares the voiceover towards the end of the film, a truth rendered all the more convincing by the speaker's personification as the station tannoy from the opening credits. But can a locomotive get tired? he also ponders, hinting at the incompatibility of industrial and biological temporalities and capacities. As Carlsen puts it, what connects *Night Mail* and *Her er Banerne* most poignantly is *'denne fælles historie om fart gennem pligtens landskab'* ('this common story of speed through the landscape of duty').[44]

A similar attention to the working classes in and on the railways characterises a Scottish film from the same year, *Waverley Steps*. Directed by John Eldridge for the Central Office of Information and the Scottish Home Department, the film's inspiration from the Swede Arne Sucksdorff's Academy Award-winning *Människor i Stad* (*'Rhythm of a City'*, 1947) was openly acknowledged.[45] *Waverley Steps* thus belongs to the 'city symphony' genre. Like Sucksdorff's short, the film weaves the paths of city dwellers together: romances, students at lectures and in pubs, tourists, within a specified timeframe of around twenty-four hours. As a contemporary commentary had it, the film is 'a study of people against the background of the streets and the bridges, the wynds and the closes of the city, done with real feeling'.[46]

But in contrast to Sucksdorff's lyrical opening shots of seagulls soaring over a sun-baked Stockholm, *Waverley Steps* opens with the scream of a locomotive whistle as the camera tracks a speeding train through the Scottish countryside. As

---

44. Carlsen 2014.
45. 'Waverley Steps: Full record.'
46. Hardy 1950: 37.

the number twenty-seven approaches Edinburgh, three crosscut perspectives ensure that the city is introduced as a complex, dynamic entity: a young woman surveys criss-crossing railway tracks from a high window, presumably a railwayman's house; the driver in the train cab teases his junior for gazing back at the woman; and schoolboys tumble and clamber up onto the fence of a bridge across the rail line through Princes Street Gardens, thrilled to be able to spot this particular locomotive. A Big Band rendition of the folk song 'Comin' through the Rye' sets the aural tone and atmosphere of late-1940s Edinburgh.

While Edinburgh is sketched as a tangle of students, tourists, solicitors, and shoppers, two trajectories through the city stand out and eventually merge at – where else? – a pub. One is a coalman whose path through the city with his horse and cart – the port of Leith, the cobbled back streets, the forgotten smithy – opens up the rhythms of working-class life. The other is a Danish sailor on shore leave, whose struggles in broken English to ask for directions draw a small crowd of helpers. As a fictional character, the Dane's presence in *Waverley Steps* gestures to the city's role as an international port but also, self-consciously, as a tourist mecca.

As Forsyth Hardy observed, when the film was screened at that year's film festival, 'the visitors who thronged Edinburgh found it fascinating to compare their impressions with those of the director'.[47] But the amateur actor himself, N.K. Strøyberg, also embodied the links between Scotland and Denmark across the North Sea at the time: he was actually a businessman's son, in the city preparing himself for a business career.[48] With his fee for his unexpected film appearance, he bought a motorbike to travel Europe.[49] Perhaps he set off around the same time as

---

47. Hardy 1950: 37–38.
48. *Slægten Obel*: 72–73.
49. 'Waverley Steps: Full record.'

the Danish documentarists arrived in Edinburgh in their little car in August 1948; certainly, they must have enjoyed the sight of their fellow Dane on screen.

## The trains run in all directions

In a wistful essay for *Kosmorama*, marking Theodor Christensen's centenary in 2014, the director Jon Bang Carlsen remembers watching *Her er Banerne* in the classroom as a schoolboy, in the flickering light of a 16 mm projector – essential school equipment in the golden age of the informational film. Carlsen reminisces that he and his friends couldn't have cared less about the facts of Fredericia's nodal status in the transport network but that the film evoked something else for them:

> '*Togene ruller i alle retninger bort fra Fredericia*', siger speakerstemmen, og det bliver et digt for os drenge i 6C, en metafor for vores egen udlængsel. Drømmen om at komme væk hakker igennem 16 mm filmfremviseren, og ingen af os lærer det, som speakerstemmen forsøger at indprente os, at Fredericia er et af Danmarks vigtigste trafikale knudepunkter. Vi er fuldstændig ligeglade med Fredericia og knudepunkter. Vi dagdrømmer kun om, om farten i de store, sorte lokomotiver deroppe på lærredet over lærerens blege ansigt kan rive os fri af de kedelige kulisser, der omgiver os dag efter dag og lukker os ude fra den virkelige verden, som det hvide ansigt under lærredet påstår filmen viser, før han trykker på knappen, og billederne starter.[50]

'The trains run in all directions from Fredericia', says the voiceover, and it becomes a poem for us boys in class 6C,

---

50. Carlsen 2014.

a metaphor for our own longing for escape. The dream of getting away cuts through the 16 mm projector, and none of us learn what the narrator's voice is trying to impress on us, that Fredericia is one of Denmark's most important transport nodes. We couldn't care less about Fredericia and transport nodes. We just daydream about whether the speed of the big, black locomotives up there on the screen above the teacher's pale face could rip us away from the boring scenery that surrounds us day after day, shutting us out from the real world, which the white face under the screen claims the film shows, before he presses the button, and the images begin.

Carlsen's is one of the most evocative accounts I have ever found of how post-war informational films were consumed by their intended audience. The intentions of the commissioning organisations, the pedagogical ambitions of the teacher, even the aesthetic efforts of the filmmakers – none of these could guarantee the successful communication of facts, nor the strategic shaping of citizens.

Tracing and evaluating the social impact of the films is nigh impossible, and was rarely attempted by the organisations which commissioned and funded them.[51] But what is more interesting is their fleeting affects, or even their more lingering influence, on a viewer's life – a crystallisation of the dream of escape, the sensation of movement, a jolt of aesthetic inspiration. Motion in a time of stasis. As we have seen, such films not only travelled the world to inform audiences about other cultures and new technological advances; they were also carriers of inspiration for other filmmakers, caught up in an ecology of aesthetic influence, professional development, exchange of equipment, and international friendships. And it was in the

---

51. Thomson 2021: 537–538, 552–553.

screening rooms – in schools, film festivals, or production companies – that encounters between viewers and films took place, eliciting boredom, learning, fascination, ambition. Every film a *landvinding*.

## Bibliography

Bang Carlsen, J. 2014. 'Togene ruller i alle retninger bort fra Fredericia'. *Kosmorama* 254. https://www.kosmorama.org/kosmorama/artikler/togene-ruller-i-alle-retninger-bort-fra-fredericia. Accessed 2 October 2021.

Boisen, I. 1977. *Klip fra en filmmands liv*. Copenhagen: Nyt Nordisk Forlag/Arnold Busck.

Christensen, T. n.d. 'Laver De ikke rigtige Film?' Speech typescript, Produktionsplaner 1945–46, Theodor Christensen Særsamling, Det Danske Filminstitut.

———. n.d. Handwritten notes on film as movement. Produktionsplaner 1945–1946, Theodor Christensen Særsamling, Det Danske Filminstitut.

———. 1947a. 'HER ER BANERNE eller VI ER BANERNE' [manuscript] 4 June 1947, Det Danske Filminstitut, Statens Filmcentral Særsamling, Filmsager, Her er Banerne, Diverse Korrespondance.

———. 1947b. [letter to Ib Koch-Olsen], 25 March 1947, Det Danske Filminstitut, Statens Filmcentral Særsamling, Filmsager, Her er Banerne, Diverse Korrespondance.

Dansk Kulturfilm & Ministeriernes Filmudvalg. 1948. 'Uddrag af anmeldelser fra forevisning den 28 februar 1948'. [Summary of press reviews]. Det Danske Filminstitut, Statens Filmcentral Særsamling, Filmsager, Her er Banerne, Diverse Korrespondance.

'Denmark Fights for Freedom'. Danmark Paa Film, https://www.danmarkpaafilm.dk/film/denmark-fights-freedom. Accessed 5 August 2022.

'Edinburgh International Film Festival Memories'. http://www.edfilmfestmemories.org.uk/timeline/home.html. Accessed 30 September 2021.

Elton, A. 1945. 'The production of a film or films on the social institutions of Denmark'. Danish Film Institute, Statens Filmcentral Særsamling, Filmsager, Socialfilmene, Diverse materiale v/ korrespondance, økonomi, materiale og forevisning af alle fem socialfilm.

'Filmdatabasen'. Det Danske Filminstitut. https://www.dfi.dk/viden-om-film. Accessed 30 September 2021.

Grierson, J. 1979. 'Documentary: A World Perspective'. In F. Hardy (ed.), *Grierson on Documentary*. London: Faber & Faber, 203–224.

Hardy, F. 1947. 'Denmark has thriving film movement today'. *Weekly Scotsman*, D I, A: Vredens Dag, 145, Dreyer Archive, DFI.

———. 1948. 'Denmark'. *Documentary 48*, 16–17.

———. 1949. 'Danish Documentary'. *Documentary 49*, 18.

———. 1950. 'The Edinburgh Film Festival'. *Hollywood Quarterly*, 5:1, 33–40. https://doi.org/10.2307/1209483. Accessed 5 August 2022.

———. 1979. 'Introduction'. In F. Hardy (ed.), *Grierson on Documentary*.

'Iran – Det nye Persien'. n.d. Danmark Paa Film. https://www.danmarkpaafilm.dk/film/iran-det-nye-persien. Accessed 5 August 2022.

'Kai Rosenberg'. n.d. 'Viden om Film'. Det Danske Filminstitut. https://www.dfi.dk/viden-om-film/filmdatabasen/person/kai-rosenberg. Accessed 5 October 2021.

Nørrested, C. and Alsted, C. 1987. *Kortfilmen og staten*. Copenhagen: Forlaget Eventus.

Sevel, O. 2006. *Nordisk Film: Set indefra*. Viborg: Aschehoug.

Richards, J. 2011. 'John Grierson and the Lost World of the GPO Film Unit'. In S. Anthony and J.G. Mansell (eds), *The Projection of Britain: A History of the GPO Film Unit*. London: BFI/Palgrave Macmillan, 1–9.

Roos, J. 1968. 'THEODOR/Set af Jørgen Roos'. *Kosmorama* 84 (April), 150–151. https://www.kosmorama.org/kosmorama/arkiv/

theodor-christensen/84-theodor-set-af-jorgen-roos. Accessed 30 September 2021.

Sargeant, A. 2011. 'Harry Watt: On Land, at Sea and in the Air'. In S. Anthony and J.G. Mansell (eds), *The Projection of Britain: A History of the GPO Film Unit*. London: BFI/Palgrave Macmillan, 53–61.

Sevel, O. 2006. *Nordisk Film: Set indefra*. Viborg: Aschehoug.

*Slægten Obel. Med særlig tilknytning til Aalborg*. Aalborg 1976. Slægtsforskernes Bibliotek. https://slaegtsbibliotek.dk/920486.pdf. Accessed 1 October 2021.

Sørensen, L.M. 2014. *Dansk film under nazismen*. Copenhagen: Lindhardt & Ringhof.

Thomsen, B.T. 2007. *Lagerlöfs literære landvinding: Nation, mobilitet og modernitet i Nils Holgersson og tilgrænsende tekster*. Amsterdam Contributions to Scandinavian Studies.

Thomson, C.C. 2018. *Short Films from a Small Nation: Danish Informational Cinema 1935–1965*. Edinburgh: Edinburgh University Press.

———. 2019. 'Screening the population: Public information films in Scandinavian tuberculosis campaigns around 1950'. *Journal of Scandinavian Cinema* 9:1, 59–74.

———. 2021. 'The Smoking Machine: Public Health Films and Public Value in Britain and Denmark, 1950–1964'. In M. Hjort and T. Nannicelli (eds), *A Companion to Motion Pictures and Public Value*. New York: Wiley & Sons, 536–557.

'Waverley Steps: Full record.' n.d. National Library of Scotland. https://movingimage.nls.uk/film/0114. Accessed 1 October 2021.

# Filmography

*Many of the Danish films can be viewed at https://www.danmarkpaafilm.dk.*

*1337 Mennesker* (*1337 People*). 1946. Film. Directed by Theodor Christensen. Denmark: Nordisk Films Kompagni for Kommunerne i Storkøbenhavn, Københavns Amt, Ministeriernes Filmudvalg.

*Danmark (Denmark)*. 1935. Film. Directed by Poul Henningsen. Denmark: Poul Eibyes Filmsteknik for Udenrigsministeriet.

*Denmark Fights for Freedom*. 1944. Film. Directed by *uncredited*. Denmark/UK/ USA: Office of War Information.

*Drifters*. 1929. Film. Directed by John Grierson. UK: New Era Films for Empire Marketing Board Film Unit.

*Germania anno zero (Germany Year Zero)*. 1948. Film. Directed by Roberto Rossellini. Italy/France: Tevere Film.

*Her er Banerne (Here are the Railways)*. 1948. Film. Directed by Theodor Christensen. Denmark: Nordisk Films Kompagni for Dansk Kulturfilm and Danske Statsbaner.

*Iran – Det nye Persien (Iran – The New Persia)*. 1939. Film. Directed by Ingolf Boisen, Theodor Christensen, Axel Lerche and Tove Hebo. Denmark: Minerva Film for Kampsax.

*Louisiana Story*. 1948. Film. Directed by Robert Flaherty. USA: Robert J. Flaherty Productions.

*Moana – A Romance of the Golden Age*. 1926. Film. Directed by Robert Flaherty. USA: Famous Players-Lasky Corporation.

*Mänrniskor i Stad (Rhythm of a City)*. 1947. Film. Directed by Arne Sucksdorff. Sweden: AB Svensk Filmindustri.

*Night Mail*. 1936. Film. Directed by Harry Watt and Basil Wright. UK: GPO Film Unit.

*Shipyard*. 1935. Film. Directed by Paul Rotha. UK: Gaumont-British Instructional.

*Social Denmark* film series. 1947. Film. Produced by Arthur Elton. Denmark: Arbejds- og Socialministeriet and Ministeriernes Filmudvalg.

    *Denmark Grows Up*. 1947. Film. Directed by Hagen Hasselbalch, Astrid Henning-Jensen and Søren Melson. Denmark: Nordisk Film Kompagni.

    *Good Mothers* (originally released as *Mødrehjælpen)*. 1942. Film. Directed by Carl Th. Dreyer. Denmark: Dansk Kulturfilm.

    *Health for Denmark*. 1947. Film. Directed by Torben Anton Svendsen. Denmark: Palladium Film.

*People's Holiday.* 1947. Film. Directed by Søren Melson. Denmark: Palladium Film.

*The Seventh Age* (*De Gamle*). 1947. Film. Directed by Torben Anton Svendsen. Denmark: Palladium Film.

*The Song of Ceylon.* 1934. Film. Directed by Basil Wright. UK: GPO Film Unit.

*They Guide You Across* (*Sikkerhed i luften*). 1949. Film. Directed by Ingolf Boisen. Denmark: Minerva Film for United Nations, Ministeriernes filmudvalg, Dansk Kulturfilm.

*Waverley Steps.* 1948. Film. Directed by John Eldridge. UK: Greenpark Productions for Central Office of Information.

# · 7 ·

# With Gratitude

## Steinvör Pálsson

I had the great good fortune to have Dr Bjarne Thorup Thomsen as my PhD supervisor from the autumn of 1999 to January 2006, when I was awarded my doctorate.

I was not your typical PhD candidate. A single parent and a former dancer by profession, I had entered the academic world somewhat late in life. But from our very first meeting, Bjarne put me at ease. His constant encouragement and interest in my work enabled me to continue with my thesis when at times I was struggling to progress with it.

In 2002, my father Hermann Pálsson died as the result of a road accident and I paused my studies for a year. I am doubtful that I would have been able to continue had it not been for Bjarne's sensitivity and patience. His insights and invaluable suggestions guided me towards the eventual submission of my thesis. I thank him for the kindness and wisdom he showed me as my PhD supervisor, and I warmly congratulate him on his retirement.

## · 8 ·

# Winter Afternoons in Buccleuch Place

## Dana Caspi

'What is Laphroaig?' I asked Bjarne one afternoon in his room. It must have been in 1996: I was a fourth-year student and the fortunate translator of Peter Høeg's phenomenal bestseller *Frøken Smillas fornemmelse for sne* into Hebrew. It was the first book I'd been asked to translate, and Bjarne very kindly offered to help me. With endless amounts of patience and encouragement, he explained every word and idiom that I struggled with, and there were many. But on that particular afternoon he seemed embarrassed by my question and didn't answer straight away.

Eventually he said: 'You don't know what Laphroaig is?'

Oh my God, I thought, it must be something really rude, and this will be awkward for both of us.

When he did eventually explain, I realised he was embarrassed on my behalf: three years in Scotland and not a clue about whisky! But I think that with his keen senses, Bjarne also realised something else about me: I was still searching; I still had so much to learn! And so it was largely thanks to him that I was able to stay on in Edinburgh and work on a PhD in Scandinavian literature, with Bjarne as my supervisor of course. The years that followed were immensely exciting and edifying. Bjarne allowed me great freedom in my explorations and yet steered me safely towards coherence and purpose.

Eventually I chose to concentrate on translation and leave the academic world, but Bjarne's invaluable advice and insights, both as a translation consultant and as my supervisor, have been with me ever since, and I am grateful for the many hours we spent discussing everything from religious awakenings and Bible interpretations to geographical discoveries and conquests. And literature of course.

Wishing Bjarne a youthful retirement, full of curiosity and joy. *Slàinte*, Bjarne!

A Literary Lens on Scandinavia

· 9 ·

# Amalie Skram as a Travel Writer

## Janet Garton

Amalie Skram (1846–1905) was a well-travelled writer – extraordinarily so according to the standards of her time and the expectations of her gender. She was born and grew up in Bergen, originally a Hanseatic seaport which was the focal point for trading along Norway's extensive western coast, and which in the mid-nineteenth century had far stronger links with other European ports than with the capital Kristiania. The rail link between the two Norwegian cities was not finished until 1894, and the people of Bergen remained fiercely independent and outward-looking.

The young Amalie Alver was the second child and oldest daughter of Mons Monsen Alver (1819–98), a shop assistant who worked his way up to become a partner in the business and buy a comfortable family house in the mercantile district. Amalie was a quick-witted and vivacious child with a love of adventure – and according to her brother Ludvig, more than a bit of a tomboy: '*som en gut mere end som en pige i sine interesser og sit væsen, altid parat til at gjøre erfaringer, nysgjerrig og vovsom og ikke ræd for at begi sig ud paa ukjendte, farlige veie*'[1] ('more

---

[1]. Letter from Ludvig Alver to Gerhard Gran, 14 August 1896. The National Library of Norway, Oslo, Brevsamling nr. 117. Unless otherwise indicated, the translations in this article are this author's.

like a boy than a girl in her interests and her being, always ready to experience new things, curious and bold and not afraid of following unknown and dangerous paths'). She would roam around the town and the harbour, observing the bustling trading scenes and eager to investigate the less salubrious areas, the narrow back streets and alleyways with their inns and snugs, their drunks and their squalor – all of it rich material for her later writing.

Despite the family's apparent prosperity, however, all was not well. They were living beyond their means; Amalie and her four brothers were educated at the town's best schools, and her father had become embroiled in increasingly unsuccessful speculations to try to make money. In 1864, he was bankrupt and promptly left for America in order to try to restore his fortunes – leaving behind his wife and five children, the oldest of whom, Wilhelm, was nineteen and studying for the priesthood, and the youngest, Bernhard, was nine (five others had died in infancy). Amalie was seventeen, and almost at once accepted a proposal of marriage; it was no doubt in part a decision taken to alleviate her mother's financial burden, but it was probably equally prompted by her desire for adventure. She had grown into a stunningly beautiful young woman and had already received a number of proposals – but the man she chose was August Müller (1837–98), a ship's captain from a respected Bergen family, who could offer her escape and new experiences.

Amalie was married on 3 October 1864, a few weeks after her eighteenth birthday, and soon her travels began in earnest.

Not long after the wedding, she set sail with her new husband on board his ship, the *Admiral Tromp*, a three-masted full-rigged sailing ship bound for exotic ports. This period was the final golden age of sailing, when a ship's captain had extensive authority to decide not only on the course he would sail but also on his cargo and destinations.

Firstly they sailed to London, where they stayed for a while to take on cargo and make preparations for a long voyage, and then they embarked on a journey which was to last for nearly nine months. Their destination was the West Indies. The full itinerary is not recorded, but from Amalie's letters home it is clear that they visited Mexico, Jamaica, and British Honduras, and spent several weeks in Belize. She recounted some of her experiences in a letter written from London in August 1865 to a friend in Bergen, fru Bacher:

> *Jamaica var et ekkelt sted, svært skummelt og smussig, og folkene var likedan. Vi hadde gudskjelov kun et opphold av 4 uker her, mens vi lå 10 uker i Belize. Det var jo skrekkelig lang tid, men så hadde vi det også så morsomt der, at jeg for min part skulle gjerne ha vært der ennu. Vi var invitert ut hver eneste dag, ja endogså til guvernøren i stor middag. Men rasende varmt var det, det er sant. Luften man innåndet var som ild, og solens stråler var stikkende. Men det var også på den varmeste tid da solen stod like i senit. Vi hadde en reise til London på 7½ uke. Det var lenge, men kunne ha vært verre.*[2]

Jamaica was a horrible place, very unpleasant and dirty, and the people were the same. Thank goodness we only stayed there for 4 weeks, whilst we were 10 weeks in Belize. It was a frightfully long time, but we had such a good time there that for my part I should be happy to be there still. We were invited out every single day, even to the governor's for a grand dinner. But it really was terribly hot. The air you breathed in was like fire, and the sun's rays were scorching. But it was the warmest season, when the sun was at the zenith. Our voyage

---

2. The letter is dated 3 August 1865 and is reproduced in Kielland 1976: 13–15 (14). Liv Køltzow's biography of Amalie Skram's early life, *Den unge Amalie Skram*, gives an extensive account of her early travels.

to London took 7½ weeks. It was a long time, but could have been worse.

By her own account, Amalie was a born sailor. She enjoyed life on board and claimed never to have been seasick. She was fascinated by the minutiae of the ship's construction and navigation; she was not a passive captain's wife who sat in the cabin and drank tea. Indeed, her husband enrolled her as a member of the crew and paid her a pound a month in wages. She was not afraid to stand on deck in a roaring gale or to haul on ropes alongside the deckhands. The arrival of the ship in foreign ports was usually an event for the local community, and August Müller enjoyed showing off his lovely young wife.

Over the next seven years, Amalie spent much of her life at sea. She had two sons, Jacob and Ludvig, in 1866 and 1868, and they travelled with her on later voyages. Australia, Peru, Cape Horn, the Mediterranean, the Black Sea, Constantinople – she experienced many different lands and peoples, and took her sons with her on a trip around the world, all the time observing and storing up experiences on which she would later draw in her writing. From 1871, she and Müller set up house in Bergen, although he continued to sail until 1876, when he sold his ship and came ashore. He bought a mill at Ask near Bergen, where the family was to settle; but it was only a year later that Amalie asked for a divorce.

Behind the exciting seafaring life and the glittering society in exotic foreign ports, Amalie and August's marriage had been problematic from the start. They were an ill-matched pair; he was a seasoned traveller, used to the rough-and-tumble of a sailor's life with its easy-going acceptance of the double standard (men have sexual adventures; respectable women remain chaste), whereas she – despite her adventurous nature – was a sheltered and immature young bourgeoise. She had no knowledge of what a husband would expect of her, and the discovery of the realities of married life was a shock from which she never fully recovered.

During their stay in Belize she had a miscarriage, and on the voyage she was often ill with what seems to have been some kind of hysterical attacks, involving hallucinations and being treated by her husband with opium. She began to find intimate contact unbearable; things were no better after they settled on land, and eventually became so bad that in 1877 she had a breakdown and was admitted to Gaustad psychiatric hospital. It was only after Müller agreed to a divorce that she began to recover.

Leaving him in Bergen, she moved to Western Norway with her two sons to live with her brothers, firstly with Ludvig in Frederikshald and then with Wilhelm in Kristiania. During these relatively settled years she began her writing career, firstly as a literary critic and then, tentatively, as a creative writer.

By the age of twenty-five, then, Amalie Müller's life as a round-the-world voyager was over. After that she never left Europe – but neither did she remain settled in her own country, content to relive her early adventures in her writing.

In August 1882, she attended Bjørnstjerne Bjørnson's jubilee celebrations at Aulestad, and there she met and fell in love with the Danish writer and journalist Erik Skram (1847–1923). There followed two years of intense letter-writing and mutual visits across Kattegat. Amalie visited Copenhagen a few times, travelling the whole way by ship if she possibly could; it was always her preferred mode of travel. Finally, in March 1884, she left Kristiania for good and set sail for Copenhagen with all her worldly goods – but without her sons – to marry Erik and live in Denmark for the rest of her life.[3]

Amalie Skram, as she then became, embarked on her writing career in earnest when she moved to Denmark; her first novel,

---

3. For an account of Amalie Skram's later life, see Garton 2011.

*Constance Ring*, was published in 1885, and over the next fifteen years she published fourteen books, as well as a number of short stories. She did not write travel books as such, but in several of her novels and stories she drew on her experiences to provide a wide variety of characters and locations for her fiction. Most of her novels are set wholly in Norway, but in two of them – *To Venner* ('Two Friends', 1887) and *Forraadt* ('*Betrayed*,' 1892) life at sea is central to the action, whereas a third, *Fru Inés* (1891), is set entirely in Constantinople. And two of the stories in *Børnefortællinger* ('Children's Stories', 1890), 'I det Asowske Hav' ('On the Sea of Asov') and 'Paa Hondurasfloden' ('On the River in Honduras') happen in far-distant climes.

The closest of these stories to the author's actual experience must be the short story 'I det Asovske Hav', which relates an incident on board ship where two small boys are travelling with their father, the ship's captain, and his wife. The story begins calmly enough with the boys quarrelling about learning their lessons while at sea, but quickly takes a dramatic turn as the captain's wife falls into the sea and is nearly drowned before being rescued. The account sounds authentic, down to the boys' wordless terror and the woman's hysterical laughter as she regains consciousness – although there is no record of it having actually happened. The setting of the scene at the beginning of the story, however, bears the unmistakable stamp of first-hand knowledge:

> Bjørgvinn *laa tilankers i det Asowske Hav et Par Mile fra Kysten sammen med mange andre Dampere og Sejlfartøjer av forskjellige Nationaliteter. Der er nemlig saa grundt Vande ved Kysten, at Skibene ikke kan gaa op til Lossepladsene, men maa bli liggende paa Dybet, hvor Ladningen føres ud i Lægtere.*[4]

---

4. Skram 1911–12, I: 325.

The *Bjørgvin* lay at anchor in the Sea of Asov a couple of miles from the coast, together with many other steamers and sailing ships of various nationalities. That is because the waters by the coast are so shallow that ships cannot tie up by the quay to load, but have to stay in deeper waters, while the cargo is ferried out by barges.

'Paa Hondurasfloden', on the other hand, seems a more fantastical account of a young European woman visiting an old English vicar and his wife, who minister to the native population in Honduras. But here again the description of the river, flora, and fauna as they are paddled along in a boat and visit a settlement are described in such realistic detail that they must derive from an alert and interested observer. At the edges of the greenish river grow jungles of reeds and enormous water lilies, and the banks are lined with calla, cacti, and palms. The river is full of crocodiles; onshore is a riot of peacocks, turkeys, and parrots; and inside the old lady's hut roam chickens and her pet deer. Sounds, sights, and smells assault the senses, and there is no attempt to prettify; the young girl is repulsed by the old lady's face with '*den sorte, fremstaaende Mund med de graablege, skorpede Læber*' ('the black, pouting mouth with its grey, crusty lips') which she is required to kiss.[5]

*To Venner* is the second volume in the series of four novels usually referred to as *Hellemyrsfolket* ('The People of Hellemyr'), which follows the fortunes of a Bergen family in Zolaesque fashion through several generations, from extreme poverty through relative affluence to an unhappy end, demonstrating the impossibility of escaping the fate predetermined by heredity and environment.[6] Most of the story takes place in the area

---

5. Ibid.: 362.
6. *Sjur Gabriel* (1887); *To Venner* (1887); *S.G. Myre* (1890); *Afkom* ('Descendants', 1898).

in and around Bergen, but this second volume is an exception; here we follow the adventures of the fifteen-year-old Sivert, grandson of the peasant farmer Sjur Gabriel, who tries to escape the family of which he is ashamed by signing on as a ship's boy and going to sea. The voyage on board *To Venner* takes him via Madeira all the way to Jamaica, where they stay for some time before returning through the Straits of Gibraltar to Marseilles, then to Lisbon to load up with salt, finally setting course to return home to Bergen. At first Sivert is dreadfully seasick and treated harshly by the crew, but gradually he finds his sea legs and starts to pull his weight, earning praise for his stamina and initiative.

The atmosphere of the busy port of Kingston is vividly brought to life in the novel. The captain hires a group of black workers to help load the wood he has bought, which includes a quantity of lignum vitae, a hardwood in which Amalie herself had invested on her first trip to Jamaica. It was a bad investment, she wrote to fru Bacher; after encouraging her to buy it, Müller was unable to sell it on their return, so they had to keep it.

The streets of the town are also described as the young Sivert ventures to explore them, with their crowd of colourful and ragged inhabitants; we see the ramshackle huts with their small parcels of land, an old woman hanging up washing on a myriad of criss-crossing washing lines, a younger woman washing clothes in a tub while her son stands naked in front of her suckling her breast. He makes his way to a brothel frequented by his fellow shipmates, where he is welcomed by the girls and led into a room which makes a pathetic attempt at finery:

> *Her fik de ham tilsæde i et Monstrum af en Straasofa, der stod i Hjørnet ved Vinduet med et raat forarbejdet Bord foran. I det modsatte Hjørne var en lignende Sofa og nøjagtig det samme*

*Bord. Paa begge Sider af Indgangsdøren var spændt to Hængekøjer tværs over Værelset med lange Touge, der var fastgjort i Væggen og slæbte henad Gulvets hullede Sivmatter. Paa en af Væggene var anbragt et skablignende Møbel, hvis Døre stod paa Klem og fremviste nogle Glas og noget brøstfældigt Stentøj, med Skuffer oppe og nede, ud fra hvilke der stak Tøjstumper og Baandstykker. Ovenover Skabet hang farvede Litografier af Dronning Viktoria og Prins Albert i Kroningsdragt samt et med Fluesnaus belagt Spejl. Paa Bordene stod der Glas og tomme Flasker, en halvspist Kokusnød laa paa en Stol, nogle afgnavede Hønseben og et Stykke Hvedebrød oppe paa Skabet. Foran Vinduerne hang der Musselinsgardiner med lange Flænger og optrapsede Kanter. To Lamper med fedtede Glas og sprukne Kupler oplyste Rummet.*[7]

Here they made him sit down on a monstrous straw sofa, which stood in the corner by the window with a rough-hewn table in front of it. In the opposite corner stood a similar sofa and an exact copy of the table. On both sides of the entrance, two hammocks were slung across the room on long ropes which were fastened to the wall and trailed along the rush matting on the floor, which was full of holes. Along one of the walls stood a kind of cupboard, its doors hanging open to show some glasses and some chipped crockery, with drawers above and below, out of which pieces of material and ribbon were spilling. Above the cupboard hung coloured lithographs of Queen Victoria and Prince Albert in coronation robes, together with a mirror covered with flyspecks. On the table stood glasses and empty bottles, a half-eaten coconut lay on a stool, and there were some gnawed chicken bones and a piece of bread on top of the cupboard. In front of the windows hung muslin curtains with long rips in them and frayed

---

7. Skram 1911–12, II: 132.

edges. The room was lit by two lamps with smeared glass and cracked globes.

The description of these seedy premises is so acute that the reader wonders whether Amalie Skram is writing from first-hand experience; if not, she must have seen something very like it.

As the ship prepares to leave Kingston, there is an addition to the company; two Frenchmen, a botanist and a zoologist, come aboard together with the specimens they have collected for Jardin des Plantes in Paris. They arrive with two large carts of luggage – not only plants but also a menagerie of living specimens, including birds, turtles, snakes, crocodiles, porcupines, fish, and tiger cubs. Their presence enlivens the journey and provides some humour in their attempts to communicate; both they and the ship's crew speak only rudimentary English. After they and their cargo have been dropped off in Marseilles, life on board is dull – until the ship is a couple of days out from Lisbon, where they run into a terrible storm.

The storm itself and the reactions of the crew as the water in the hold rises and the pumps fail is described with frightening intensity; the lamps are smashed, the masts snap, and the tiller and helmsman are washed overboard as Sivert is posted to keep watch – and finally catches sight of an approaching steamer. The novel ends as the surviving crew launch the lifeboat and row towards their salvation. That is the end of Sivert's adventures at sea.

There are many testimonies to the fact that Amalie Skram knew what she was talking about when she described life on board a sailing ship, perhaps none more heartfelt than that from an old sailor in Bergen, who thirty years later borrowed the novel from Amalie's son Ludvig Müller and returned it with the following words of praise: '*Og* To Venner!!! *Vet De, Møller*

*– der er ikke en eneste manøvreringsfeil i hele boken! Hvorledes tror De, det vilde gaa med skutene i «sjøromanerne» ellers? De vilde søkke ner paa hver eneste sides vildene hav!*[8] *('And To Venner!!!* You know, Møller – there isn't a single navigational mistake in the whole novel! How do you think things would go with sailing craft in "sea novels" otherwise? They would be scuttled on every page of stormy seas!'*)*

A quite different life at sea is portrayed in the novel Amalie Skram published five years later, *Forraadt*. The ship, however, is of the same kind, the one she had sailed with and knew intimately, a three-masted full-rigged sailing bark. The *Orion* is captained by Captain Adolph Riber from Bergen, a bluff and good-natured sailor who has done well for himself and decides it is time to complete his good fortune by taking a wife. He marries for love, choosing a very young and beautiful girl who he thinks will be easy to mould into the supportive companion he seeks. She is to be a captain's wife on board ship, and straight after the marriage they set sail for London, before crossing the Atlantic to America.

It is easy to see from the descriptions in the novel that Amalie Skram had been in London in 1864 with August Müller. Fashions and places in the city in the mid-nineteenth century are brought vividly to life, as Riber and Aurora (Ory) visit the Alhambra theatre, eat oysters in Maiden Lane, go shopping near St Paul's Churchyard and finally go on board in Victoria Docks. The decor of the boarding house in which they stay in Cheapside, with its Irish landlady with the false hair braids and the rasping voice, sounds depressingly familiar:

> [...] *at sidde her hele Dagen, stængt inde i dette frygtelige Værelse, med denne beklumrede, engelske Stenkulslugt, hvor der altid var*

---
8. Müller 1917.

*halvmørkt, hvor Hestehaarsmøblerne ganske sikkert aldrig havde været banket eller luftet ud, og hvor Stolene var saa tunge og store, at hun maatte bruge begge Hænder for at flytte dem.* [...] *Ikke engang Kaminen, hvis blanke Marmorgesims og skinnende Messinggelænder Ory straks var blit saa indtat i, havde hun mere nogen Hygge af at se paa. Ikke engang naar der var Ild i den som nu. For det store, forgyldte Spejl ovenover var saa fedtet og plettet, at ikke engang Gaskronen, som hang nedover Midtbordet, kunde spejle sig ordentlig i det, og de kunstige Blomster og brogede Fugle paa Gesimsen var saa støvede og smudsige, at man ikke kunde se, hvad de var gjort af.*⁹

[...] sitting here all day, cooped up in this awful room filled with suffocating English coal fumes, where it was always half-dark, where the horsehair furniture had probably never been beaten or aired, and where the chairs were so massive and heavy she had to use both hands to move them. [...] Not even the fireplace with its gleaming white marble mantelpiece and shiny brass fender, which Ory had liked so much at first, pleased her any more. Not even now with a fire blazing. The large gilt mirror above it was so greasy and spotted that even the reflection of the gas chandelier hanging over the centre of the table was blurred, and the artificial flowers and multicoloured birds on the mantelpiece were so grimy and dusty that it was hard to tell what they were made of.¹⁰

The less salubrious side of London life is also much in evidence here, as Riber conducts Ory around the dance halls and public bars, keen to show off his lovely wife – whereas what she notices is his easy familiarity with the scantily clad and brazen

---

9. Skram 1911–12, I: 386–387.
10. Skram 2018: 25–26.

women who cross their path, as she begins to suspect that there is a part of his life which is quite different from the respectable façade he maintains back home in Norway.

When they finally set sail for America, more than halfway through the novel, we follow in detail Ory's observations of life on board ship. The characters of the seamen are boldly drawn, from the quarrelsome first mate to the eager but clumsy ship's boy Halfdan – a lad Ory remembers from school. And the overall design of the ship, from rigging to messrooms, is minutely described. Ory's first impressions of the captain's sleeping quarters, with its nautical flavour and economical use of space, are drawn from life:

*Gulvet var bedækket af storrudet Voksdug i graa og røde Farver, Magen til den i Kahytten. Paa den ene Langvæg var der en høj Seng, bygget fast i Væggen med 3 Rader Skuffer under, og en Tophimmel, hvorfra der faldt ned mørkegrønne Sirtsgardiner med hvidblomstret Mønster. Paa Tværvæggen tæt ved Sengen en Egetræsservante med Laag, og en høj Chiffoniere. Paa den anden Langvæg ligeoverfor Sengen stod nede ved Gulvet en lang, smal Kasse. Ory løfted paa Laaget og saa, at den var fuld af sammenrullede Søkort. Paa den fjerde Væg fandtes, foruden den portierebehængte Indgang til Salonen, et højt, fladt, hvidlakeret Skab med en Klap paa Midten og Skuffer oppe og nede.*[11]

The floor was covered with oil cloth, a checkered pattern of large grey and red checks, the same as in the day cabin. Against one wall was a high bed, secured to the wall, with three drawers underneath and a canopy above, draped with dark green calico curtains that had a white floral pattern. On the short wall right next to the bed was an oak washstand

---

11. Skram 1911–12, I: 429–430.

with a lid and a tall chiffonier. Against the wall across from the bed was a long, narrow chest. Ory lifted the top and saw that it was full of rolled up navigation charts. On the fourth wall there was, besides the curtained doorway to the day cabin, a tall, slim white lacquered cabinet with a leaf in the middle and drawers above and below.[12]

Like Amalie, Ory is a good sailor, unperturbed by wind and storms. What sends her into a state of shock is discovering that Riber is not the chaste and clean-living man she had believed him to be but a reprobate who has had mistresses in several ports and even been previously engaged. Her determination to discover the details of his past excesses, at the same time as she denies him any sexual release, drives him into increasingly desperate bafflement and frustration. Meanwhile, as if in a mirror image of the stagnation of their relationship, the *Orion* becomes becalmed in Florida Bay. Tension rises in the oppressive heat and stillness, as the couple, trapped day after day in the narrow confines of the vessel where neither can find any refuge from the other or even space for a brief respite from enforced cohabitation, become estranged to the point where the only way out is overboard.[13]

In *Fru Inés*, the protagonist is again an unhappily married woman, this time a Spanish Levantine who is the wife of von Ribbing, the Swedish consul in Constantinople. Her husband is an irascible and much older man, and Inés has taken to banter and flirting with several admirers in order to surround herself with an illusion of gaiety to disguise her inner desolation. She embarks on an affair with a young Swedish businessman in an effort to experience the happiness of sexual fulfilment of

---

12. Skram 2018: 78–79.
13. There is a fuller exploration of the novel's themes and conflicts in the Afterword to my recent edition of the novel, Skram 2021: 131–167.

which she has heard; but the inexperienced Arthur Flemming is unable to satisfy her. Broken-hearted when she rejects him, he takes his own life, leaving her pregnant and searching desperately for a way out.

Absorbing as the human conflicts are, in many ways it is the city itself which is the protagonist of this novel. Constantinople, with its rich gallery of human characters of many ethnicities and backgrounds, its ancient buildings and crowded streets, is more than just a backdrop to the story; it is an essential part of it.

Whilst she was writing the novel in the spring of 1891, Amalie Skram wrote to her publisher, Paul Langhoff, in order to explain why it was taking her so much longer than she had promised; it was because of the effort involved in recalling to mind all her impressions from the time she'd spent there:

*Jeg slider mere med dette arbejde end jeg* nogensinde *tidligere har gjort. Det er fordi historien foregår i Konstantinopel og fordi jeg må grave og grave i min hjerne for at få levende frem for mig byen, folkene, livet, atmosfæren o.s.v. Det er ikke fordi det nu er 12 år siden, jeg var der sidste gang, men det er fordi alting der er så tusenfold broget og sammensat, så fuldt af farver og rigdom.*[14]

I'm struggling more with this work than I have ever done before. It is because the story takes place in Constantinople, and because I have to dig and dig in my brain in order to bring to life the city, the people, the life, the atmosphere etc. It is not because it is now 12 years since I was last there, but everything there is so enormously multifaceted and complex, so full of colour and richness.

---

14. Letter to Paul Langhoff from March 1891, in Garton 2010: 90.

There are many different settings in the novel, reflecting the differences of wealth and class of its inhabitants. It begins in the quiet luxury of a hotel on Prinkipo Island in the Sea of Marmara where Inés and her entourage are staying, and then moves to her city residence in the Grande Rue de Pera with its balcony supported by Ionic columns, set in a spacious garden with a lawn, fountains, and tropical plants, and an allée of acacias. Inés and Flemming stroll through the streets, take the funicular up to the higher part of town, eat in the restaurant pavilion in Bosphorus Park, and visit the silent cemetery with its hundred-year-old cypresses. All around them, meanwhile, is the crush and clamour of the streets where an exotic mêlée of people and animals jostle for space:

> *De begyndte langsomt at stige opover de ujevnt slidte Stentrin, hvor pustende Fodgjængere i Turbaner og Tyrkebukser, i græske Nationaldragter, i armeniske Præstekitler ased ivej mellem guldbroderte Albanesere og mørkklædte Europæere med Fez og tvilsomme Damer. Et Par kaade Ryttere kom sprængende i Galop paa styrtefærdige Lejeheste. En af dem strøg saa tæt forbi Inés, at Flemming hurtig maatte rive hende til Side, for at hun ikke skulde blive rendt overende. Straks efter fik hun et Puf i Ryggen af nogle tyrkeklædte Portechaisebærere, der lakonisk gik videre med sit forgyldte Bur, fra hvis Vindu et tilsløret Kvindeansigt titted ud.*[15]

They began to climb slowly up the uneven, worn stone steps, where puffing pedestrians in turbans and Turkish trousers, in Greek national costumes, and in Armenian clerical robes were struggling along among gold-embroidered Albanians and dark-clad Europeans with fezzes and questionable women.

---

15. Skram 1911–12, I: 155.

A couple of reckless horsemen came racing at a gallop on horses ready to drop from fatigue. One of them brushed past Inés so closely that Flemming had to hastily pull her aside so she wouldn't be knocked down. Shortly afterwards she was nudged in the back by some Turkish sedan chair bearers who laconically kept walking, bearing their gilded cage from whose window a veiled woman was peeking.[16]

As the novel proceeds, the luxurious upper-class districts in which most of the first part is set are gradually replaced by more squalid lower-class environments, mirroring the change in Fru Inés from the over-privileged, haughty consul's wife into a haunted and desperate figure. In a horrifying scene, she watches a pack of stray dogs, of which the streets are full, turn on an outcast dog and rip its skin off; in her feverish imagination, she becomes that dog, mutilated and suffering, looking for a peaceful place to die: '*Nu vidste hun det. Hun var Hunden, og hun skulde dø som den.*'[17] ('Now she knew. She was the dog and she would die like it had.'[18]) When she sinks down in a doorway, overcome by cramps, she is helped by the silent, veiled native women with whom she would otherwise have had no contact.

Amalie Skram's efforts at teasing out her memories have produced so much information in this short novel that it could almost be used as a travel guide to the city and the area around it, much of which would still be recognisable today.

After her move to Copenhagen in 1884, Amalie Skram's own travels were mostly limited to visits home to Norway. She went back fairly often, either to visit one of her two sons – Jacob, who had become a student in Kristiania but rapidly gone off the rails and required urgently rescuing from penury and

---

16. Skram 2014: 65.
17. Skram 1911–12, I: 197.
18. Skram 2014: 139.

drunkenness, or Ludvig, who had started work in Bergen in his uncle Tobias Müller's business and was isolated and unhappy – or to undertake research for her novels, most of which are set in Norway.

Over the years, her opinion of the two countries changed; from being an ardent Norwegian patriot who in her early letters to Erik extolled the sterling virtues of her countrymen as opposed to the weak and unprincipled Danes, she came to appreciate the superiority of Copenhagen as a cultural centre and complain about the backwardness of Norwegians, whom she described in a letter to her German translator Marie Herzfeld in 1893 as a horde of barbarians and parvenues.[19] It was in Denmark and not in Norway where her books were appreciated, and the Danes who eventually awarded her a writer's stipend.

Eventually, in 1901, she published a pamphlet, *Landsforrædere* (*'Traitors'*) in which she declared unequivocally that her loyalties lay with her adopted country. Not for nothing had Georg and Edvard Brandes been writing down here for a generation; it was here that her books had received the kind of recognition which gives an author the courage to carry on writing. And in an article published in Norway a couple of years earlier she had demanded that the words inscribed on her tombstone should be '*Dansk Ægtehustru, dansk Borger, dansk Undersaat og dansk Forfatter*' ('Danish wife, Danish citizen, Danish subject and Danish author').[20] With the omission of 'Danish wife' – since she was by that time separated from Erik – this was done.

In the 1890s, Amalie Skram undertook two final extended trips, one east and one west. In February 1894, after a mental breakdown caused by a combination of writer's block and

---

19. Letter to Marie Herzfeld 18 October 1893. The National Library of Norway, Oslo, Brevsamling nr. 64.
20. 'Et Par Ord fra Amalie Skram'. *Verdens Gang* 26, 31 January 1899.

tensions in her marriage, she agreed to be admitted to the psychiatric ward of Copenhagen Hospital under the care of the physician Knud Pontoppidan. The rest and healing she had hoped for did not materialise; instead she claimed she was treated like a dangerous lunatic, and it was only after two months of unremitting struggle that she was discharged. Normal life could not be resumed straight away; instead, thanks to her devoted friend Ane Cathrine Achen, who collected donations for her from their circle of acquaintances, she was able to undertake a sea voyage to recuperate.

Sofie Horten, a well-known feminist, was about to depart for Finland and suggested to Amalie that she should accompany her, which she did. On 8 May 1894, they sailed on the steamship *Vasa* and were away for several weeks, first in Helsinki and then in St Petersburg, travelling home via Stockholm. We can follow her travels through her letters home to Erik. The largest part of the letters is taken up with describing her own emotions, her sadness at being away from her four-year-old daughter and her unresolved conflicts with her husband. In between, however, she tells of animated social gatherings with cultivated hosts, and above all of her pleasure at being on her travels again:

> *Har havt en aldeles storartet rejse. Sejlladsen på Østersøen var som i Pasaten. Fuldstændig! Brilliant kaptejn, hyggeligt rejseselskab, ikke at tale om min rejsefælle, som er udmærket. Kom igårmorges torsdag, kl. 9 til Åbo, den forrige hovedstad. Blev så af kaptejnen inviteret til at gå i land og bese staden, kjørte afsted i to vogne, var allevegne, også ombord på 'Vasa', der kl. 4 om eftermdg skulde afgå til Helsingfors. Blev der presenteret for kaptejnen, der viste sig at være lige så prægtig som ham på 'Estræa' [...]*[21]

---

21. Letter dated 11 May 1894. See Garton 2002, III: 301.

Have had an absolutely wonderful voyage. Sailing on the Baltic Sea was like going through the Straits. Exactly! Brilliant captain, pleasant company, not to mention my companion, who is excellent. Yesterday morning, Thursday at 9.0, we arrived in Åbo, the former capital. Were invited by the captain to go ashore and see the town, drove off in two carriages, went everywhere, also on board the *Vasa* which was to sail for Helsinki at 4 pm. Were presented to the captain, who turned out to be just as splendid as the one on *Estræa* […]

Just over a year later, at the end of October 1895, Amalie Skram's travels took her the other way – to Paris, where she was to stay for three months. Paris was at that time a cultural centre and a magnet for Scandinavian writers and artists; the Norwegian writers Bjørnstjerne Bjørnson, Camilla Collett, and Knut Hamsun, and the artists Frits Thaulow, Harriet Backer, and Edvard Munch, were among the many who studied and worked there.

Amalie Skram intended to enjoy the cultural activities, socialise with the Scandinavian circle (prominent among whom were the writer Jonas Lie and his wife Thomasine), seek out new material for her writing – and get away from her husband, with whom the conflicts continued. However, the trip was fraught with difficulties from the start – and prompted her one and only published travelogue, '*Rejseuheld*' ('Travel Accidents'), which appeared in *Politiken* on 9 December 1895. In it she recounts incidents from her journey by boat to Kiel and then by train via Altona, Bremen, and Cologne to Paris. The different nationalities she meets on the way behave in typical fashion; fat German ladies eat continually, whereas arrogant Frenchmen take up all the space and tread on everyone's toes. Misfortunes befall the traveller continually; Amalie Skram was well-known for being absent-minded and forgetful, and the letter is a tragi-comedy of forgotten garments, lost keys, missed appointments, and untraceable addresses.

Amalie Skram did not enjoy her stay in Paris; intended as recuperation, it became a daily struggle. She was continually short of money in an expensive city, felt cheated by landladies, and was robbed at the Moulin Rouge; she had to write begging letters home for advances and loans. The invitations and theatre trips she had expected did not materialise, and the Lies, on whose hospitality she had reckoned, did not include her in their social group – they were tired of being plagued by visiting countrymen, she was told. Just about her only contact with other Scandinavians during the months she was there was with Arne and Hulda Garborg; the former had written supportive reviews of her books, and the latter, with whom she took French lessons, was to become a faithful friend in her last years. She changed addresses frequently, searching for lodgings which were cheap, warm, and clean – and was continually disappointed; the changes of address also meant that letters and money orders went astray. Once she thought she had found an ideal room to rent, together with a couple of friendly Norwegian girls – but then had to move out again in a hurry when they received letters from home instructing them not to remain under the same roof as *such* an author.

Her stay in Paris can be followed through her letters, especially those she wrote home to Erik, from various different addresses and recounting the vicissitudes of her daily struggles. But as was the case with her letters home from the Finnish trip, far more space is devoted to analysing her feelings about him and their life together back in Denmark than to descriptions of Paris and her activities there. They can hardly be called travel letters. Erik complains that she says so little about where she is living and what she is doing, he has had to get out an old map to try to find the street and imagine her surroundings. Why can she not tell him more about her experiences there, about what Paris means for her? It has not meant anything, she replies:

> *Hvad Paris har vært for mig? Paris har vært* Dig *og småen og sorgen. Nu først, efter at dine dejlige breve har skabt lys omkring mig, begynder Paris at bli Paris. Og nu må jeg rejse. Det er vanvittigt at bli her længere.* [...] *Jeg har brugt så forfærdelig mange penge, ikke fordi jeg har brugt dem, men fordi jeg er blet snydt og bedraget og bestjålet. Franskmændene er verdens griskeste folk. Det er jeg vis på.*[22]

What Paris has been for me? Paris has been *you* and Baby and sorrow. Only now, after your lovely letters have created light around me, does Paris begin to be Paris. And now I must leave. It's crazy to stay any longer. [...] I have used a dreadful lot of money, not because I have used it, but because I have been deceived and cheated and robbed. The French are the world's most avaricious people. *I am certain of it.*[23]

A few days later Amalie travelled by train to Le Havre – visiting Erik's brother Tyge on the way – and boarded ship for the long voyage to Copenhagen. Her unsuccessful bid to find creative stimulus in Paris, as others of her countrymen had done, was over.

Whenever possible, as in this instance, Amalie Skram would avoid travelling by train and go by sea instead. Her dislike of trains amounted to '*togskrekk*' ('train phobia'), which was confirmed when in July 1897 there was a train crash in Gentofte in which thirty-six people were killed; she should have been

---

22. Letter dated 20 January 1896. Garton 2002, III: 405.
23. Garton 2003, 408–409.

on that train, she told Erik, had she not been so absorbed in her writing that she missed a dinner to which she had been invited.[24] She was always far more sanguine about danger at sea, perhaps because she knew what she was facing. Sea travel had been a formative part of her life, as it became an integral part of her fiction.

## Bibliography

Garton, Janet (ed.). 2002. *Elskede Amalie. Brevvekslingen mellom Amalie og Erik Skram 1882–1899*. I–III. Oslo: Gyldendal.

———. (ed. and trans.). 2003. *Caught in the Enchanter's Net. Amalie and Erik Skram's Letters*. Norwich: Norvik Press.

———. (ed.). 2010. *Amalie Skram. Brevveksling med forlæggere*. Copenhagen: Det Danske Sprog- og Litteraturselskab.

———. 2011. *Amalie. Et forfatterliv*. Oslo: Gyldendal.

Kielland, Eugenia (ed.) 1976. *Amalie Skram. Mellom slagene*. Oslo: Aschehoug.

Køltzow, Liv. 1992. *Den unge Amalie Skram. Et portrett fra det 19. århundre*. Oslo: Gyldendal.

Müller, Ludvig. 1917. 'Amalie Skram som sjømand'. *Tidens Tegn* 143, 27/5.

Skram, Amalie. 1901. *Landsforrædere*. Copenhagen: Gyldendalske Boghandels Forlag.

———. 1911–12. *Samlede Værker. Mindeudgave*. I–III. Kristiania: Gyldendalske Boghandel, Nordisk Forlag.

———. 2014. *Fru Inés*. Katherine Hanson and Judith Messick (trans.). London: Norvik Press.

———. 2018. *Betrayed*. Katherine Hanson and Judith Messick (trans.). London: Norvik Press.

———. 2021. *Forraadt*. Janet Garton (ed.). Danske klassikere. Copenhagen: Det Danske Sprog- og Litteraturselskab/Gyldendal.

---

24. Letter dated 12 July 1897. Garton 2002, III: 473.

· 10 ·

# Flying Lessons with Bjarne

## Anna Bohlin

Kindness is undoubtedly a cardinal academic virtue. We are often encouraged to think the other way around: that only greed, envy, and pride will further our academic careers. Nothing could be more misleading. Kindness is often mistakenly opposed to criticism; while criticism is essential to academic thought, it may be offered kindly or unkindly. How would a new idea ever develop into a theoretical argument if not received with kind appreciation? How would new ideas ever come up in the first place, if not through kind consideration of others' thoughts? How could we ever survive academic institutions, systems, applications, and publishing policies, if kind fellowship was nowhere to be found? Many of us travel to work in other countries, and we would be lost – physically and existentially – without the kindness of academic colleagues. We simply cannot do without it. Intellectual achievements hinge on kindness, and Bjarne Thorup Thomsen has that virtue in abundance.

When does it happen that literally all the contributors of an anthology explicitly ask you, as the editor, to convey their sincere gratitude to the anonymous peer reviewer? Only when Bjarne is your peer. When is your (as the Swedish expression goes) fifty-eleventh email full of endless revisions and tedious practicalities for the contributors still met with generous words of appreciation for *your* hard work, instead of grunting reminders of the author's own workload? Only when Bjarne is the author. And when do you reach out to a researcher you barely know to ask for support for an application – and immediately get an enthusiastic reply and an invitation to present the research project at the University of Edinburgh? Only when you reach out to Bjarne. I have a lot to thank Bjarne for.

The reason for that email asking for support, was Bjarne's brilliant study *Lagerlöfs litterære landvinding. Nation, mobilitet og modernitet i Nils Holgersson og tilgrænsende tekster* (2007). He challenged the predominant view of Selma Lagerlöf's *Nils Holgersson's Wonderful Journey through Sweden* (1906–07) as advocating a regionalist nationalism, by investigating transitions, transgressions, tensions, and fragmentations on different levels of the literary text. *Nils Holgersson* in Bjarne's interpretation is a text where the nation is defamiliarised and recognised anew. Furthermore, the main protagonists – that is the hybrid flock of different species binding the nation together – are analysed in relation to the hybrid novel form. *Lagerlöfs litterære landvinding* is a study of directions: literary form in relation to represented forms and movements. To fly with Nils, guided by Bjarne Thorup Thomsen, taught me to pay attention to horizontal and vertical axes, orientation and mobility, centrifugal and centripetal movements.

The centrifugal and the centripetal in Bjarne's work may pertain to the novel's outlook on the world, as seen in an article on the topography in another of Lagerlöf's novels, *Jerusalem* (1901–02), or to forces that distinguish the representation of the nation.[1] As he noted in yet another illuminating article, *Nils Holgersson* and *Jerusalem* are both 'governed by a tension between what might be termed centrifugal and centripetal

---

1. On the centrifugal novel, see Thorup Thomsen 2005; 2021b.

forces, between fragmentation of place and cohesion of place'.² In *Lagerlöfs litterære landvinding*, Bjarne stresses how centripetal and centrifugal movements structure the literary text simultaneously. The representation of Stockholm as the home of the entire nation in *Nils Holgersson* works through a coordination of centripetal and centrifugal forces, while homecoming in a later sketch is characterised by a contradictory logic: '*Selv de centrifugale kræfter får en centripetal funktion.*'³ ('Even the centrifugal forces acquire a centripetal function.') That helped me to spot the simultaneous centrifugal and centripetal forces in the Swedish novels of the 1840s that preceded Lagerlöf's quest to map the nation. Contrary to the use of nature in the novels of the 1830s, the landscape in several of the popular novels of the 1840s was part of a nationalist cartographic enterprise. However, the logic of Romantic nationalism simultaneously pulled the different provinces together into unity and split them apart.⁴

Bjarne's exploration of territorialities has also encouraged me to watch out for coordinates in vertical and horizontal directions. *Nils Holgersson's* 'horizontal up-down or north-south axis', Bjarne writes, 'is supplemented by a vertical top-down axis'.⁵ These axes may refer to the narrative's direction or to the gaze in the narrative, but they may also refer to nationalist ideas being vertically earth-bound or horizontally community oriented, or to sacral versus earthly representations of the landscape.⁶

---

2. Thorup Thomsen 1998: 131.
3. Thorup Thomsen 2007: 80, 95.
4. Bohlin 2016: 69. This article was published within the research project 'Enchanting Nations: Commodity Market, Folklore, and Nationalism in Scandinavian Literature 1830–1850'. The application was supported by Bjarne Thorup Thomsen and the project subsequently financed by Riksbankens Jubileumsfond 2016–18.
5. Thorup Thomsen 1998: 136.
6. See e.g. Thorup Thomsen 2007: 22, 81.

Bjarne states that 'the vertical axis of landscape is a treasured dimension [...] in [...] both *Jerusalem* and *Nils Holgersson*, but in varying forms'.⁷ One way in which they differ is the perspective: in *Jerusalem*, 'a spiritually loaded topography', a 'vertical openness', is perceived from the ground, while Nils Holgersson looks down on a transcendent earth with a bird's-eye view.⁸ These are indeed directions worth tracking back to the beginning of the nineteenth century and the inception of Romantic nationalism. Those flying lessons with Nils and Bjarne Thorup Thomsen will continue to inform my investigations of what he calls 'a dialogic notion of nationhood and an awareness of the contingent nature of nation space'.⁹ His kindness gave my research project wings, both in terms of theoretical inspiration and in terms of support for the application that secured the project's finances. I am immensely grateful.

## Bibliography

Bohlin, Anna. 2016. 'Den svenska 1840-talsromanen som nationell kartografi'. *Samlaren* 137, 58–86.

Thorup Thomsen, Bjarne. 1998. 'Terra (In)cognita: Reflections on the search for the sacred place in Selma Lagerlöf's Jerusalem and Nils Holgerssons underbara resa genom Sverige'. In Louise Vinge (ed.), *Selma Lagerlöf Seen from Abroad*. Stockholm: Kungl. Vitterhets Historie och Antikvitets Akademien, 131–141.

———. 2005. 'Om topografin i Selma Lagerlöf Jerusalem, del I.' L. Vinge (trans.). In M. Karlsson and L. Vinge (eds), *I Selma Lagerlöfs värld. Lagerlöfstudier*. Stockholm: Symposion & Selma Lagerlöf-sällskapet, 166–181.

---

7. Thorup Thomsen 1998: 139.
8. Ibid.; ('en andligt laddad topografi', 'denna vertikala öppenhet' author's trans.), Thorup Thomsen 2005: 177.
9. Thorup Thomsen 2021a: 90–91.

———. 2007. *Lagerlöfs litterære landvinding: Nation, mobilitet og modernitet i Nils Holgersson og tilgrænsende tekster.* Amsterdam: Amsterdam Contributions to Scandinavian Studies.

———. 2021a [2007]. 'Nordic National Borderlands in Selma Lagerlöf'. In Bjarne Thorup Thomsen (ed.), *Centring on the Peripheries: Studies in Scandinavian, Scottish, Gaelic and Greenlandic Literature.* London: Norvik Press, 79–93.

———. 2021b. 'Outreach, Invasion, Displacement: Denmark's Disputed Southern Borderland as Negotiated through Strategic and Affective Aspects of Space in Novels by Andersen and Bang'. In A. Bohlin et al. (eds), *Nineteenth-Century Nationalisms and Emotions in the Baltic Sea Region: The Production of Loss.* Leiden: Brill, 164–191.

# · 11 ·

# Feminism, Interplay, and Cooperation: A Comparison of Selma Lagerlöf's 'Hem och stat' and Karen Blixen's 'En Baaltale med 14 Aars Forsinkelse'

## Barbara Tesio-Ryan

Selma Lagerlöf and Karen Blixen are two of the most prominent Nordic authors in world literature. While both authors are widely recognised as prolific storytellers, they both expanded their talents to a wide production of non-fiction prose, often in the form of essays and speeches. This paper is going to compare Selma Lagerlöf's 'Hem och stat' ('Home and State', 1911)[1] and Karen Blixen's 'En Baaltale med 14 Aars Forsinkelse' ('Oration at a Bonfire', 1951).[2] While the two authors had different public views on the subject of feminism, when comparing these two speeches it becomes evident that their thoughts on interaction and cooperation between the sexes are strikingly similar. Both speeches were written by Lagerlöf and Blixen at a time in their writing career when they were famous well beyond the Scandinavian literary market, and recognised as skilled storytellers and public speakers.

---

1. Lagerlöf 1911a; 1911b.
2. Blixen 1965; Dinesen 1979.

## Home and State and Oration at a Bonfire

'Hem och stat' was given as a speech by Selma Lagerlöf in 1911 during the 6th Congress of the International Woman Suffrage Alliance (IWSA) in Stockholm.[3] Having won the Nobel Prize for literature two years earlier, she was at the height of her celebrity status and thus the most prominent guest of the Congress. 'En Baaltale' was initially commissioned in 1939, on the occasion of the International Women's Congress in Copenhagen. As Blixen herself recalls in her '*Baaltale*', however, she eventually presented it for the first time in 1953, first at a Danish teachers' seminar and then as part of a series of radio programmes that she broadcast on Danmarks Radio.[4] 'En Baaltale' was then published in *Det Danske Magasin* in 1953.[5]

Already this brief contextualisation allows us to identify an interesting similarity. Both speeches were commissioned by the most prominent women's organisation of the time, from the most prominent woman author in Scandinavia at the time. The historical context of conception, however, varies significantly.

In 1911, the central request of the Women's Alliance was that of universal suffrage, while in 1939, when Blixen's speech was originally commissioned, the major issues for the women's movement regarded equal pay and equal rights.[6] In the space of less than thirty years, the world had changed with the First World War, and the concepts of class and gender were being reshaped and readapted. When 'En Baaltale' was eventually delivered in 1953, the Second World War had forever changed the physiognomy of Western society, and 1949 had also seen

---
3. Stenberg 2014: 28–48.
4. Stecher 2014: 39.
5. Blixen 1953: 64–82.
6. See International Alliance of Women 1939.

the publication of the seminal work of Simone de Beauvoir, *Le Deuxième Sexe*,[7] which effectively started what is considered as the second wave of feminism.

Elaine Showalter divides the seminal part of the literature of women into three stages:[8] Feminine, Feminist, and Female. The Feminine phase, dated by Showalter from 1840 to 1880, is the phase where women were writing to 'equal the intellectual achievements of the male culture'.[9] The Feminist phase, dated between 1880 and 1920, is the phase that coincides with women winning the vote: 'women are historically enabled to reject the accommodating postures of femininity and to use literature to dramatise the ordeal of wronged womanhood'.[10] In the Female phase, started in 1920 and ongoing, 'women reject both imitation and protest – two forms of dependency – and turn instead to female experience as the source of an autonomous art'.[11]

According to Showalter's classifications, we could place Lagerlöf's writing, and specifically 'Hem och Stat', within the Feminist phase of women's writing. In fact, as Lisbeth Stenberg has noted, 'the women's movement at the turn of the twentieth century provided an important part of the context and preconditions for Selma Lagerlöf's authorship. After being awarded the Nobel Prize for Literature in 1909, Lagerlöf actively engaged in the campaign for female suffrage'.[12] On the other hand, Karen Blixen can be placed within what Showalter defines as the Female phase. Contrary to Lagerlöf's experience, she was never politically engaged with the women's movement of her time.

---

7. de Beauvoir 1949.
8. See Showalter 1978.
9. Showalter 2016: 35.
10. Ibid.
11. Showalter 2016: 36.
12. Forsås-Scott et al. 2014: 24.

However, despite the difference in their political agenda and the socio-historical context of reception, both speeches contains similar opinions on gender, as well as similar style and rhetorical devices. The most important similarity between the speeches is the concept of mutual collaboration. In 'Hem och stat', Lagerlöf illustrates how society is based on two pillars, namely the Home and the State. While the creation of the Home is due to the work of women, the creation of the State is the invention of man. The difference in the genesis and consolidation of those two institutions, according to Lagerlöf, lies in how the collaboration between sexes has shaped them. While in the case of the Home, women have been, when needed, supported by men, in the creation of the State, men have only worked on their own and never reached for the collaboration of women. This, according to Lagerlöf, explains the fallacy of State as an institution versus the longevity of the Home.

In 'En Baaltale', Blixen illustrates her reasoning for the necessary existence of the two sexes and justifies it with the concept of interplay and interaction. According to Blixen, a functioning society will work when the two sexes are interacting and cooperating – that is, when they both are fully aware of their own individuality and able to respect each other. A further interesting similarity between the two authors is the concept of storytelling, and the following section will discuss how both authors employ storytelling and humour as rhetorical devices to convey their opinions on gender.

## Storytelling, style, and humour

Throughout their writing careers, both Blixen and Lagerlöf were widely recognised as, and presented themselves, as storytellers. At the time in which their respective speeches were composed and delivered, they were world famous and experienced public speakers. They had both practised and perfected their performative roles as storytellers, Lagerlöf with her renowned Nobel speech and Blixen with her public storyteller persona of Isak Dinesen. They were both able and confident speakers in a language other than their own, and both employed storytelling as a founding feature of their writing.

Eric Johannessen has underlined the inextricable connection between their formative years and the influence of storytelling: 'in view of their background it is not surprising that both Selma Lagerlöf and Isak Dinesen have become storytellers, because both grew up in an environment in which the story reigned supreme'.[13] Because of their popularity, however, the receiving focus of their speeches was on their performance rather than the content. As Stenberg notes in the case of 'Hem och stat': 'Lagerlöf's celebrity and performance had defused her message'.[14] In the case of Karen Blixen instead, what had made her 'En Baaltale' rather controversial at the time in which it was presented, and in consequent Blixenian criticism, was her opening statement *Jeg er ikke Kvindesagskvinde* ('I am not a feminist').[15]

Storytelling as a rhetorical device to capture the audience's attention, as well as a technique to present their arguments, is present in both speeches. Interestingly, both Blixen and Lagerlöf use similar techniques, imageries, and even style structure. For example, both papers start with the authors acknowledging their audience and thanking them for the invitation to speak. Both Lagerlöf and Blixen underline how writing these speeches has given them an opportunity to actually reflect upon the subject of feminism and the women's movement. For Lagerlöf, this is an opportunity to publicly declare her political alliance:

---

13. Johannesson 1960: 20.
14. Forsås-Scott et al. 2014: 29.
15. Blixen 1965: 73; Dinesen 1979: 66.

> *Och i detta mitt tack ligger inte bara ett erkännande av den heder, som uppdraget innebär, utan jag vill tacka också därför, att Ledningen genom att göra mig till talsman för rösträttssaken har nödgat mig att för min ringa del söka komma till rätta med den skiftande och törhända världsomvändande företeelse, som heter kvinnorörelsen.*[16]

In making me a spokesman for the Suffrage Cause, they have not only conferred an honour upon me, but they have also impelled me to try to get a clearer comprehension of the ever changing and mayhap world transforming event called the Woman's Movement.[17]

Blixen also takes the opportunity to situate herself within the political panorama of feminism by stating: '*Idet jeg nu taler om Kvindesagen, maa jeg begynde med at sige, at det er en Sag som jeg ikke forstaat mig paa, og som jeg aldrig af egen Drift har beskæftiget mig med*'[18] ('In speaking about feminism I must begin by saying it is a matter which I do not understand, and which I have never concerned myself with of my own volition')[19] and that '*Jeg er ikke Kvindesagskvinde*'[20] ('I am not a feminist').[21]

The Danish word used by Blixen for feminist is '*kvindesagskvinde*', and, as Marianne Stecher has pointed out,[22] it refers specifically to the Danish Women's Movement, from which Blixen is here distancing herself, and throughout her speech she will explain her reasoning.

---

16. Lagerlöf 1911a: 3.
17. Lagerlöf 1911b: 1.
18. Blixen 1965: 72.
19. Dinesen 1979: 65.
20. Blixen 1965: 73.
21. Dinesen 1979: 65.
22. See Stecher 2014.

It is relevant to underline that both Blixen and Lagerlöf are using a similar technique here, namely that of presenting themselves as non-experts, or as Brigitte Mral underlines in her analysis of Lagerlöf's speech, 'the gently ironic mask of a deeply uncertain suffragette'.[23] By doing this, both Blixen and Lagerlöf are presenting themselves as non-threatening to the audience. As Stenberg notices, Lagerlöf had already used this technique in her Nobel speech 'in which she had told a story with her father as the central character. She had thus established herself as non-threatening to the conservative gender hierarchy, which consisted on that occasion of the all-male Swedish hierarchy.'[24] Blixen achieves her non-threatening status with the use of humour, by stating how her invitation to speak at the International Women's Congress *'vistnok fremkom under forkerte Forudsætninger'*[25] ('presumably was given upon mistaken assumptions'),[26] and how, rather than actually attending the congress, she had gone to the theatre: *'Levede jeg en Uge [...] i en Shakespeare'sk Verden, og naar jeg hørte forkyndt: "Svaghed, Dit Navn er Kvinde!" – tænkte jeg ikke paa at protestere, mend tog det med.'*[27] ('I spent a week [...] in a Shakespearean world, and when I heard it proclaimed "Frailty, thy name is woman!" it didn't occur to me to protest; I accepted it as a matter of fact.')[28]

She then explains how she declined her invitation to the organiser of the congress:

*Jeg takkede Fru Hein mange Gange, men svarede: 'Jeg kan ikke paatage mig denne Opgave, for jeg er ikke Kvindesagskvinde.'*

---

23. Mral 1999: 168.
24. Forsås-Scott et al. 2014: 28.
25. Blixen 1965: 72.
26. Dinesen 1979: 65.
27. Blixen 1965: 72–73.
28. Dinesen 1979: 66.

> *'Er Du da imod Kvindesagskvinde?' spurgte Fru Hein.*
> *'Nej,' sagde jeg, 'det kan jeg heller ikke sige at jeg er.'*
> *'Hvordan staar Du da i Virkeligheden til Kvindesagen?' spurgete Fru Hein mig igen.*
> *'Ja, det har jeg ikke tænkt over,' svarede jeg.*
> *'Saa tænk over det nu,' sagde Fru Hein.*[29]

> I thanked Mrs Hein warmly but said, 'I cannot accept this assignment, for I am not a feminist.'
> 'Are you against feminism?' asked Mrs Hein.
> 'No,' I said, 'I can't say that I'm that, either.'
> 'How do you stand upon feminism?' asked Mrs Hein again.
> 'Well, I never thought of it,' I answered.
> 'Well, think of it now,' said Mrs Hein.[30]

In Blixen's speech, the employment of storytelling is similar to her entertaining narrative fiction and fitting to the context in which it was eventually delivered – namely a series of radio speeches. Lagerlöf's speech, on the other hand, is conscious of the historical importance of its delivery and clearly adapted to a defined political agenda, and to a politically engaged audience.

## Home – domesticity as the sphere of femininity

Both Lagerlöf and Blixen structure their speeches around answering a pivotal question, and each of those questions exemplarily represents the historical context in which they were delivered. Lagerlöf, in 1911 in front of the audience of

---

29. Blixen 1965: 73.
30. Dinesen 1979: 66.

the International Woman Congress asks: '*Vi kvinnor fordra rösträtt. Vad ha vi då att åberopa oss pa som kan berattiga oss att ta del i rikstyrelsen?*'[31] ('We demand Suffrage. What plea can we advance that will entitle us to a voice in the Government?')[32] Blixen, in 1953, perhaps mirroring de Beauvoir's existentialism, asks '*Hvorfor er der to Køn?*'[33] ('Why are there two sexes?')[34]

Lagerlöf engages her audience by questioning the exclusion of women from the political life of the State: '*Men ha vi då ingeting gjort, som kan berättiga oss till samma fordringar pa tillvaron som mannen? [...] Vår tid har varit lång pa jorden, lika lång som hans. Har den gått spårlöst forbi?*'[35] ('Have we done nothing which entitles us to equal rights with man? Our time on earth has been long – as long as his. Has it left no trace in passing?')[36] The main contribution of women, Lagerlöf will argue, is the creation of the Home as the founding structure of society.

> *Vår gåva til mänskligheten har varit hemmet, detta och intent annat. Vi ha byggt på denna lilla byggnad sedan vår moder Evas tid. Vi ha ändrat planen, vi har experimenterat, vi ha upptäckt nytt, vi ha återvänt till gammalt, vi ha anpassat oss sjalva, vi ha gått ut och tämt dem bland de vilda djuren, som hemmet behövde, vi ha bland markens växter sokt ut sädesslagen, de fruktbärande träden, de välsmakande bären, de skönaste blommorna. Vi ha klätt vårt hem och prytt det, vi hat utarbetat dess seder, vi har skapat uppfostringskonsten, trevnaden, hövligheten, det glada, behagliga umgängessättet.*[37]

---

31. Lagerlöf 1911a: 6.
32. Lagerlöf 1911b: 2.
33. Blixen 1965: 73.
34. Dinesen 1979: 66.
35. Lagerlöf 1911a: 6.
36. Lagerlöf 1911b: 3.
37. Lagerlöf 1911a: 8.

Our gift to humanity is the Home – that, and nothing else. We have been building upon this little structure ever since the time of our Mother Eve. We have altered the plan; we have experimented; we have made new discoveries; we have gone back to the old; we have adapted ourselves; we have gone forth and tamed such among the wild beasts as were needed in the Home; we have selected from the growths of the earth fruit bearing trees, luscious berries, seeds, and the choicest flowers, we have furnished and decorated our Home; we have developed its customs; we have created the art of child training, comfort, courtesy, and pleasant social intercourse.[38]

Notice here the ironic use of '*detta och intent annat*' ('that and nothing else'), and the following listing of accomplishment necessary to the development of human civilisation. Lagerlöf then questions whether this accomplishment has ever been recognised: '*Är denna kvinnans insats i kulturen ringa eller värdefull? Är den uppskattad eller föraktad?*'[39] ('Is this woman's contribution to civilisation inconsiderable or valuable? Is it appreciated or despised?')[40] And the answer, according to Lagerlöf, can be found in her current society: '*Hun har den mannen kunnat bära alla sina olyckor? Det är därför, att hans hustru alltid har berett honom ett gott hem.*'[41] ('How has that man been able to bear up under all his misfortunes? Because his wife has always eased his burden by making a good Home for him.')[42] Because of this support, Lagerlöf explains, man has been able to create the State: '*Mannens främsta gåva till kulturen* är *den välordnade,*

---

38. Lagerlöf 1911b: 5.
39. Lagerlöf 1911a: 9.
40. Lagerlöf 1911b: 6.
41. Lagerlöf 1911a: 9.
42. Lagerlöf 1911b: 5.

*starka, skyddande staten.'*⁴³ ('Man's greatest contribution to civilisation is the well-organised, strong and protecting State.')⁴⁴ This concept of the Home and the domestic sphere as a woman's domain, as opposed to a man's external realm of action, is present in Blixen's speech as well:

> *Mandens Tygdepunkt, hans Væsens Gehalt, ligger i, hvad han i Livet udfører og udretter, Kvindens i, hvad hun er [...] dette vil da sige, at Manden skaber Værket af, men udenfor, sig selv [...] Kvindens Virke er at udvide hendes eget Væsen.*⁴⁵

> A man's center of gravity, the substance of his being, consists in what he has executed and performed in his life; the woman's in what she is [...] that is to say, the man creates something by himself, but outside of himself [...] the woman's function is to expand her own being.⁴⁶

In her speech, Blixen refers to the time she spent in Kenya to depict the interaction between the feminine domestic sphere with the masculine external activities:

> *I Øst-Afrika, der i min Tid var et Pionerland, blev den Kvindens Virksomhed, hvorom jeg har talt, hendes Udvidelse af hendes eget Væsen, paaskønnet i en Grad, som man vistnok herhjemme vanskeligt kan forestille sig. En Blomsterhave eller Blomsterbuket føltes, tror jeg, af de Mænd, som ko mind fra haardt Arbejde i Marken eller paa Ekspeditioner, som en Gve, ja, som en Velsignelse. De spurgte os: Har I nu faaet Lavandler til at gro? Men ingen Mand derude fandt i min Tid paa selv at anlægge*

---

43. Lagerlöf 1911a: 14.
44. Lagerlöf 1911b: 9.
45. Blixen 1965: 80.
46. Dinesen 1979: 73.

> *en Blomsterhave. I Virkeligheden tror jer, at Blomsterhavens Tilstedeværelse for Mændene derude havde sin egentlige Værdi deri, at den udtrykte eller betød vor egen Tilstedværelse for Mændene derude havde sin egentlige Værdi deri, at den udtrykte eller betød vor egen Tilstedeværelse. Til Gengæld vurderede vi, I Samspillet mellem os, Mændenes Arbejde og Daad langt højere, end Kvinder I Europa kunde gøre det.*[47]

In East Africa, which in my time was a pioneer country, the woman's activity about which I have spoken became an extension of her own being, valued to such a degree that we here at home would find it difficult to imagine. A flower garden or a bouquet was, I believe, felt by those men who came in from hard work in the fields or from expeditions to be a gift, yes, a blessing. They asked us, have you been able to grow lavender? In my time, no man out there undertook to plant a flower garden. In reality I believe that there the existence of a flower garden had for men its real value in that it expressed or represented our presence, in recompense we valued the interplay between us, the work and deeds of man, far higher than women in Europe could or do.[48]

## Work, inclusivity, and cooperation

Conscious, perhaps, of how reactionary her views might sound to her radio listeners, before going ahead to develop her theory of cooperation and interaction, Blixen introduces in her speech a crucial reference to the previous generation of the women's movement:

---

47. Blixen 1965: 85.
48. Dinesen 1979: 78.

*Jeg ved, i hvad Gæld jeg staar til de gamle Kvindesagskvinder I deres Grav. Naar jeg selv i mit Liv har kunnet studere, hvad jeg vilde og hvor jeg vilde, naar jeg har kunnet rejse alene Verden rundt, naar jeg frit har kunnet faa mine Ideer frem paa Tryk, ja, naar jeg i Dag kan staa paa en Talerstol, saa skylder jeg disse Kvinder det.*[49]

I know in which debt I stand to the older women of the women's movement now in their graves. When I myself in my lifetime have been able to study what I wished, and where I wished, when I have been able to travel around the world alone, when I have been able to put my ideas freely into print, yea, when I today can stand here at the lectern, it is because of these women.[50]

It is interesting to underline that this intergenerational reference appears in Lagerlöf too:

*Jag ställer mig framför Rembrandts gamla borgarkvinna, hon med de tusen rynkorna i det kloka ansiktet, och jag frågar henne, varför hon har levet [...] Vi läsa svaret i hennes milda och goda leende: 'Jag har ingenting annat gjort än skapat ett gott hem' [...] Vi veta, att om vi fragade mannen, om vi kunde ställa upp dem släktled efter släktled, tusental och milliontal efter varandra, skulle ingen komma på den tanken att svara, att de ha varit för att skapa ett hem. Det har varit kvinnans sak. Det finns ingen man, som gör anspråk på äran att ha skapat hemmet.*[51]

I place myself before Rembrandt's old peasant woman, she of the thousand wrinkles in her intelligent face, and ask

---

49. Blixen 1965: 86.
50. Dinesen 1979: 79.
51. Lagerlöf 1911a: 7–8.

myself why she lived [...] We read the answer in her calm and kindly smile: 'All that I did was to make a good Home' [...] We know that if we were to ask the men, could line them up, generation after generation, thousands and millions in succession, it would not occur to one of them to say that he had lived for the purpose of making a good Home. That has been woman's affair. No man assumes the honour of having founded the Home.[52]

Stenberg notes how the employment of Rembrandt's portrait and the reference to previous generations of women 'lends women's work an eternal, almost mythical significance'.[53] Lagerlöf argues for more inclusivity in the workplace, urging women to enter the job market: *'Var övertygad framför allt, att det har varit nödvändigt! Du maste in överallt, du maste finnas till hands överallt, om staten en gång skall kunna bli älskad som ett hem.'*[54] ('Be assured that it is necessary work! You must enter all fields; you must be on hand everywhere, if the State is ever to be beloved like the Home. Be certain that your services, now so despised, shall soon be sought after.')[55] Lagerlöf reasons that the State will never function effectively, unless it includes women.

To explain the necessity for cooperation between the sexes, Lagerlöf describes how the success of the Home, and its everlasting strength, are the result of collaboration: *'Jag har vågat säga, att hemmet är kvinnans skapelse, men jag har aldrig sagt, att hon har skapat det ensam. Till lycka för henne och för alla har hon alltid där haft mannen bredvid sig. Husbonde och matmor har*

---

52. Lagerlöf 1911b: 4–5.
53. Forsås-Scott et al. 2014: 31.
54. Lagerlöf 1911a: 19.
55. Lagerlöf 1911b: 13.

*suttit sida vid sida.'*⁵⁶ ('I have been bold enough to state that the Home is woman's creation. But I did not say that she alone created it. Fortunately for her and for all of us, she has ever had the man with her. Master and mistress have sat side by side.')⁵⁷ And while not all Homes are perfect, across all society and classes they do function and they continue to provide the foundation of society. She underlines that in the creation of the State:

> *Har mannen stått ensam. Det har stått en drottning vid kungens sida under kröningspällen, men hon har inte varit med som drottning, bara som hustru. Intet har tvungit mannen att föra kvinnan med sig i domssalen, i ämbetsverket, i varumagasinet, han har strävat sig fram ensam med sina svåra värv.*⁵⁸

> [M]an has stood alone. Nothing has impelled man to take woman with him into the hall of Justice, into the Civil Service Department, into the House of Commerce. He has forged his way alone.⁵⁹

The success of his endeavour is questionable, according to Lagerlöf: *'Vad vittna hatet mellan samhällsklasserna? Vad vittna de dova ropen nedifrån, allt hot om omstörtning? Vad vittnar all klagan från arbetslösa? Vad vittnar utvandringen.'*⁶⁰ ('Witness

---

56. Lagerlöf 1911a: 17.
57. Lagerlöf 1911b: 12.
58. Lagerlöf 1911a: 17–18. Notice that *'Det har stått en drottning vid kungens sida under kröningspällen, men hon har inte varit med som drottning, bara som hustru'* is absent from the English translation. It could be argued that less than a decade after the death of Queen Victoria, the translator would consider this sentence difficult to contextualise for an English-speaking readership.
59. Lagerlöf 1911b: 12.
60. Lagerlöf 1911a: 18.

the hatred between the classes; witness the stifled cries from beneath, all the threats of revolutions. Witness the complaints of the unemployed; witness emigration!')[61] Including women in the State, and admitting the necessity of cooperation, would mean, according to Lagerlöf, the creation of the ideal State:

> *Ack, vi kvinnor äro inga fullkomliga varelser, ni män äro inte fullkomliga mera än vi. Hun skola vi nå fram till det, som är stort och gott utan att hjälpa varandra? Vi tro inte, att verket skall gå fort, men vi tro, att det vore synd, och dårskap att avvisa vår hjälp. Vi tro, att Guds vind för oss. Det lilla mästerverket, hemmet, var var skapelse men mannens hjälp. Det stora mästerverket, den goda staten, skall skapas av mannen, då han på allvar tar kvinnan till sin hjälpare.*[62]

Alas, we women are not perfect beings! You men are no more perfect than we are. How are we to attain that which is great and good unless we help each other? We do not think that the work can be accomplished at once, but we do believe that it would be folly to reject our help. We believe that the winds of God are bearing us onward, that our little masterwork, the Home, was our creation with the help of men. The great masterwork, the State, shall be perfected by man when in all seriousness he takes woman as his helper.[63]

## Under the disguise – reclaiming a feminine discourse

At the time of writing her '*Baaltale*', and having witnessed the gradual achievement of women's emancipation, for Blixen the

---

61. Lagerlöf 1911b: 12.
62. Lagerlöf 1911a: 19–20.
63. Lagerlöf 1911b: 14.

matter is now that of reclaiming women's essential difference from men. Blixen argues that it is now time for women to reassess their own individuality, to not act like men but as themselves. Blixen's critique of the first generation of feminists, indeed, is that of making their way into the masculine world of the workplace by adopting male disguises: '*Thi de gamle Kvindesagskvinder var ikke alene retsindige, tapre og urokkeligt tro – de var ogsaa listige!* [...] *Eller de gjorde deres Indtog i Forklædning, i en mental og psykisk Mandssragt*'[64] ('The early women of the women's movement were not only just, courageous, and unswervingly loyal – they were also sly! [...] that is, they made their entrance in disguise, in a costume which intellectually or psychologically represented a male'),[65] and she is now encouraging women to act differently: '*Men i Dag er jo Kvinden ude af Lemmen i Træhesten og indefor Citadellernes Mure. Og hun har vistnok faaet saa fast Fodfæste i de gamle Borge, at hun frejdigt kan opslaa sin Ridderhjelm og vise Verden, at hun er Kvinde og ingen formummet Skælm.*'[66] ('But today, woman has sprung out from the wooden horse and walks within the walls of the citadels. And she has certainly such a firm footing in the old strongholds that she can confidently open her visor and show the world that she is a woman and no disguised rogue.')[67]

Referring again to Showalter's distinction, the Female phase is the time to reject the two forms of dependency – imitation and protest – and reclaim the female experience. Anticipating post-war French feminism, Blixen seems to be suggesting that to reach true emancipation, women should be owning their own discourse and distance themselves from a male one: '*Under Forklædningen er vi, hvad vi er, og hvad vi gennem Tiderne har*

---

64. Blixen 1965: 87.
65. Dinesen 1979: 80.
66. Blixen 1965: 87.
67. Dinesen 1979: 80.

været. For vi har, i fuld Troskab mod vort kvindelige Væsen, og med fuld Overholdelse af vor kvindelige Værdighed.'[68] ('Under the disguise we are what we are, and what we have been throughout time. With complete loyalty towards our female being and in complete accord with our female dignity.')[69] Blixen also notices that although women are still kept away from the higher roles of the workplace, the feminine element is present in all the grounding figures of the patriarchal Western society:

*For dem, der holdt paa, at Kvindeligheden maa skurre paa Prækestolen of i Dommersædet, vil det være værd at lægge Mærke til, at de mandlige Sagkyndige, der saa selvfølgeligt har indtaget deres Pladser der, gerne – ligesom drevene af et særligt Instinkt – har ændret deres Apparition hen imod den kvindelige. Vor Præstekjole med den hvide, pibede Krave er jo en smuk og værdig Kvindedragt, Lægerens og Husmødrenes Kilter har meget tilfælles, og de høje Dommere bærer i Funktion folderige Klæder og forhøjer i nogle Lande deres Værdighed med langlokkede, krusede Parykker.*[70]

For those who have believed that femininity would grate in the pulpit and on the bench, it is worth observing that the male experts who have, as a matter of course, taken their places there have, driven as it were by a special instinct, willingly changed their appearance somewhat towards the womanly. Our clergyman's robe with its white ruff is a beautiful and noble woman's costume; the physician's and housemother's white coats have much in common; high-ranking judges wear flowing robes when on the bench and in some countries enhances their dignity with long, curly wigs.[71]

---

68. Blixen 1965: 88.
69. Dinesen 1979: 81.
70. Blixen 1965: 91.
71. Dinesen 1979: 84–85.

Both Blixen and Lagerlöf identify the feminine element as the essential missing element in a patriarchal society. To be effective, society, or State, must acknowledge the necessity of including women and the feminine element. The feminine in both authors represents a strong grounding element – in Lagerlöf it is embodied in the Home as the foundation of the State, in Blixen in the way its representation is worn and used by the founding figures of Western society, such as church and justice. It is the essential grounding aspect of the feminine that is necessary for the development of society in Blixen:

> *vor eget Samfund, – i hvilket Menneskene er naaet saa vidt i hvad de kan udrette og i de konkrete Resultater de kan vise,- det trænger til Mennesker, som er. Ja, selve vor Tid kunde siges at behøve at omlægge sin ambition fra at udrette mere, til at være* [...] *'thi jeg vil lægge Tidens Kvinder lige saa vel som dens Mænd dette paa Hjerte: ikke blot at tænke paa, hvad de vil udrette, men dybeste at vide, hvad de er.*[72]

> precisely our small society – in which human beings have achieved so much in what they are able to do and in what concrete results they can show – needs people who are. Indeed, our own time can be said to need a revision of its ambition from doing to being [...] I wish to insinuate into the minds of the women of our time as well as those of the men, that they should meditate not only upon what they may accomplish but most profoundly upon what they are.[73]

In both Blixen and Lagerlöf, the ultimate aim of their speeches is not to argue for one gender's superiority against the other, but

---

72. Blixen 1965: 92–93.
73. Dinesen 1979: 85–86.

rather to advocate the necessity of interplay and interaction of both in order to establish a healthy and strong society. Lagerlöf reasons '*Ack, vi kvinnor äro inga fullkomliga varelser, ni män äro inte fullkomliga mera än vi. Hun skola vi nå fram till det, som är stort och gott utan att hjälpa varandra?*'[74] ('Alas, we women are not perfect beings! You men are no more perfect than we are. How are we to attain that which is great and good unless we help each other?')[75] and, as if completing this consideration, Blixen writes '*Jeg selv anser Inspiration for at være den højeste menneskelige Lykke. Og Inspirationen kræver altid to Elementer [...] Ja, jeg tror at jo mægtigere denne gensidige Inspiration virker, jo rigere og mere levende vil et Samfund udvikle sig.*'[76] ('I myself look upon inspiration as the greatest human blessing. And inspiration always requires two elements [...] Yes, I think that the more strongly the mutual inspiration functions, the richer and more animated a society will develop.')[77]

## Conclusive thoughts

This paper was inspired by Bjarne and by his research into Selma Lagerlöf, especially his work in *Re-Mapping Lagerlöf: Performance, Intermediality and European Transmissions*, which he co-edited with Helena Forsås-Scott and Lisbeth Stenberg. This paper was also inspired by Bjarne's lecturing work and, on a more personal note, by his invaluable guidance as a supervisor while writing my doctoral thesis on Karen Blixen.[78] In celebration of his long and admirable career, and in everlasting

---

74. Lagerlöf 1911a: 19.
75. Lagerlöf 1911b: 14.
76. Blixen 1965: 77.
77. Dinesen 1979: 70.
78. See Tesio-Ryan 2019.

gratitude of what his academic support has meant to me, I thought it fitting to write about two of his, and my, favourite women writers of all time.

When Bjarne kindly gave me a copy of *Re-Mapping Lagerlöf* and I first read Lisbeth Stenberg's chapter on Lagerlöf's 'Hem och Stat', I immediately thought of Karen Blixen's 'En Baaltale'. At the time, I was a tutor in Danish Literature and my classes were designed around Blixen's 'En Baaltale', her conceptualisation of femininity, the impact of her years in Kenya in the development of so many of her female characters, and her understanding of gender and social roles.

'En Baaltale' always triggered lively discussion in the class – Blixen's approach to gender, the idea of interaction and inspiration, seemed to be very relevant still to this day. However, because the life of a part-time PhD student is doomed to always be a hectic affair, I never actually had the time to explore how Blixen's and Lagerlöf's thoughts on feminism and the feminine compared – and even worse, I never fully discussed the topic with Bjarne during our supervisions. Hence, I took the opportunity to write this paper to finally do it. Bjarne himself has compared Lagerlöf to another iconic Dane, Hans Christian Andersen, in his paper 'Comparative Considerations: Lagerlöf, Andersen and the British Perspective', where he observes 'some notable similarities and direct influences between texts'.[79]

In comparing 'Hem' and 'En Baaltale', I was struck by the similarities between them. Despite their stylistic differences, as well as the notable historical distance, I found it compelling that both authors had such similar approaches to the subject of gender. While Karen Blixen was certainly a Lagerlöf reader – which can be seen from the several annotated copies of Lagerlöf

---

79. Thomsen Thorup 2011: 2.

novels among her library holdings in Rungstedlund[80] – it is not clear whether she had the opportunity to read 'Hem och Stat', making a direct correlation between the two papers difficult to establish. Yet, in comparing the two texts, I had the impression that they somehow complemented each other, as if they were, in a way, dialoguing. The post-suffragette, almost existential consideration of gender in 'En Baaltale' could be read as a commentary to 'Hem och Stat'. Perhaps it could be considered as Karen Blixen's way to finally repay the debt she knew she owed to those *'gamle Kvindesagskvinder'* with an oration which aims to inspire a new generation to reconsider their roles and adapt them to an evolving and developing society. I believe that those two papers demonstrate that both Lagerlöf and Blixen were not only remarkably brave, versatile, and accomplished authors, they were also original thinkers and, each in their own way, very ahead of their time.

## Bibliography

Blixen, Karen. 1965. *Essays*. Rungstedlundfonden, København: Gyldendal, 64–82.

Bondesson, Pia. 1982. *Karen Blixens bogsamling på Rungstedlund, En katalog*. København: Gyldendal, 207–208.

de Beauvoir, Simone. 1949. *Le Deuxième Sexe*. Paris: Gallimard.

Dinesen, I. 1979. *Daguerreotypes, and Other Essays*. W.D. Paden and P.M. Mitchell (trans.). Chicago: The University of Chicago Press.

Forsås-Scott, Helena et al. 2014. *Re-mapping Lagerlof: Performance, Intermediality, and European Transmission*. Lund: Nordic Academic Press.

International Alliance of Women. 1939. *Report of the Thirteenth Congress Copenhagen July 8th to 14th 1939*. Ashford: International Alliance of

---

80. See Bondesson 1982: 207, 208, entries: 903–907.

Women. https://lse-atom.arkivum.net/uklse-dl1if010030010085. 12 September 2022.

Johannesson, Eric O. 1960. 'Isak Dinesen and Selma Lagerlof'. *Scandinavian Studies* 32:1, 18–26.

Lagerlöf, Selma. 1911a. *Hem och stat. Föredrag vid rösträttskongressen den 13 juni 1911*. Stockholm: Bonnier. https://litteraturbanken.se/f%C3%B6rfattare/Lagerl%C3%B6fS/titlar/HemOchStat Accessed 12 September 2022.

———. 1911b. *Home And State.* V. Swanston Howard (trans.). New York: The Woman Suffrage Party. Source: Library of Congress and Sewall-Belmont House and Museum, Washington, D.C.

Mral, Brigitte. 1999. 'The Public Woman: Women Speakers Around the Turn of the Century in Sweden'. In Christine Mason Sutherland and Rebecca Sutcliffe, *The Changing Tradition: Women in the History of Rethotic*. Calgary: University of Calgary Press, 168.

Showalter, Elaine. 1978. *A literature of their own.* London: Virago.

Showalter, Elaine. 2016. 'Towards a Feminist Poetics'. In Mary Jacobus (ed.), *Women Writing and Writing about Women*. London: Routledge, 35.

Stecher, Marianne. 2014. *The creative dialectic in Karen Blixen's essays: on gender, Nazi Germany, and colonial desire.* Copenhagen: Museum Tusculanum Press, 39.

Tesio-Ryan, Barbara. 2019. 'Reassessing Karen Blixen's Gengældelsens Veje/The Angelic Avengers: a novel challenging gender, totalitarianism and colonial practices'. Unpublished PhD thesis. University of Edinburgh.

Thomsen Thorup, Bjarne. 2011. 'Comparative Considerations: Lagerlof, Andersen and the British Perspective'. *Northern Studies* 42, 2.

· 12 ·

# Selma Lagerlöf's Transnational Terrains

## Lisbeth Stenberg

In 2014, a scholarly volume in the English language presenting the Swedish world literature author Selma Lagerlöf appeared. *Re-Mapping Lagerlöf. Performance, Intermediality, and European Transmissions* focused on new interdisciplinary research in three areas: Lagerlöf as a celebrity; films inspired by her texts; and her texts in relation to other cultures. Many of the chapters in the anthology were developed from papers given at the international Lagerlöf conference held in 2011 at University College London. On that occasion, the three first volumes of 'Lagerlöf in English', a series of new English translations, were launched by Norvik Press.

Both the conference and the book were initiatives of UCL's Professor Helena Forsås-Scott, who was also responsible for the Norvik Press 'Lagerlöf in English' series. She involved Bjarne Thorup Thomsen and this author in the organising of the conference and the editing of *Re-Mapping Lagerlöf.* In these projects, Bjarne was always on hand, doing his part without much ado. He was a perfect, reliable team player.

The release of the book took place in the celebration hall at the Swedish Academy in Stockholm on 17 May 2014. It was arranged thus in memory of the two first women to take chairs in the Academy: Selma Lagerlöf in 1914, and Elin Wägner in 1944. At the release, we editors were there lending a hand. Gunilla Blom Thomsen also made a considerable contribution, and getting to know her made me see that she was as dedicated as her husband in her efforts to promote Selma Lagerlöf's authorship.

The conference and the English-language presentation of current research was of vital importance for the Swedish Lagerlöf scholars who participated. Helena Forsås-Scott and Bjarne Thorup Thomsen, both working in British institutions, were at the centre of the international scene and had key contacts around the world. By creating spaces where we could meet both in person and in texts, they initiated further international contacts. In the years to follow, symposiums were held in Tokyo, Moscow, and Berlin to try to build networks in countries where Lagerlöf had been highly recognised in her time but from which no one had participated in the 2011 conference.

While Bjarne Thorup Thomsen opened up Lagerlöf research internationally, in his own research on Lagerlöf he brought attention to the way she used marginal places and positions. She sought – in his term – 'peripherality' when depicting the nation, and in this way she uncovered transnational terrains. In his chapter in *Re-Mapping Lagerlöf,* Bjarne illustrated these transnational terrains with great elegance by beginning with a little known utopian text from 1888 written at Landskrona – on the border with Denmark. By focusing on two central texts, *Nils Holgersson* and *The Outcast,* he deepened his analysis and showed Lagerlöf's efforts to avoid limitations and exclusions in creating a national identity. He finally presented a totally unknown text, 'Lapland–Schonen' from 1918. Lagerlöf was commissioned to write it as a piece to be read by German war prisoners being transported by train from Russia through Sweden, from Lapland in the north to Schonen in the south.

The readers are invited to remember their own local homeland ('*hembygd*') and compare it to parts of Sweden. The feeling for a landscape, the '*hembygd*', is a common experience. Bjarne understands 'Lapland–Schonen' as 'an important internationalisation of the idea of the wonderful journey'.

That Lagerlöf's authorship won international acclaim during her lifetime is well known: she was then translated into around forty languages. She was to a large extent promoted by the international women's movement, an important context and precondition for her authorship. Today, the publication of new translations makes it possible for readers across the globe to access her works. The values imbedded in Lagerlöf's authorship, of democratisation and the value of every human being, are still needed in the world today. With his research, Bjarne Thorup Thomsen has helped us understand the way that Lagerlöf in her art brought a true internationalism to life.

## Bibliography

Forsås-Scott, Helena, Stenberg, Lisbeth, and Thorup Thomsen, Bjarne (eds). 2014. *Re-Mapping Lagerlöf: Performance, Intermediality and European Transmissions*. Lund: Nordic Academic Press.

· 13 ·

# Olof Högberg's Analogy for the Colonisation of the North of Sweden

## Anders Öhman

I first met Bjarne Thorup Thomsen at the conference *Centring on the Peripheries* held at the University of Edinburgh in 2002. The theme of the conference was important to me. It tried to acknowledge the significance of literatures from parts of Northern Europe that had been marginalised as coming from peripheries. The conference showed that there could be surprising literary alliances and historical parallels between literatures from the northern parts of Scandinavia, Scotland, and Greenland. The different papers presented at the conference showed that the participants had similar experiences concerning the relation between periphery and the national centres in their countries.

It was Bjarne who understood these similarities between the northern regions and invited researchers and authors to share their experiences with each other and discuss the problems and the opportunities of belonging to a periphery. A few years later, Bjarne edited a volume, published by the Norvik Press, which contained several of the papers, including mine, delivered at the conference. This was an important step in my research of the novels from the northern part of Sweden, Norrland, which tried to talk back to the national centre of Sweden. Therefore, I am still much obliged to Bjarne for inviting me to Edinburgh and for making me see the similarities between the history of northern Sweden and other parts of Northern Europe.

In this article, I want to discuss a novel by Olof Högberg, one of the first writers who reacted against what he saw as the exploitation of Norrland by companies and authorities from the south of Sweden. Olof Högberg, who, together with his contemporary colleague Pelle Molin, is regarded as one of the first writers coming from and writing about Norrland. I argue that, in this rather unknown novel from the early twentieth century, Högberg found a way to discuss the consequences of colonisation. He did this, as I will try to show, by writing a chronicle of the colonisation of a fictive land in South America. The consequences consist of the creation of social, religious, and ethnic hierarchies, the subordination of indigenous people, and, not least, the exploitation of nature. These were issues concerning the relation between the south of Sweden and Norrland, which he had previously treated in novels, lectures, and articles.

Olof Högberg was born in the parish of Högsjö, located between the cities of Härnösand and Sundsvall, in 1855 and died in his home of Njurunda outside Sundsvall in 1932. Around 1900, he worked as a journalist at the newspaper *Sundsvalls-Posten* but left shortly before he made his debut as a writer with the novel *Den stora vreden* ('The Great Wrath'), which is the first great epic of Norrland. Chapters from the novel was rewarded with the journal *Idun*'s novel prize in 1905, and the complete edition of more than 1,200 pages was published in 1906.

Högberg has an aura of eccentricity surrounding him. He studied at Uppsala University for a long time without completing his exam, but that does not mean he was an idle student. He took an active part in different radical associations at the university devoted to discussions of problems of contemporary society, not least the question of the exploitation of land and forests in Norrland.

His childhood in the surroundings of Sundsvall and Härnösand meant that he grew up in what was considered the very centre of the violent industrialisation of the northern parts of Sweden. At close range he could watch how several forest industries threatened to decompose and ruin his childhood tracts. In his suite of novels *Från Norrlands sista halvsekel* ('*From Norrland's Last Half Century*'), published between 1910 and 1912, he gives a graphic picture of the rapid transformation of nature which followed in the steps of the forest industry:

*Här omkring sträckte sig nu det ändlösa skogsriket, där marker såldes, köptes och kalhöggs, skogsdomäner och millionförmögenheter skapades, millioner timmer flottades och millionbolag bildades. [...]. Alla foro fram som utbölingar från rus och i rus, utan hejd, utan vett, utan återhåll, utan tanke på en morgondag.*

Around here the endless forests laid, where land was sold, bought, and clear-cut, forest domains and fortunes of millions were made, timber in millions were log-driven and million-companies were formed [...]. Everyone ravished like outcasts from drunkenness and in drunkenness, with no stopping, no sense, no restraint, without any thought of tomorrow.[1]

Högberg saw through the contemporary rhetoric about Norrland as a land of the future. The promise of the future was associated with the exploitation of the natural resources in the north. There wasn't any reflection about what we today would call a sustainable development; it was more like devastation. At

---

1. Högberg, 1912: 89 (author's translation).

least, it seemed like that for Högberg. In a lecture script from the 1890s, he described the inhabitants of the north as unaware of the real worth of the natural resources, and thereby letting other people take care of them. These people didn't have any feeling for their real worth and meaning.

In another lecture script from around the turn of the century 1900, Högberg writes in the mode of satire about the colonial dimension in the south of Sweden's relation towards Norrland:

> *Vi ha gubevars många gånger hört omtalas att Norrland blifvit upptäckt på det ena eller andra viset. På 1850-talet upptäcktes det af skogspatroner. […] På sista tiden har landet upptäckts af geologer, kartografer, konstnärer, turister, vattenfalls- och grufspekulanter, mormonprofeter och alla möjliga sorters värfvare. […] I alla tider har Norrland på olika vis varit upptäckt. Och så pass djupt och mångtydigt är detta land att detta eviga upptäckande skall fortgå i evärdliga tider.*
>
> We have, goodness me, many times heard that Norrland has been discovered in one way or the other. In the 1850s it was discovered by forest bosses. […]. Lately the country has been discovered by geologists, cartographers, artists, tourists, waterfall- and mine-speculators, Mormon prophets, and all sorts of recruiters. […]. At all times, Norrland has in different ways been discovered. And so deep and versatile is this land that these constant discoveries will go on forever.[2]

Högberg seems to be saying that Norrland is not a virgin wasteland you can treat in any way you like. This is probably the reason why it is so crucial to Högberg that the people

---

2. Högberg, Olof Högbergs arkiv, vol 9, Landsarkivet i Härnösand, 'Kung Sverres genomtåg till Norges eröfring', MS (author's translation).

living in Norrland become aware that they have a history, a culture, and a nature which surrounds them with importance and meaning. And it is the role of the intellectuals to create such an awareness and cultural identity. As Högberg wrote in the journal *Idun* as a comment on what his motives were for writing *Den stora vreden*: '*Om detta land icke har en historia, en saga, så måste landet få en sådan!*' ('If this land does not have a history, a story, then the land must get one!')[3]

Therefore, it was the ambition to give Norrland a history, a cultural identity, which made it take so long to write *Den stora vreden* ('*The Great Wrath*').

Ingeborg Nordin-Hennel, who wrote the first study of Högberg's novel, claims that he was working on the novel at least since the end of the 1870s.[4] Mainly this had to do with the problem of finding a suitable form to contain all the stories and tales that Högberg had gathered and wanted to incorporate in his novel. In the end, it was the genre of the adventure novel, combined with that of the chronicle, which became the form that could solve his problems of composition. The adventure concatenated the different stories with each other and brought the plot forward in the long novel.

The novel, with the mythic Gråe Jägarn ('The Grey Hunter') and his godson Svarte-Mickel ('Black-Michael') as two of the main heroes, was mainly about how Norrland for a short period of time in the beginning of the eighteenth century was liberated from the oppression which had been the cause of its sufferings. For a while there is a kind of utopian equality in the north, but after a couple of years, the Swedish crown regains its power and the rebel leader and his wife, Mäster-Sara ('Master-Sara'), take their refuge in subterranean caves in the mountains.

---

3. Högberg: 1906 (author's translation).
4. Nordin-Hennel: 1976.

I have previously also mentioned the role of the chronicle in Högberg's novel in an article in the scholarly journal *Samlaren*, where I focused on the importance of the adventure plot to construct a Norrlandic cultural identity.[5] The chronicle functioned above all to contribute with descriptions and legends about events and relations in the past in the novel.

It is remarkable that Högberg's choice of the chronicle as a form originated from his interest in the colonisation of South America and the different chronicles which dealt with this. During his time as a student in Uppsala, he learned both Portuguese and Spanish to be able to read the old writings. One of the main influences for *Den stora vreden* probably was the Spanish writer Antonio de Solis y Rivadeneira's chronicle on the conquest of Mexico from 1691, *Historia de la conquista de Mexico*.

Thus, it seems that the chronicles on the different colonial powers' conquest of the continent of South America had a strong attraction for Olof Högberg. It seems not too far-fetched to imagine that he, in the Spanish nation's relation to the colonised parts of South America, could recognise a parallel to the colonisation of his own Norrland. Although Ingeborg Nordin-Hennel brings up the chronicle on the conquest of Mexico as an important influence for Högberg's *Den stora vreden*, she does not mention the novel that came out in 1915 and which I take as Högberg's attempt at writing a novel completely in the genre of the chronicle. That novel is *Under Jesu bröders' spira* ('*Under the sceptre of "The brothers of Christ"*').

The chronicle as a genre consists of, as its name indicates, chronological accounts for historical events. The perspective of the genre is mainly to report on conditions of a society and the changes of these. Therefore, it is not principally depicting how different characters are psychologically developed and changed

---

5. Öhman: 2015.

or how a hero acts as in the plot of an adventure novel; rather it is occupied with the description of events.

For this reason, Högberg's novel is also interesting from an ecocritical perspective. Many scholars with an ecocritical point of view have discussed other descriptive genres, like for example the pastoral, as distinctive for an early awareness of man's relation to nature. Graham Huggan and Helen Tiffin, in their *Postcolonial Ecocriticism*, argue that it is nature's impact on man which is usually the focus of these descriptive genres: 'The emphasis of pastoral or romantic elegy has generally been on the impact of the environment on the human rather than the other way round.'[6]

However, in Högberg's *Under Jesu bröders' spira* it is also described how the human affects nature. Högberg shows how certain men with their lust for power colonise other people and their land. In the process, this also upset the order of nature, even if the consequence regarding nature is only suggested in the text. It is interesting how the colonisation and its consequences are depicted in the novel about a fictitious nation in South America, and how this also has bearing on what you can call the Norrlandic question.

The novel begins with a foreword written by the narrator, the fictive last 'archduke of Mitácan, the last name vassal on the Andean wall, Fernán Diégo de Huèlvas'.[7] The chronicle about the history of Mitácan is directed his excellency General Don Carlos de Sucra of Orinóco, to whom Fernán Diégo escaped when Mitácan had gone under due to the rebellion of the indigenous people.

The perspective of the narrator Fernán Diégo is the view of the conqueror. He is the descendent in the third generation of

---
6. Huggan and Tiffin 2010: 16.
7. Högberg 1915: 3. [The novel has not been translated to English and all quotations are translated by this author.]

the knights that by coincidence happened to arrive at the realm that became Mitácan. He writes that in front of his paternal grandfather, who founded Mitácan as a fiefdom, '*låg som oftast El dorado, bakom dem alla rivna broar, se där en enkel geografi.*' ('mostly there lay El dorado, behind them all the demolished bridges, look, what a simple geography!').[8] That is, it is by coincidence that these Spanish knights arrive at Mitácan in the new world and occupy a land which they consider to become a vassal state to the Spanish crown. However, Castile and later Spain do not know of its existence, initially because they don't know how to get into contact with Spain, and later because the Jesuit priests make sure that no news between the old and the new world is transmitted.

By the way, this is an analogy to one of Högberg's arguments in *Den stora vreden*, regarding the unawareness of the royal power in Sweden of how its power was exercised in a harmful way in Norrland by both the clergy and the king's trustees.

Fernán Diégo describes Mitácan in the beginning as a paradise which made it seem like an El Dorado to the conquerors. There was the mighty mountain Atamináco, which irrigated the plateaus and made the land a fertile paradise. But he also contemptuously calls the inhabitants that populated the land to which the Spaniards arrived 'redskins', 'barbarians', and 'savages'. Also, he is ambivalent towards the role of the Jesuit priests in the making of Mitácan. They and their high-handedness, intolerance, and viciousness are the reason that Mitácan finally perishes, but, on the other hand, it is their structural engineering and craftmanship that made Mitácan one of the richest cities in the new world.

The leader of the rebellious indigenous people against the Jesuits and the other people of Mitácan was, according to the

---

8. Ibid.: 5.

chronicler, a *'rasförgäten vit ledarhand'* ('race-oblivious white leaderhand'), that is, a white man for whom the colour of the skin or ethnicity didn't matter:

> *Personen röjde nog för våra ögon tycke av en castilian, men icke så den främmande tonen i hans castilianska, om även denna flöt ledigt från hans mun. Staben utgjordes till största delen av nordiskt blonda män. De talade ett strävt men ej missljudande språk, där ett ofta återkommande ord var fan eller möjligen vad holländaren skriver som van.*

> That person seemed to our eyes to have the resemblance of a Castilian, but not so the foreign tone of his language, even if this flowed freely from his mouth. His staff consisted mainly of Nordic blonde men. They talked a rough but not dissonant language, where a frequent word was fan or perhaps what the Dutch people writes as van.[9]

It is this leader of, supposedly Swedish, men that Mauritz Edström in an essay declares to be none other than the hero from *Den stora vreden*, Svarte-Mickel ('Black-Michael'), the godson of Gråe Jägarn ('The Grey Hunter') and the liberator of Norrland.[10] And of course, it will be he who comes to liberate Mitácan from its colonial masters, whether these represent the secular or the spiritual powers.

However, the story of Mitácan does not begin with Fernán Diégo's paternal grandfather, the Jesuit priests, or the other Castilians. Those who, apart from the Iquitos, constituted the inhabitants of Mitácan from the beginning in the sixteenth century were refugees from the oppressive tyranny of the

---

9. Ibid.: 6–7. (*Fan* is a Swedish swear word for the devil.)
10. Edström 1981.

old world. They came to the continent of South America in the hope of creating a new home for themselves. Until the Castilian knights arrived, this was a home depicted as a new kind of Eden. The unique aspect of these refugees was that they represented all three great religions in their time. They were Jews, Christians, and Muslims that had been forced together on the ships to protect their lives and escape from oppression.

Because they were people in exile, they didn't have any claims on the unknown territory to which they arrived. From the start, the native Iquitos were suspicious and sought to question the newly arrived about what they were looking for in their land. Those answered that they only wanted nourishment for themselves and their families. It was an answer that satisfied the Iquitos who therefore chose to *'bevilja främlingen från havet en broderlig landrätt jämsides med sig själva i detta paradisiska land'* ('grant the strangers from the sea a brotherly right of land alongside themselves in this paradisiac land').[11]

The chronicler reflects on the nature which surrounds the first refugees and declares that it constitutes an eternal background to the development of Mitácan from its greatness to its downfall:

> *Och bland dessa högslätter, som aldrig skulle svika första stundens löften om ett paradis, hamnade omsider fäderna i sitt eget valda klimat å södra basen till Nevádan de Ataminácо. Allt framgent skulle detta urverk skifta deras dagars stunder med teckenspråk i rosenrött och guld, violett och liljeskärt [...]. Och sedan, utan att behöva vite mäns beundrande aktgivelse, skulle Nevádan vidare, lika oförtruten som förr i världens tider, avdela året, skifta timmar, flöda och välsigna landet, pålitlig, god och härlig endast genom fri betingelse i sitt eget väsen.*

---

11. Ibid.: 17.

And among these plateaus, who never would betray its first promise of a paradise, the fathers ended at length in their own chosen climate at the south base to the Nevâda de Ataminâco. Henceforth, their clockwork would divide the moments of their days with a sign language in rose and gold, violet and pink […]. And then, without the need for the admiring attention of white men, the Nevâda would, just as tireless as before in the times of the world, divide the year, change the hours, flow, and bless the land, reliable, good, and lovely only through free conditions in its own being.[12]

There are similarities with the views of nature which Huggan and Tiffin say characterise the pastoral. Nature affects man through its cyclical movement, but it stays eternal and unaffected by her.[13] It is a view of nature that Timothy Morton in his *Ecology without Nature* calls a traditional ecological view where man is placed besides the so called 'nature'.[14]

This is also, interestingly, a view of nature that the first refugees in their daily practice does not include. They live in and with nature. They do not use it as scenery, or a pastoral background, which becomes clear when the first knights of Castile arrive and threaten the Edenic condition. As the knights disappointedly observe when they first enter the city: '*Den stora slätten tedde sig för sviket spanande ögon som ett huvudsakligt åkerbruks- och betesland.*' ('The great plain looked, to disappointedly searching eyes, as mainly a pasture and agricultural land'.)[15] That is, just like Norrland, it was not an exotic virgin land but settled, cultivated, and inhabited.

In the society which the first refugees created, and in which Josua Cazár became the natural leader, the hierarchies of the old

12. Ibid.: 22.
13. Huggan and Tiffin 2010.
14. Morton 2007.
15. Högberg 1915: 36.

world vanished. Cazár understood how to '*rikta krafterna på den omgivande rika naturens många möjligheter, hålla trogen fred och vänskap med iquiterna och angelägnare* än *allt tygla kolonisternas inbördes troshat*' ('turn their energies to the surrounding fertile nature's many possibilities, to maintain a loyal peace and friendship with the Iquitos and, more important than anything else, curb the settler's mutual hatred of belief').[16] Their relation to the Iquitos is also, I think, an analogy to how Högberg imagined the northerners' relationship with the Sami people should look like.

It is nearly a utopian society that is established in the new continent, though it is a society that does not bear the stamp of exotism or idealisation. It is a concrete and pragmatic society, something of the kind Högberg thought about the society of Norrland. Cazár and the chief of the Iquitos became close friends, and their unison lasted for three generations. And, as the chronicler observes, quarrels between different religious beliefs were forbidden:

> *Den ständigt värnade friden medförde, att kärleken allt som oftast slog enande bryggor mellan olik troende och utjämnade skiljaktligheten till en viss fördragsamhet.* [...] *Man började småningom tycka, att både Christus, Moses och Muhámmed kunde vara bra på olika vis* [...]. *Ja, märkligt nog icke heller hedningen befanns så dum i alla delar, när man väl och vackert kom på vänlig fot med honom. Religionerna försmälte, raserna likaså till en ny folkstam.*

> The constant protected peace entailed that love most often resulted in unifying bridges between different believers and flattened out disputes to a certain tolerance. [...] One began to think that both Christ, Moses, and Muhammed could be

---

16. Ibid.: 23.

alright in different ways [...]. And yes, strangely enough, not even the heathen was seen as all that foolish, when one became friends with him. The religions fused, and so did the races into a new racial group.[17]

Indeed, the original Mitácan was a kind of Eden because its foundation was built on unanimity and the mixing of racial group, religion, and nature, and the fact that it did not contain any hierarchies. But it was also a society that lived and functioned in a continuous pragmatic and concrete exchange between nature and culture. Nature was work and nourishment, not a projection surface for exotic and pastoral ideas or exploitation for the sake of profit.

This certainly will change when the first knights of Castile arrive. It is significant that the refugees do not have a particular name for the city where they have lived in peace for some generations. They just call it the Castle and are genuinely surprised when they hear that it is called Ciudád Mitácan by the knights. The leader of the refugees, Cazár, wants to know why the knights think that Ciudád Mitácan is so famous. The answer from one of the knights points to the difference between the two groups of colonisers. His answer is that it '*helt naturligt* är, *att man föga vet om en stad, som* ännu *ingen sett*' ('is quite natural that one know so little about a city no one yet have seen'), and continues by saying that, in the same way people were searching for the holy grail, lately they have been looking for '*El Dorado eller Ciudád Mitácan i alla riktningar av Nya världen*' ('El Dorado or Ciudád Mitácan in all directions of the new world').[18]

In the eyes of the knight, the castle is something that, by virtue of being unknown, may function as a projection surface

---

17. Ibid.: 24.
18. Ibid.: 32.

and a momentum for ambition and conquest. The knight also does not care about the people who already live in the city – for him it is an unseen city. It is a view that is exoticising and which transforms the world of the refugees into an empty virgin place to colonise, almost like a blank paper to write upon.

In the discussion with Cazár, the knight finally asks if they are allowed to call the place Ciudád Mitácan. In view of the future, a name is needed, he says, and continues: '*Ett stort och lysande namn, som framtiden helt säkert skall rättfärdiga! För övrigt, här kunde både geografer och kronister komma på besök; sådana måste ju hava namngivna städer för sina kartor och böcker.*' ('A great and brilliant name which the future surely will justify! Moreover, both geographers and chroniclers could come visiting. Those must have named cities for their maps and books.')[19]

The talks between Cazár and the knights arriving ends in the knights' primary business, which is that Mitácan in the future will be the property of the crown of Castile. Admittedly, the refugees are granted tax exemption and freedom of religion for a period of one hundred years, but after that they must obey the king. The chronicler and narrator comments that the refugees were happy being discovered and gave their approval to everything the knights suggested.

This is one of the places where one can perceive the author Olof Högberg's argument through the discourse of the chronicler: '*Ingen mindes längre de gömda fädernas vedermödor under hans katolska majestät av Castilien, ty ett folk utan liv i sin egen historia vandrar fram genom tiderna med sina dyrbaraste skatter i bottenslarvig säck å ryggen.*' ('No one no longer remembered the hardship of the hidden fathers under the reign of the Catholic majesty of Castile, because a people without spirit in their own history wanders through time with their most precious treasures in a sloppy

---

19. Ibid.: 32.

bag on their back.')²⁰ This is a clear reference to what, according to Högberg, has happened to Norrland. As he wrote in the journal *Idun*: '*Om detta land icke har en historia, en saga, så måste landet få en sådan!*' ('If this land does not have a history, a story, then it must obtain one!').²¹ It is a reference to the way Norrland had become a projection surface for all kinds of exoticism, but also a criticism towards the northerners themselves for not having cherished the memory of their history. Thereby, they had been exposed to the colonisers' exploitation of their land and their culture.

The arrival of the knights is also the beginning of the end of Mitácan, even if the continuation of their story is what Högberg's novel mainly consists of. The important thing for my discussion, however, takes place in the first forty pages. The rest of the chronicle consists of a slowly increasing perversion of power and an early vision of what Timothy Morton would call a dark ecology, i.e., everything and everyone is interconnected as if in a loop.²²

First, it affects the relations between the people of Mitácan and the Iquitos, and then the freedom of religion. The Jesuit priests, who arrive in Mitácan shortly after the knights, are skilled craftsmen and builders, but they also strive towards both spiritual and secular dominance. They execute the leaders of the Iquitos because they do not accept God as their Lord and as heathens insists on worshipping nature and especially the mountain Atamináco.

Gradually it becomes clear to the chronicler Fernán Diégo that the Jesuit priests have constructed a veritable factory in the underworld of the city of Mitácan to, in an industrial way, take care of the inhabitants' bodies after they died. However, to increase the production rate, they also accelerate death through an ingenious irrigation system which, in an orbit of birth and

---
20. Ibid.: 36.
21. Högberg 1906.
22. Morton 2016.

death, produces both manure and plague of the dead so that they infect the living, besides manufacturing other products from their bodies. It is a depiction of hell that prefigures testimonies from the concentration camps of the Second World War. During the siege of Mitácan, Fernán Diégo and his closest men discover the death factories of the Jesuit priests underneath the city. The chronicler and the others open a door and enters a room that

> [...] *tycktes innesluta något slags fabrik.* [...] *Vad kunde detta vara? På en hylla i grannskapet anträffades fosfor i massor. Åh, man gjorde fosfor av våra dödas ben, när de äntligen avskalats i pesthärden.* [...] *I nästa avdelning funno vi ett garveri med fina, vita människohudar å stängerna. I ett hörn tillverkades i massa våra överdådiga 'handskar av Sverige'! Sista avdelningen visade oss en kokare förblekning av de dödas hår, som hängde fullt på stänger i skrumpnade skalper* [...] *Alltså, vad allting var det nu, som 'Herrens bröder' tillverkade av oss? Peruker, handskar, såpa, tvål, lim, fosfor, gödsel och pest!*

> [...] seemed to contain some kind of factory. [...] What could this be? On a shelf nearby a lot of phosphorus was to be found. Ah, they made phosphorus of the bones of our dead when they had been peeled off in the plague. [...] In the next section we came upon a tannery with fine, white human hide on bars. In one corner a large amount of our luxurious 'gloves of Sweden' were manufactured! In the last section a boiler showed us the bleaching of the hair of the dead, hanging from the bars in withered scalps [...]. Thus, what was all this that 'the brethren of the Lord' made from us? Wigs, gloves, soap, glue, phosphorus, manure, and plague![23]

---

23. Högberg 1915: 186–187.

It seems that Högberg, through the chronicler/narrator, wants to show the consequences when power becomes abstract with no connection with concrete nature and the people who organically work with it.

From a postcolonial ecocritical perspective, the original Eden in Högberg's novel is a place where things *are* and are *made*. This is the reason that it makes no sense to create a distance between men themselves or between men, animals, or nature. There exists no awareness of the fall, no projections or wishful thinking, only active work. Unfortunately, it also makes the refugees vulnerable because they lack awareness of their own history. This was the same as in the case with the culture and nature of Norrland that Olof Högberg was an early and eager spokesman of, and which the fictitious colony of Mitácan in many ways reflect.

The story of the conquest of the fictive South American city of Mitácan is, in the genre of the chronicle, an allegory of the history of Norrland. From the beginning, Norrland was an egalitarian and near utopian part of the country, where there was no aristocracy or priesthood and where the inhabitants lived in unison with each other and with the indigenous Sami people. At least, that was what Högberg imagined and wanted to highlight with his writing. To this aim he especially, so it seems, added an aversion towards the clergy.

According to Högberg, after this Edenic condition in the history of Norrland, the explorers and the exploiters arrived and broke the egalitarian relations and ravished nature for the greedy sake of profit. It was with a depiction like this that Högberg wanted Norrland to write back to the authorities in the south of Sweden.

There were several reasons for his choice to disguise his critique of colonisation. He had already written two novels that took place in Norrland, but none of them seemed to create any reaction against what he saw as the exploitation of Norrland. I think that his reading of the chronicle of the conquest of Mexico gave him the idea that he could make his critique more profound by writing a chronicle. He clearly saw the analogies between the conquest of South America and Norrland – why shouldn't other people see it? Also, in *Den stora vreden* ('*The Great Wrath*') he had partly used the form of the chronicle to retell stories and legends that he had heard, and I believe it suited his way of writing. He was more inclined towards storytelling than in creating dialogue and dramatic conflicts between his characters.

You can certainly say that Högberg failed with his novel's ambition. I have not found a single review of the novel, only an article that says he is going to publish the novel, and I presume that only a few people might have read the novel since it was published. Despite this, it is an interesting book, not least in the way it foreshadows an ecological consciousness and relates this to a postcolonial problematic. Also, it shows how an intellectual and a writer in Norrland in the early twentieth century reacted against what he considered to be a colonisation and exploitation of the nature and culture of the north of Sweden. Even if the novel itself was not a success, Olof Högberg's writing in general had a great impact on successive Norrland writers – he was an inspiration to authors such as Albert Viksten, Kerstin Ekman, and Sara Lidman in their writing about the nature and culture of Norrland and its complex colonial relation with the south of Sweden.

## Bibliography

Edström, Mauritz. 1981. 'Svarte-Mickels återkomst'. In I. Nordin-Hennel and M. Edström (eds), *Drömmen om Norrland och världen*. Bjästa: CeWe förlaget.

Huggan, Graham and Tiffin, Helen. 2010. *Postcolonial ecocriticism. Literature, animals, environment*. London: Routledge.

Högberg, Olof. 1906. 'Den stora vreden och dess författare'. *Idun* 4.1.

———. 1912. *Från Norrlands sista halvsekel III. Utbölingar*, del 1, Stockholm: C.E. Fritzes bokförlag.

———. 1915. *Under Jesu bröders' spira. Ur nya världens romantik, en förgången stats historia, ett samhälles väg till döden*, del 1, Stockholm: C.E. Fritzes.

Morton, Timothy. 2007. *Ecology without Nature. Rethinking environmental aesthetics*. Cambridge, Mass: Harvard University Press.

———. 2016. *Dark Ecology. For a logic of future coexistence*. New York: Columbia University Press.

Nordin-Hennel, Ingeborg. 1976. *Den stora vreden. Studier i Olof Högbergs prosaepos*. Umeå: Acta Universitatis Umensis.

Öhman, Anders. 2015. 'Olof Högbergs Den stora vreden och skapandet av Norrland'. *Samlaren. Tidskrift för forskning om svensk och annan nordisk litteratur*, Årgång 136.

The Many Faces of Denmark

· 14 ·

# The Right Stuff: Gösta Winkler, Akademisk Skytteforening, and Churchill's 'Danish Demand'

## John Gilmour

On the day of the liberation of Denmark from the five-year German occupation, 5 May 1945, twenty-six-year-old Gösta Winkler found himself on duty with a detachment of other resistance volunteers in central Copenhagen. Standing guard outside the Danish *Rigsdag* ('Parliament'), Gösta Winkler was unaware on that day that he stood at the intersection of several long-running strands in Scandinavian, Danish, and European history. What had brought him there and how was that connected to Winston Churchill? This article will look at Gösta Winkler's resistance membership, the notable organisation that he joined, the training that he received, and how that came to be used in 1945.[1]

The research is based on a wider-ranging review of social, cultural, and political influences on middle-class motivation

---

1. I am grateful to Gösta Winkler's daughter, Anne (and to her husband Prof. Pierrick Pourchasse) for her recollections of her father and for access to his wartime papers, hereafter AWC – Anne Winkler Collection. I am additionally grateful to Prof. Claus Bundgård Christensen, Prof. Jonas Frykman, and Dr. Bjarne Thorup Thomsen for their help and advice.

to participate in one of the many groups that comprised the Danish Second World War non-communist resistance movement (*borgerlige modstandsbevægelse*) and the view that many of the same influences had created and maintained a specific group, *Akademisk Skytteforening (AS)*, to provide resistance participation and motivation. Additionally, the research looks at Danish and British fears of a post-occupation Soviet takeover in Denmark, and how that affected the role and deployment of *AS*.

The results indicate that membership of *AS* was attractive to patriotic, non-socialist urban males due to an emphasis on service to the nation, firmly rooted in traditional values that were reinforced by symbols, ceremonies, songs, and social bonding which were inherited from an earlier era. The *AS* military structure and culture facilitated professional combat training for civilians who were expected to risk their lives.

The British, through SOE-support for *borgerlige modstandsbevægelse*, approved the policy, promulgated by the Danish army leadership, to hold themselves in readiness for the liberation. This resulted in *AS*'s deployment to protect the capital city from the communists, with British encouragement and approval, rather than engaging in pre-liberation guerrilla warfare with the German occupiers. The *AS* research complements Peter Birkelund's excellent study of *borgerlige modstandsbevægelse* which concentrates on another associated resistance group, *Studenternes efterretningstjeneste* (see below).[2]

Gösta Winkler was born on 18 March 1919 in Copenhagen, Denmark, the child of two Swedish parents who had settled there. After graduating from high school, he joined another Swedish family's firm, Sonessons, before branching off with a colleague to start up Anderson & Winkler. The company

---

2. Birkelund 2000.

specialised in selling machinery, tools, chains, and the like. In 1936, Gösta Winkler and a friend, John Hornbech, travelled south to Berlin for the Olympic Games, which the new regime there intended as a showcase for their Nazi state and its policies. Gösta Winkler recalled later that while there, he formed his view that Hitler was an evil and dangerous man.

The invasion and occupation of Denmark by Germany began on 9 April 1940. Gösta Winkler later wrote a thirty-page Swedish manuscript narrative (undated) of the events between 1940 and 1945, drawing on a sixteen-page Danish manuscript narrative (also undated).[3] While these two texts are in themselves accurate and informative, they replicate countless similar general narratives at the expense of the insight that we would have gained if Gösta Winkler had set down more of his own experiences and feelings throughout these momentous years. Fortunately, there are one or two glimpses of his adventures, but like many of his contemporaries, he presumably felt that what he experienced was less important to record than the deeds of civil and military leaders, and we consequently are the losers. 'I will not bore you with all the different activities and events during these months [...]'[4] However, it is not the intention here to recount the developments during the years of occupation while there are several excellent histories available as background.[5]

The Danish reaction to occupation was initially stunned and then muted. The neutrality that had protected Denmark during the First World War had been brutally discarded by Hitler, and Danish leaders accepted a 'protective' occupation that allowed life in Denmark to continue much as before.

---

3. *AWC Danmark under ockupationen* (sic) *1940–1945* (hereafter *DUO*). *Erobringen at Danmark & Norge* den 9 april (hereafter *EDN*).
4. *DUO*: 26.
5. Olesen 2013; Christensen 2013.

Except that it could not, and unease became criticism. However, Gösta Winkler wrote that in 1941 '[t]here was not as yet any resistance movement', but he joined a Copenhagen group called *Akademisk Skytteforening (AS)* – 'Academic Shooting Association' in English.[6] This was to be a decisive step in Gösta Winkler's life, becoming member number 386 in the *terrainsportsafdelingen* or field sports section.[7] As another member joining *AS* at this time, Arne Børge Sejr, recalled,

> I joined *AS to* learn to shoot [...] in 1940 when I became a student [...] *AS was in reality the first group that had the advantage of being ready to fight the Germans.*[8] [author's italics]

Sejr went on to establish *Studenternes efterretningstjeneste (SE)*, 'Students' Intelligence Service', a movement that would play a significant part in the resistance movement and would involve Gösta Winkler in one of the most memorable events of the occupation.[9]

Unlike *SE*, *Akademisk Skytteforening* was not formed in response to the occupation. Its origin was much more complex, and its place in Danish society was more deeply rooted and influential. Gösta Winkler had become a member of an historic organisation that had decades of service behind it and had retained many – but not all – the features of its earlier background. *AS* has its origins in the civilian volunteer quasi-military corps formed in Sweden and Denmark in the mid-nineteenth

---

6. *DUO*: 11.
7. Erling Heidler, AS Editor, 8 October 2019, email.
8. Sejr 1995.
9. 'Arne Sejr'. http://denstoredanske.dk/Dansk_Biografisk_Leksikon/Medier/Journalist/Arne_Sejr. Accessed 12 April 2020.

century to support national defence.[10] Three common driving forces stimulated their formation in both countries.

Firstly, growing national identity and the influence of 'Scandinavianism' was combined with national humiliation on the battlefield leading to a loss of territory. For Sweden, this was the victory of Russia in the east during the Finnish War (1808–09). The result was that Finland, an integral province of the Swedish kingdom, became a grand duchy of the Czarist Empire. Despite the new Swedish Bernadotte dynasty refocusing to the west, unsurprisingly, there was a mid-century pushback from the *Storsvenskar* (Greater Sweden) activists against the old enemy, Russia.[11] In Denmark, following the disastrous Second Schleswig War of 1864 against expansionist Prussia and the loss of 40% of Danish territory with the population reduced from 2.6 million to 1.6 million, the civil movements that had formed from about 1861 to defend the country became a wave of shooting associations with encouragement from military professionals.[12] A citizens' army under Garibaldi had demonstrated that even against a powerful force such as the Austrian army, it could be more effective – which interested the politicians. In Sweden, in 1861, a journal article stated that with armed citizens, '[n]ot even our most powerful neighbour (i.e. Russia) with its numerous army would benefit from attacking [...]'[13]

Secondly, there was a growing concern among the middle classes about the political and social ambitions of the rural peasant class and growing urban working class. Long before the Bolshevik revolutionary movements, the middle classes feared the effects of education, literacy, and increasing

---

10. Bendixen 2009.
11. Björnsson 1980.
12. Bendixen 2000: 17.
13. Enefalk 2009: 105, n.1.

incomes on their class inferiors. The mid-century revolutions of 1848, a series of republican revolts against European monarchies, beginning in Sicily, and spreading to France, Germany, Italy, and the Austrian Empire, had seriously alarmed the Danish and Swedish bourgeoisie. In Sweden, there was talk of the threat of an 'inner Russia'.[14] It appeared to them that the minions were on the rise and might have to be tamed by armed force.

Thirdly, the changes in mid-nineteenth-century society had created a cadre of young, educated lower-middle-class men who were motivated to join the corps by the prospect of social engagement and advancement, in addition to responding to the foreign and class threats to their country. A patriotic movement in which they could find like-minded individuals seeking to establish a position in the rapidly changing class structure of mid-nineteenth-century Scandinavia could attract those young men who were travelling hopefully on the social mobility highway.

The movement peaked early in Sweden with a high point of 40,000 members by 1867. Constitutional reform of the *Riksdag* ('Parliament'), which had been postponed by the 1848 events, was now enacted in 1866 abolishing the four estates and introducing a bicameral assembly. This reform, which addressed the 'inner Russia' together with an economic recession and the realisation after the defeat of France by Germany in 1870 that little Sweden – even with a citizens' army – could never compete with a major modern military state seems to have deflated the ambitions of the corps movement. Most of the shooting associations were dissolved, but they left a residue of patriotic debris in society and in schools in particular well into the next century. Denmark was different.

---

14. Ibid.: 106.

Danish self-esteem had been badly dented by the 1864 defeat, but instead of accepting the implications for future conflicts, the Danish shooting corps were given the adrenalin shot of revanchism. The patriotism of the membership was combined with the military leadership's defensive passion. Many of the shooting corps carried banners with the motto 'The campaign goal is to win (back) South Jutland'.[15] Unlike Sweden, this revanchism fuelled a continued interest in, and support for, the shooting corps.

Political struggles also resonated in the development of the shooting corps. The Danish constitutional changes in 1849 had created a bicameral constitutional monarchy, and by the 1870s, political parties emerged broadly as conservative or right wing and liberals or (non-socialist) left wing. The lower house, *Folketinget*, was liberal-leaning, while conservatives dominated the upper *Landstinget*. Regarding national security, the conservatives wanted to maintain strong defence, while the left wished less expenditure on defence to ease the burden on taxpayers. This issue was one of the causes of tension between conservatives and the liberals up to the First World War.

Militarised volunteer corps were only permitted in Copenhagen, the right's power base. They became more militarised with uniforms and regular exercises, unlike those in the regions, due to encouragement from military officers who welcomed their defensive spirit rather than the appearance of a citizens' army. Against this highly charged situation, the *Academisk Skyttekorps (ASK)* was founded in 1866 as a student contingent force in case of war.[16] In the 1880s, the political tensions between right and left motivated the left to attempt to take over the shooting corps. They partly succeeded in the

---

15. Bendixen 2000: 17.
16. Ibid.: 18.

provinces but not in Copenhagen. *ASK*, composed of students, was exempt from this move, but the successful retention by the right of their brother associations in Copenhagen must have influenced the political orientation of *ASK* towards conservatism.

The left now began to set up rifle associations in the provinces with armed intervention in mind, thus provoking the formation of more armed corps such as the restoration in 1885 of the *Kongens Livjæger Korps* (*KLK*). The *KLK*'s remit was first, to help defend Copenhagen; second, to guard the king and royal family; third, to maintain order in the capital. We shall see these duties again in 1945 in connection with Gösta Winkler and the *AS*. The patriotic symbolism of the involvement of the head of state in the *KLK*'s title for an organisation later described as 'politically a little fanatical' cannot be overstated.[17]

Although the right saw defence as an existential patriotic issue – dying for 'God, King and Fatherland' – the left regarded it more as a utilitarian means to maintain neutrality in a European war. Both left and right were agreed that Denmark should be defended and that shooting associations and volunteer corps had a role in that. This broad consensus was maintained up to the end of the First World War in 1918. By then the Social Democrats had emerged as a political force on the left and the Russian revolution had terrified the upper classes throughout Europe and not least in Denmark. Twelve hundred members of the *ASK* had been part of the August 1914 response to the outbreak of war, and it was with great disappointment that they were demobilised after a few months and returned to their studies when no threat to Denmark materialised in Copenhagen. The unity created among these

---

17. Ibid.

*ASK* members in the face of possible death however was much longer lasting.[18]

The revolutionary virus from Russia that afflicted Germany never infected Denmark, but politicians and the military prepared for the eventuality of civil war leading to the involvement of the *ASK* in national politics. The prospect of regaining South Jutland from the enfeebled German state was also a contributory factor. By 1919, the year of Gösta Winkler's birth, after over fifty years of existence, *ASK* alumni formed an influential national network in business and politics, which attracted the army's intelligence service. Its chief, Erik With also became head of *ASK* until 1917 when, for continuity, his intelligence successor replaced him. Significantly, With went on to become Army Commander in 1931 until 1939 and promoted connections between the scouting movement and volunteer corps.[19]

In November 1918, one hundred *ASK* members had acted to disrupt a talk arranged by energised leftist students inviting a speaker who had recognised German sovereignty in formerly Danish South Jutland.

> [...] we were a motley crew [...] feeling a disturbing failure in ourselves, a hidden fear for what would happen and first and foremost a new and fresh adoration for the Fatherland [...] we were in opposition to the prevailing sentiments.[20]

Part of that opposition was a scepticism of democratic government and hatred of red revolution. Several *ASK* members joined a voluntary corps formed to support the anti-communist Whites in the brutal Finnish civil war. The political consensus supporting volunteer corps now broke down because the left

---

18. Ibid.: 37.
19. Ibid.: 28.
20. Ibid.: 39.

feared, with the example of the Finnish corps in mind, that the right-wing paramilitary violence, which characterised post-war Europe and Germany in particular, could now transfer to Denmark against workers' groups. The left believed that the state alone and not armed volunteers should have the monopoly on violence in the form of democratically accountable army and police. Yet, secretly, the army in 1919 had taken steps in concert with the volunteer corps in Copenhagen, including *ASK*, to mobilise their members into the army in case of civil disorder. Some, however, presciently recognised the threat to the existence of volunteer corps if the movement that was founded to defend the country against external threat was now used internally against a section of the population. It would instead be used against the left government of Prime Minister C.Th. Zahle in the 1920 'Easter Crisis'.

Zahle had, in the eyes of Erik With and other military, political, and public figures (including many *ASK* alumni), demonstrated insufficient zeal to secure the return of the lost territory of South Jutland to Denmark. Zahle wanted to fulfil the Versailles Treaty obligation according to a democratic plebiscite result to exclude the return to Denmark of the Danish-speaking minority areas around Flensburg in central Schleswig. This outraged the right, including With's group of *ASK* alumni who pressurised the king. Zahle was dismissed for refusing to include central Schleswig. The left retaliated by threating a general strike, and faced with a potential workers' revolution, the king backed down and appointed a compromise prime minister.

Now began a long political campaign by the socialist left to rein in the volunteer corps that in their view threatened both Danish democracy and Danish workers, culminating in their prohibition through a change to the law in May 1937 and ending the formal connection with the army.[21] Significantly, while *ASK* was never aligned with a political party, its membership was notable for the number of senior army officers included.[22]

That political campaign has been examined in detail in Thomas Bendixen's thesis and is not central to Gösta Winkler's story except perhaps in one respect. The pressure and criticism exerted by the left surely hardened attitudes, solidified opinions, and reinforced a sense of siege and fellowship within the corps movement, including *ASK*. When Gösta Winkler joined its successor, *Akademisk Skytteforening* (*AS*) in 1941, these sentiments prevailed within the organisation. While the left could eliminate the corps movement, it could not eradicate the solid cultural underpinning that was evidenced in rank structure and uniforms, pride in past service, regular meetings, and training that reinforced group identity, and commitment to future sacrifice for 'God, King and Fatherland'. All of these would strengthen *AS*'s ability to contribute during the German occupation.

The annual report of *AS* for 1937 contains several pages solemnly describing the demise of *ASK* as if a member of royalty had died.[23] A uniformed parade had taken place in June attended by royal family members and senior officers, including With. Speeches were made regretting the passing '[...] bitter [...] sorrow in the heart [...] deep sadness' and with military ceremony, the corps' flag '[...] sewn seventy years ago by Danish women [...]' was handed over to the university rector.[24] The report also demonstrates that while the law would be observed,

---

21. Lov. Nr. 112, 7.5.1937. Hærlov §88: 'Private associations of people, organised, trained or equipped for military purpose, may not continue.'
22. Bendixen 2000: 88.
23. *Akademisk Skytteforening Aarsberetning for 1937*. (Hereafter ASA 1937.)
24. ASA 1937: 10–12.

*ASK* would metamorphose into *Akademisk Skytteforening* and the association's constitution adjusted accordingly.[25]

The quasi-spiritual loyalty of the *ASK* members, past and present, was evident in the speeches and ceremony of the dissolution. This indicates that the organisation meant more to its members than simply military training, competition, and service, a cultural importance that would carry over in 1937 from *ASK* to *Akademisk Skytteforening* and to which Gösta Winkler would subscribe fully from 1941. How was this culture originated, developed, inculcated, and used?

As early as 1859 in Sweden, the patriotic poet Viktor Rydberg was urging that not only should adults be encouraged to join armed civilian corps but also that physical and military characteristics should be nurtured in Swedish youth.[26] This was a broader ambition than simply forming militias; this was a manifesto to militarise the nation through education and linking physical prowess with military competence. A campaign to introduce this approach into schools succeeded when in 1863, the government instructed that military exercises were to be instituted in senior schools.[27] Alongside these curricular changes, there was a torrent of song compositions as reinforcement, which together with the exercises persisted until 1918 – long after the corps had been disbanded. The songs combined patriotism with sacrifice, a feature that also became prominent in Danish corps' songs. One of Rydberg's most famous works, 'The Song of the Athenians' was set to music by Sibelius. It contains expressions such as '[s]weet is death [...] die for your town and your home [...] see the elders bleed and die [...]'[28] These sentiments did not survive in Britain after the war poets'

---

25. ASA 1937: 4–5.
26. Enefalk 2009: 108.
27. Ibid.: 109.
28. Ibid.: 118.

assaults on the sickening contrasts between noble, patriotic sacrifice and modern, technological warfare as exemplified in Wilfred Owen's *'Dolce et decorum est'*. However, they survived after 1918 in neutral Denmark to foster part of the *AS*'s culture.

The cultural similarities between the Swedish initiatives for the patriotic militarisation of youth and the activities of *ASK* are striking. Firstly, there was an emphasis on gymnastics and fitness. The 1937 annual report notes eight different teams each training on two evenings per week including horizontal bar, rings, and parallel bars. Competitions and meetings with other clubs were frequent.[29] Military activity training was not merely limited to shooting – rifles and pistols – but also to bayonet combat, cyphers, leadership, and cycling. However, while there is little mention of singing in the 1937 annual report, the 'flag-song' written by Carl Ploug for *ASK* in 1867 does feature. Its stirring words were sung at each hoisting and lowering of the corps flag beginning 'Fly high, fly proud and free, our flag'.[30]

Songs were certainly a feature of *ASK*. This is evidenced by the large collection of *ASK* songbooks left to the Danish State Archives by alumnus Judge Asger Christian Emil Gøtzsche.[31] Gøtzsche graduated in 1917 and his songbooks include works from May 1914 ('Slumber sweet in Schleswig's earth, dearly bought by You [...] Beautiful is death that thou hast, nothing finer found [...]'); a recruitment leaflet ('Forward my friends, to the fight undaunted, with Youth's jubilant mood'); and a recruitment dinner programme dated 1915 ('Our chief is hewn from granite, not plaster, and thereby is he fair'). These songs

---

29. ASA 1937: 34–37.
30. 'Vaj højt, vaj stolt og frit vort flag'. https://da.wikipedia.org/wiki/Vaj_h%C3%B8jt,_vaj_stolt_og_frit_vort_flag. Accessed 13 April 2020.
31. Rigsarkivet 0280–144 Gøtzsche, Asger Christian Emil, lansdommer: Samling vedr. Academisk Skyttekorps 1915–42.

were written to be sung at gatherings, which underlines the social nature of the *ASK*. Their style and content was intended to cement collective commitment around specific values of patriotism, sacrifice, courage, and corps identity. Gösta Winkler's song collection from twenty years later reveals similarities – with one significant difference – as will be seen.

There were two other social mechanisms to bind the membership together: get-togethers at the *ASK* property outside Copenhagen at Høje Sandbjerg and annual outings in the countryside.

Høje Sandbjerg lies in lush countryside about 22 km north of Copenhagen with fine views over Øresund to Sweden. The barracks and accommodation were basic and maintained by the members, and Group Leader Winkler was part of the 1942 maintenance team.[32] The facility was used for residential training, competition, and exercises, often with other groups. Annual outings (*'Stortur'*) were held in other country properties made available to *ASK* by well-heeled owners and provided further opportunities for members to assemble, train, and socialise.

Gösta Winkler joined the *ASK* successor, *Akademisk Skytteforening* (*AS*), in 1941 to serve Denmark during the occupation. As we have seen, *AS* maintained continuity with its historic predecessor's purpose, values, organisation, facilities, and connections with the army. These would all shape Gösta Winkler's wartime training and deployment within *motstandsbevægelsen*, the Danish resistance movement, in addition to cementing his lifetime commitment to the organisation. How had *AS* fared after the occupation in 1940?

The rebranding of *ASK* to *Akademisk Skytteforening* in 1937 also extended to its activities. Outwardly, it toned down the

---

32. AWC. 1942. *Medlemsblad for Akademisk Skytteforening* 9, 110.

emphasis on military-related training such as weapon handling and emphasised 'field sports'. The close links with the army continued nevertheless. The records of *AS* for the occupation years in the Danish national archives are disappointingly sparse, and there is nothing at all after 1943. This is perhaps not surprising given the advice from *SE* in October 1942. '[…] move all membership records and important papers. No names should be left […] Make sure to have a place that naturally lies outside the reach of the Germans and Nazis; send the papers there […]'[33] This clear indication that the *AS* was an adversary of the occupiers and collaborators was camouflaged up to 1943.

On the surface, *AS* activities continued as normal within the new circumstances. Clearly, the possession of firearms and ammunition made the authorities nervous. Shooting was banned on 11 April 1940 and ammunition confiscated later that month. Nevertheless, a summer 1940 student recruitment leaflet was resolutely optimistic. After defending its self-evident failure '[…] to defend the Fatherland […]' it went on:

> When the war is over and the foreign occupying forces have left, the *Akademisk Skytteforening* will stand ready to create a Denmark where there is no place for self-resignation.
>
> In the hard times we face, *Akademisk Skytteforening* sees its remit to unite Danish students in affection for Denmark, to strengthen Danish students' will to regenerate broken ideals and to create a student spirit that sets the freedom to resist over the whole country.

---

33. RA Akademisk Skyttekorps Korrespondance 1940–43, hereafter *RA ASK*. SE to *Akademisk Skytteforening* kontor, 7 October 1942. I am grateful to my friend and colleague, Bjarne Thorup Thomsen, for his help in deciphering some of the handwritten contents.

> *Akademisk Skytteforening* will address this remit through physical work, gymnastics and sport, performed communally [...] shooting is currently forbidden.[34]

This was the manifesto that Gösta Winkler signed up for, and it is remarkable for its inspiring language and defiant tone.

Shooting began again, albeit to a limited extent in September when ammunition was again available from the regulating authority, the Danish Shooting, Gymnastic and Sports Association, in which retired General With was an office holder.

Gösta Winkler's reaction to the invasion was predictably negative but he was not sure how he could respond. However, the twenty-year-old student was approached and recruited at Copenhagen University in late 1940 by the *AS*, who he described as 'a little volunteer army of academics with uniforms, weapons and equipment under military discipline'.[35] Recruitment into a resistance group was cautious due to the need for secrecy and mutual reliability, both operationally and politically. This explains why the Danish communist party (DKP) formed an early group in resistance, but the political right also had advantages as Gösta Winkler's recruitment demonstrates. They used existing networks such as scout troops and sports associations, particularly field sports, as conduits into resistance activities, which, as far as the cohabitation government was concerned, were illegal.[36]

Gösta Winkler's training began in the bitter winter of January 1941. At Høje Sandbjerg, out of sight of the occupiers, the first day's training began with three to four hours' continuous running up and down a slope in -20°C through

---

34. RA ASK *Russer af 1940!*
35. AWC *DUO*: 16.
36. *Danmark besat*: 382–383.

snowdrifts. The twenty recruits 'puffed and moaned but none gave up' although Gösta Winkler thought he would die.

He survived and quickly got fitter. 'Discipline was hard and if you didn't turn up without an excuse or notice, you soon realised you were unwelcome.' This was not a pastime; it was deadly serious.

Gösta Winkler had begun a two-year training period to become an *AS* Group Leader in what he later described as '[…] the first large organisation that consciously began to operate in the resistance command structure'. The long-standing connections with the army leadership, now under Gørtz, were maintained, and his predecessor Erik With was the *AS* chairman.[37]

Evidence of the direction for leadership training is documented in the archives.[38] The approach emphasises the importance of both physical and attitudinal development in candidates of 'the right stuff'. Danish history as well as natural history was important to create a patriotic spirit. Much of this would reflect the thinking of Gösta Winkler's instructors.

However, *AS* was a victim of its own recruiting success. In March 1941, With had to write a letter to Tuborg Brewery's board seeking funds to maintain *AS*, noting that the field sports section had increased from fifteen to 180 and emphasising that the aim was to '[…] create patriotic Danish, healthy and willing young students […]'[39]

Songs were still an essential part of creating patriotism, and the *AS* songbook was even publicised in a national newspaper.[40] The writer rhapsodised about the '[…] beautiful, manly, corps songs […]', but as the songs in Gösta Winkler's

---

37. RA ASK Letter to With 30 October 1940.
38. RA ASK *Lederskole* September 1940.
39. RA ASK With to Tuborg 15 March 1941.
40. RA ASK Berlinske Tidende 19 March 1941.

papers demonstrate, the nineteenth century's nationalist death-wish sentiments of Gørtsche's 1914 collection had given way to more optimistic and adversarial feelings. The wave of spontaneous mass community singing involving 740,000 participants that occurred throughout Denmark in summer 1940 was an expression of patriotic opposition to the occupation, for example with songs such as 'In Denmark am I born'.[41]

The Danish communal song-tradition, similar to *AS*, had its roots in the nineteenth century, often ascribed to the Christian reformer N.F.S. Grundtvig, but arguably even earlier to late-eighteenth-century men's clubs in Copenhagen, where the city's gentry gathered to sing, debate, socialise, and drink. Community singing developed with nineteenth century nationalism and adopted those patriotic themes which the occupation reinvigorated.[42] Some of Gösta Winkler's *AS* songs were more pointed than patriotic.

> We've got no uniforms, And no more rifles too, Round the field we storm, In civilian clothes.
> We can't do manoeuvres, And parade as a corps, We can't do much more, But do what we can.
> Take another way? No, no, no, no, […].[43]

One song promotes unity round the campfire at Høje Sandberg.

> If we are many, the flame grows together, Otherwise the bonfire dies.
> If we are friends, our innermost shines, That's the bonfire's message.

---

41. *Danmark besat*: 179–181.
42. Mikkelsen 2008.
43. AWC *Kantate*, 14 November 1942.

Another typed, copied sheet expresses a much more hostile and personalised message.

> Hitler has a branch so dear, whereon the victory hangs.
> But when he gets close, he can't take hold.
> What you want you just can't get, now it goes the other way.
> Before long he, himself, will on the branch hang.[44]

Songs were (and are) a major feature of *AS* social gatherings and not only promoted *esprit de corps* but also reinforced collegiate and cultural values. 'Our songbook always has permanent fixtures, and many of the old, well-known songs are sung over and over again.'[45] Gösta Winkler's papers clearly indicate his wholehearted adherence to these values and participation in singing with his colleagues that sustained him for the difficult years of his resistance duty in the *AS*.

The development of Danish resistance was neither straightforward nor inevitable due to a variety of related factors; the cohabitation of the government with the occupiers and consequent reluctance to create opposition; the gradual 'bottom-up' growth of politically and socially diverse resistance organisations; the fear of reprisals; the humiliation of 1940 and the continuation of the Danish armed services until 1943; the objectives of Britain and its subversion organisation, SOE, in Denmark; growing anti-German opposition; and the activities of German paramilitary collaborators.

Beginning with 9 April 1940, With's successor as army chief, Prior, had been the only military leader at the key meeting with the king and government politicians to press for continued resistance to the invaders, but the prospect of

---
44. AWC Loose songs sheets.
45. 'Lidt om Traditionerne'. http://www.akademiskskytteforening.dk/index.php/om-foreningen/traditioner. Accessed 20 April 2020.

further deaths in a hopeless fight with the superior Germans carried the meeting. Prior recalled: 'A deep feeling of sorrow, bitterness and shame filled me', but the factor of losing Danish lives needlessly dominated resistance thinking until liberation in 1945.[46] The policy of the SOE was to force a break between the cohabitation government and the Germans, but the SOE was not aiming to support sabotage in Denmark until 1943 (although the first two SOE parachutists had been dropped in late 1941).[47]

Nineteen forty-one was the key year in the development of resistance because the German attack on Russia freed European communists from their uncomfortable defence of the 1939 German–Soviet alliance and allowed them to resume their offensive against their Nazi ideological enemies. In Denmark, the communist party (*DKP*) was banned and communists arrested, but in 1942, *DKP* formed *BOPA* ('Peoples' Partisans') and from 1943, non-communists also joined. Gösta Winkler noted that the arrests '[…] unfortunately created (communist) martyrs […] and sympathy far outside their own circles'.[48]

Both *BOPA* and amateur groups such as the schoolboys of Aalborg's 'Churchill Club' carried out sabotage actions throughout 1942 without significant SOE resources. While groups like the 'Churchill Club' had only patriotic intentions, the same could not be said of the conspiring, power-hungry communists, who saw resistance participation as a means to help them achieve their objective to 'improve' or 'develop' Danish parliamentary democracy.[49] The 1942 sabotage actions led to Prime Minister Buhl's September broadcast under German

---

46. Christensen et al. 2005.
47. Bennet 1966.
48. AWC *DUO*: 11.
49. *Danmark besat*: 382.

pressure condemning these 'serious crimes' and warning of dire consequences. The reality was that no amount of sabotage would end the occupation of Denmark. Only the defeat of the Third Reich would achieve that, so the April 1940 question again arose. 'Why risk Danish lives needlessly in a pointless struggle?'

The Danish army, which was not disbanded and interned by the Germans until August 1943 when German direct rule began, had an answer to this question, and they persuaded the British to alter their sabotage policy. The conservative senior army officer cadre, as we have seen, long feared left-wing revolution, and by autumn 1940, a group known as 'the League' in great secrecy had developed the *P-plan* (*Pålidelig* or 'reliable') that could mobilise a reliable (i.e. non-communist) force in case of civil disorder. This thinking was of course entirely consistent with *AS* origins, culture, and leadership.

*P-plan* required that the cohabitation status quo be maintained in Denmark and sabotage with likely reprisals would only complicate the army's task of building the force. *AS* was part of this force.

New army chief Ebbe Gørtz, himself an *AS* alumnus, gave a speech in May 1942 to its members in which he set out the army's expectations of them *inter alia* to be the guardians of being Danish, freedom, and independence. He also urged them to demonstrate leadership: '[…] if we are passive, we will go with the flow and let others lead'. This was a coded reference to the communists.[50]

*P-plan* was revealed to an enthralled SOE in March 1942 with the attraction that this secret army could be mobilised at short notice in the service of the Allies – 8,000 men in four hours. The army had captured SOE's strategy and now it

---

50. RA ASK Stenografisk Referat af General Gørtz' Tale 21 May 1942.

took control of SOE's weapons supplies and rationed them to the resistance.[51] The communists would not get many SOE arms.

Gösta Winkler had completed his Group Leader's course 'after two years' hard training' in the autumn of 1943 when 'we got strict orders not to undertake any kind of other illegal activity (for example, sabotage) for they dare not risk that the Germans could destroy the whole of our organisation if someone was arrested and subjected to torture'.[52] Gösta Winkler was now unknowingly part of *P-plan*.

These orders did not prevent Gösta Winkler and his troops taking part in one of the famous events of the Danish occupation – the transfer by resistance groups of 7,000 Danish Jews to safety in Sweden in October 1943. Arne Sejr and *SE* were the primary organisers of the rescue, which may explain why *AS* were approached. 'The Jewish operation was atypical. It was not an organised resistance group. Everyone possible got involved.'[53] First, the Jews had to be taken to ports on Sjælland where they could embark to Sweden. Gösta Winkler was ordered to go to Vordingborg to arrange for Jews there to travel to Sweden. After successfully getting them away, the next day, he took six Jews by tram and train from Copenhagen to Korsør. The train stopped at Roskilde, and German soldiers got on to go to Slagelse. Gösta Winkler's quick-thinking response was to engage them in friendly conversation to divert their attention away from the Jews in the compartment. They were so delighted that a Dane would talk to them instead of the normal 'cold shoulder' that Gösta Winkler's ruse worked. An incident two days later underlined the reality that not all Germans were Jew-hating anti-Semites.

---

51. *Danmark besat*: 460–463.
52. AWC *DUO*: 19.
53. Birkelund quoted in Højsgaard.

Gösta Winkler and his troops were in the woods at night near Køge, south of Copenhagen, with several hundred Jews when the operation went wrong and a German patrol boat detected one of the rescue vessels. The German garrison was mobilised and the *AS* troops had to commandeer cars, taxis, and lorries to escape with the Jews in a detour to embark from Gilleleje, north of Copenhagen. Gösta Winkler found himself in a taxi with five Jews when they were stopped by a German patrol at 1.30 in the morning.

> I thought that now it was over for both the Jews and me; the Germans began to shine torches into the vehicle but completely inexplicably after a couple of minutes they waved the driver on. Fortunately, it was Wehrmacht and not an SS patrol and I am convinced that they understood what it was about. Perhaps they were sick of the war or felt sorry for the Jews – I never got to find out.

Gösta Winkler continued to Gilleleje, and most of the Jews were embarked that night and next morning to Sweden a few miles across Øresund. The risks that Gösta Winkler and his men took were significant as a collaborator contacted the Gestapo and thirty-seven remaining Jews hidden in the church in Gilleleje were arrested that day.

In late 1943, resistance groups formed a Freedom Council (*Frihedsråd*) to coordinate the diverse resistance activities, and senior army officers, now freed from internment and with the full confidence of SOE as 'responsible circles' (i.e. non-communists) began to prepare for Liberation. They had also persuaded the Swedish government to train and arm so-called 'police troops' in Sweden. This Danish Brigade was a substantial force and was intended to cross into Denmark at Liberation to secure the country from renegade Germans and communist plotters.

Gösta Winkler was told that he and his *AS* colleagues were now part of a larger military organisation and that they could expect combat with a less than 50% chance of survival. This prospect deterred a few, who left, but for the remainder, a period of intensive training began, which included marksmanship, close combat, street fighting, and so on.[54] Gösta Winkler's papers contain some of his training notes: twenty pages in his own quite summarised writing on leading an armed group, eight pages of copy-typed notes headed 'Urban warfare', and a printed pocket booklet with much of the same text entitled 'Summarised Rules for Urban Warfare'.[55] There is no doubt that Gösta Winkler was being primed for street combat and house-to-house fighting with a variety of weapons from pistols to knives.

One of the most striking items in Gösta Winkler's papers is a quarto page with detailed pencil scale drawings on both sides; on one side is a German hand grenade and a Danish hand grenade Type M23: on the other is a British 'Mills Bomb' hand-grenade – all annotated clearly with a breakdown of the parts. The correlation between Gösta Winkler's notes and the 1944 SOE training manual for street fighting indicates that SOE was the likely source of the combat techniques.[56] The prospect of taking a knife to an adversary's throat clearly affected Gösta Winkler.

> For me and many of my colleagues, a mental change took place. One became tough and the Germans were no longer seen as humans but only as enemies. Shoot first otherwise

---

54. AWC *DUO*: 25.
55. AWC.
56. 'How to be a Spy'. https://archive.org/stream/the-wwii-soe-training-manual-rigden/the-wwii-soe-training-manual-rigden_djvu.txt. Accessed 17 April 2020. 280 SOE SYLLABUS, STREET FIGHTING, January 1944.

you would be killed. If one attacked a sentry post, you could not use a firearm so jump on them and either cut their throats or stick a knife in their hearts.

Gösta Winkler's training exercises in street combat were '[...] some of the hardest and most thankless I have ever experienced'. With increased German and collaborator surveillance, Gösta Winkler had to be careful.

Often, we had to go under-ground and hide weapons in different places with the continuous risk of being reported by '*stikkere*' (collaborators) and we knew that possession of weapons meant the death penalty.

This was no trivial risk. Captain Ahnfeldt-Mollerup, military officer, commander of *AS*, and army contact with the Freedom Council, was arrested by the Gestapo in February 1945. He died in the famous RAF raid on the Gestapo building in March 1945, during which many resistance members escaped. In the confusion after the raid, near the family business, Gösta Winkler helped a fugitive gunman evade capture by five *HIPO* paramilitary, uniformed collaborators who lined up Gösta Winkler and his staff and threatened to shoot each one if the fugitive's hiding place was not divulged.[57] None answered and the *HIPO* men left empty-handed.[58]

The day of liberation arrived on 5 May following the German surrender and was to take effect from 08.00. The following narrative is compiled from Gösta Winkler's record and a detailed history of his *AS* detachment, *Kompani Nord*

---

57. *Besættelsens Hvem Hvad Hvor*. 1985: 137. See also Lundtofte 2014.
58. AWC *DUO*: 26–27.

*(KN)* – omitting names – of the events of 4–20 May.[59] (The unit is also known as the *Slotsholm Detachement* and as the *Christiansborg-bataljon*.)[60]

Mobilisation orders went out at 01.30 to *Kompani Nord (KN)* to assemble according to plans formulated in September and October 1944. They faced not only 20–30,000 Germans but also several thousand armed collaborators. The latter were to cause more trouble than the Germans, but after German Commander Lindemann had warned on 15 April that Denmark would be defended '[...] against every attack [...] to the last bullet and to the last breath', Gösta Winkler's twelve-man platoon had to prepare mentally and physically for a fight to the end.[61] 'We were ready to fight and die [...]' *KN* was part of the 425-strong *Christiansborg-bataljon* and consisted of ninety-six officers and men armed with sixty rifles, ten pistols, and sixty-six grenades. These weapons were supplemented by private arms, and each man carried a knife. 'I handed out machine guns and rifles plus (identification) armbands which were obligatory. Everyone had Danish army steel helmets [...] some had old army uniforms [...]'

The day before, a pair of his men had boldly 'organised' a local authority lorry, filled it with petrol taken from a collaborator, and the platoon boarded it to drive through the suburb of Hellerup and celebrating crowds. The platoon assembled the next day (5 May) to receive orders at 07.00 to march into central Copenhagen and guard the government buildings and

---

59. A.W.C. Petersen, V. Kaj, *Beretning om Kompagni Nords Deltagelse i Danmarks Frihedskamp*, 4 May 1946. Hereafter *BKND*. This document is anonymous but the accompanying letter to Gösta Winkler is signed KP. Police officer Kaj Petersen was a staff officer in *Detachement Slotsholm*. The style and content is typical of a police report of events with witness statements (also anonymous.)
60. Friheedsmuseet modstandsdatabas; Gøsta Emil Winkler.
61. *Danmark besat*: 587.

the *Rigsdag* (Parliament) on Slotsholm island. Once there at 09.50, Gösta Winkler's platoon took up position, guarding access points, particularly the connecting bridges. There was no trouble from the Germans, but some *HIPO* collaborators had seized vehicles and attacked the area near the bridge connecting Slotsholm. Gösta Winkler's platoon exchanged fire and they gave up and retreated. There were no casualties, and the platoon set up barriers and firing positions.

All that night and for the next three nights, *HIPO* men were heard firing in the streets around the centre. There was a stream of collaborators detained, and the platoon lorry was commandeered to take them away. In a reversal of circumstances, *AS* troops had to step in to protect collaborators from angry crowds.

At 17.00 on 6 May, the first motorised British troops passed, and the Danish Brigade arrived from Sweden at 20.00. Other than this, Gösta Winkler was not involved in further hostilities and continued to mount guard on Slotsholm for another two weeks until guard duties were taken over by the regular army, police, and the Danish Brigade.

The question arises: from whom were the *AS* guard protecting the country's key buildings? The obvious answer is of course the Germans who might have seized or destroyed them in a last-ditch action, possibly with help from renegade *HIPO* collaborators. Otherwise, we need to go back a few days to a one-line demand sent by Winston Churchill on 3 May to the Foreign Office: 'What are the facts about Denmark?'[62] The war in Europe was about to end so why was Churchill concerned about Denmark?

Reacting on 4 May, the senior official in the Foreign Office asked for more information 'as we may at any moment be

---

62. NA FO371/47222 WSC to FO 3 May 1945.

faced with a puppet Government in Copenhagen set up by the Russians [...]' revealing fears about the role of the communists on the Freedom Council and their relationship with Moscow.

These fears had reached Churchill.[63] British Ambassador Halifax in Washington on 1 May had alerted the Foreign Office to the behaviour of the Freedom Council's representative in Moscow '[...] which is likely to give the Soviet Government the impression that the Danish Freedom Council wish Soviet Government to intervene in Danish affairs', i.e. the post-liberation government.[64] The Foreign Office noted: 'But is not any danger of Russian intervention in Denmark now greatly reduced by the advance of (Montgomery's) 2nd Army to Wismar?' to which another official noted: 'Reduced but not I think eliminated.'[65]

Unsurprisingly then, Gösta Winkler and the *AS* had been moved into position to prevent the type of 'popular government' that the Soviets had practised in their takeover of the Baltic States in 1940 and were to do throughout eastern Europe over the next few years.[66]

The reassuring reply that the Foreign Office gave to Churchill was based on the past few years. 'The resistance movement in Denmark [...] to a great extent organised by SOE. The Danish C.-in-C. [Commander-in-Chief] [...] for long been in touch with us through underground channels.'[67] Therefore, Churchill's concerns about a communist coup had been dealt with by the Danish army 'League' who, sharing similar concerns, had ensured through *AS* commander

---

63. NA FO371/47222 Orme Sargent to Northern Dept. 4 May 1945
64. NA FO371/47222 Washington to Foreign Office 1 May 1945.
65. NA FO371/47222 File Note N4901G 4 May 1945.
66. Christensen 2017.
67. NA FO371/47222 Orme Sargent to Prime Minister, 6 May 1945.

Ahnfeldt-Mollerup and his successor that *AS* would be deployed and in position to forestall any such move in Copenhagen.[68]

On 9 May, there was a further confirmation of *AS*'s importance in the liberation. The old *ASK* flag that had been so reluctantly given to the university in 1937 would now be retrieved by former corps members '[a]fter the Detachment's request to the Government and the Army High Command [...]' It was flown at the parade for the king on 10 May in which *AS* lined the route then was handed over by the old corps to the new *AS*.[69] The reputation of *AS* had been symbolically restored.

*AS* had now acted in the role envisaged earlier by *ASK*; first, to help defend Copenhagen; second, to guard the king and royal family; third, to maintain order in the capital. The post-liberation government of Prime Minister Buhl was a broadly based administration that contained communists, but although the left gained in the October 1945 election, the election demonstrated the continuity of traditional parliamentary government rather than a version instigated from Moscow.[70]

Gösta Winkler's presence at Christiansborg on those historic days in May 1945 was primarily a result of his duty to his country. However, his *AS* service unit had been shaped by political forces reaching back into the 1800s, by defending Danish identity and democracy against challenges from new and foreign ideologies, by military leadership asserting influence on Danish politics, and by great power interests in Northern Europe. His commitment had been sustained by the supportive culture in *AS* with its emphasis on *esprit de corps*, on symbolic traditions such as singing and socialising, on physical prowess developing fitness and military skills, on duty and

---

68. *Danmark besat*: 463.
69. AWC *DUO*: 17, 23.
70. *Danmark besat*: 693.

responsibility to Denmark and its people, and on a reverence for the past's flags and distinguished alumni. By volunteering, training, and putting their lives at risk, Gösta Winkler and his men had campaigned to secure Denmark from totalitarian Nazism and communism.

## Bibliography

*Akademisk Skytteforening Aarsberetning for 1937.* 1938. København: Poul Petri's Bogtrykkeri.

'Arne Sejr'. http://denstoredanske.dk/Dansk_Biografisk_Leksikon/Medier/Journalist/Arne_Sejr. Accessed 12 April 2020.

Bendixen, T. *En undersøgelse af de danske frivillige korps 1918–1937.* 2000. Unpublished speciale. Københavns Universitet, Historisk Institut, Juli 2000. Consulted in Det Kgl. Bibliotek | Royal Danish Library.

Bennet, J. 1966. *British Broadcasting and the Danish Resistance Movement.* Cambridge: CUP.

*Besættelsens Hvem Hvad Hvor.* 1985. Copenhagen: Politikens Forlag.

Birkelund, P. 2000. *De loyale oprører. Den nationalt-borgerlige modstandsbevægelses optåen og udvikling 1940–1945. En undersøgelse af de illegale organisationer De Frie Danske, Studenternes Efterretningstjeneste og Hjemmefronten.* Roskilde: University of Southern Denmark.

Björnsson, A. 1980. *Mot det inre och yttre Ryssland: dokument från folkbeväpningskampen i Sverige under 1800-talet.* Stockholm: Ordfront.

Christensen, C.B. et al. 2005. *Danmark besat: krig og hverdag 1940–45.* København: Høst.

Højsgaard, L. 2015. 'Studerende førte an i modstandskampen'. 2015. https://www.magisterbladet.dk/magasinet/2015/magisterbladet-nr-10-2015/studerende-foerte-an-i-modstandskampen. Accessed 20 April 2020.

'How to be a Spy'. https://archive.org/stream/the-wwii-soe-training-manual-rigden/the-wwii-soe-training-manual-rigden_djvu.txt. Accessed 17 April 2020.

'"Hurtiga gossar blir raska, modiga soldater". Något om folkbeväpningstanken i och utanför skolan från och med 1860-talet'. 2009. In A. Berg and H. Enefalk (eds), *Det mångsida verktyget. Opuscula Historica Upsaliensia* 39. Uppsala, 105–121.

'Lidt om Traditionerne'. http://www.akademiskskytteforening.dk/index.php/om-foreningen/traditioner. Accessed 20 April 2020.

*Medlemsblad for Akademisk Skytteforening 9*, November 1942. København: Poul Petri's Bogtrykkeri.

Mikkelsen, M. 2008. Den danske sang er enstemmig og hjemmestrikket in *Kristeligt Dagblad*, 23 January.

Olesen, N.W. 2013. 'The Obsession with Sovereignty' and Christensen, C.B. 2013. '"The Five Evil Years": National Self-image, Commemoration and Historiography in Denmark 1945–2010'. In J. Gilmour and J. Stephenson (eds), *Hitler's Scandinavian Legacy. The Consequences of the German Invasion for the Scandinavian Countries, Then and Now*. London: Bloomsbury.

Petersen, V. Kaj. 1946. *Beretning om Kompagni Nords Deltagelse i Danmarks Frihedskamp*, 4 May.

Rigsarkivet 0280–144 Gøtzsche, Asger Christian Emil, lansdommer: Samling vedr. Academisk Skyttekorps 1915–42.

Sejr, A. 1995. *En kamp for frihed: Studenternes Efterretningstjeneste 1940–45*. Copenghagen: Hans Reitzels Forlag.

'Vaj højt, vaj stolt og frit vort flag'. https://da.wikipedia.org/wiki/Vaj_h%C3%B8jt,_vaj_stolt_og_frit_vort_flag. Accessed 13 April 2020.

· 15 ·

## 'Jeg er ikke bange for dig': Elements of the (Anti)Hero's Journey in Two Classics of 1970s Danish Children's Literature

### Guy Puzey

## Introduction

Leif Esper Andersen's *Heksefeber* (1973) and Ole Lund Kirkegaard's *Gummi-Tarzan* (1975) are vastly different texts with regard to subject matter, style, and tone. At first glance, the clearest commonalities between the two texts might be that both have a young male protagonist and both prominently feature witchcraft. *Gummi-Tarzan* is – at face value – a lighthearted yet also downbeat text, aimed at early readers, with a contemporary setting and about a boy who is teased for being physically weak. Through an alliance with a witch he happens to encounter, the boy finds a way to reverse his fortunes, at least temporarily. *Heksefeber*, meanwhile, is a short historical novel in which a boy, having seen his mother burned at the stake for witchcraft, must begin a new life.

The contrast is visible in the illustrations too: the humour of *Gummi-Tarzan* is magnified by the author's playfully drawn illustrations, while the generally bleak tone of *Heksefeber* is enhanced by Mads Stage's evocative and skilfully integrated sketches, with a threatening portrayal of nature that was quite atypical of illustrations in most Danish children's literature up until that point.[1]

The texts could also appear to contrast each other thematically. *Heksefeber* embraces heroism, whereas *Gummi-Tarzan* appears to focus on antiheroism. These two concepts are ostensibly opposed, but since the main difference lies purely in the relative presence or absence of heroism, these themes could perhaps be regarded as two sides of the same coin. An analysis of this point of contact may shed more light on shifting models or socio-cultural understandings of heroism, while also showing a way in which traditional conventions have been subverted in literature for young people.

I first encountered these texts on Bjarne Thorup Thomsen's course dedicated to Scandinavian Literature for Children and Young People, alongside many other classic works, from Gretha Stevns' [Eilif Mortansson's] *Susy Rødtop* (1943) and Astrid Lindgren's *Pippi Långstrump* (1945) to Thorbjørn Egner's *Folk og røvere i Kardemomme by* (1955), Klaus Rifbjerg's *Kesses krig* (1982), and Torill Thorstad Hauger's *Ravnejenta* (1989). The present chapter is an updated and expanded version of an essay I wrote for that course, as a fourth-year undergraduate student, in 2005–06. With Bjarne's clear course design, coupled with his inclusive approach to students and to the subject matter at hand, that course transformed my understanding of literature, and I am sure many other former students would say the same.

The course also demonstrated the high quality of writing for children and young adults in the Nordic region, which is in no small part tied to the enormous care and thought that goes into the production of children's literature in those countries, as well as the fact the target age group is taken seriously, perhaps

---

1. Glistrup 1992: 130.

more so than in many other parts of the world. For a complex of social and educational reasons, Nordic authors and illustrators have over many decades shown a tendency not to underestimate children and to show children and young adults great respect as readers. The two primary texts to be considered here are, to my mind, fascinating examples of this trend. Although *Heksefeber* is still quite a didactic text, it tackles a dark period of history with great sensitivity, while *Gummi-Tarzan* is a subversive expression of solidarity with the oppressed, showing that there is more than one way to be heroic.

Both texts were published in the mid-1970s, in a decade that saw a huge transformation of social attitudes in Denmark, as in many other parts of the world. A wave of politically engaged activism sought to confront long-established power structures in the home, in education, and indeed across society. Many authors of books for children and young adults took on the task of expressing these ideological perspectives to young readers and providing new alternatives to the outdated viewpoints found in many older works, thereby highlighting the role of literature in reflecting, discussing, informing, or even shaping contemporary values. This is most obvious in realist texts tackling social issues in up-to-date settings, such as Bent Haller's *Katamaranen* (1976), which caused considerable controversy at the time of its publication. Ideological messages can, however, be found in all genres, from historical novels such as *Heksefeber* to humoristic texts such as *Gummi-Tarzan*, both of which are characteristic of their time in their problematisation of authority. In *Heksefeber*, this critique of authority emerges primarily in relation to the historically situated subject matter, albeit with clear parallels to contemporary debates. *Gummi-Tarzan*, meanwhile, is significant in challenging the authority associated with traditional understandings of heroism.

## Quantifying and qualifying heroism (and antiheroism)

In order to consider the themes effectively, an understanding is needed of what is signified by the terms *heroism* and *antiheroism*, and how these ideas have been contemplated in the past.

One of the best-known general works on heroism is Joseph Campbell's *The Hero with a Thousand Faces*, originally published in 1949 and revised and expanded in a 1968 second edition. Campbell applied the techniques of psychoanalysis to the study of myths, folk tales, and legends, although he generally conflated these as *myth*. This conflation of narrative types is among the many points in Campbell's analysis that have been criticised by others, such as folklorist Alan Dundes, who also posited that the purported universality of Campbell's approach has been complicit in the dilution of folklore studies.[2] Dundes referred to Gregory Hansen, who had lamented the blurred borders of folklore now encompassing 'topics ranging from letters in *Penthouse Forum* to washing dishes in Denmark'.[3] It is not my intention to suggest that *Heksefeber* or *Gummi-Tarzan* are necessarily artefacts of folklore in that sense. While fully recognising the valid criticisms of Campbell's work, not least from the perspective of folklorists, I look to Campbell's work for its insights on the concept of heroism. It is useful in this regard, in spite of its other defects, precisely because of its wide readership and hence close relationship with popular understanding of what constitutes heroism in tales (or 'myth'), as this is ultimately a socio-cultural construct. Furthermore, *Gummi-Tarzan* is in some respects a striking counter-example

---

2. Dundes 2005.
3. Hansen 1997: 99.

to Campbell's analysis, demonstrating sharply how heroism has traditionally been defined through hegemonic power structures, while also challenging Jungian archetype models.

In what could be seen as a consolidation of Freudian and Jungian ideas, Campbell claimed that, if dreams are 'symptomatic of the dynamics of the psyche', then 'myth' is a representation of the shared dreams of an entire society, with symbols that are readily identifiable by all, deriving from the collective unconscious.[4] Campbell considered heroism to be a major recurring theme present in the folk tales and legends of all cultures.

Central to Campbell's treatment of what he called the monomyth are archetypes, which possibly constitute the oldest, most instinctive, and most thoroughly cross-cultural *topoi*.[5] Campbell points out that his focus on archetypes was certainly not new, attributing the major development of the subject to Carl Gustav Jung.[6] Jung, in turn, had borrowed the term from writers of antiquity such as Cicero and Pliny, and he acknowledged the work of Friedrich Nietzsche, amongst others, on this 'theory of preconscious, primordial ideas'.[7] Archetypes are fundamentally various standard categories of characters that appear to be instantly recognisable as fulfilling a particular role, as if prior familiarity with these characters were innate to all humans. In terms of their preconscious nature, Nietzsche had suggested that many frequently occurring conclusions drawn in modern-day dreams are the same as those that 'for many millennia mankind also drew *when awake*'.[8] Dundes describes

---

4. Campbell 2004 [1968]: 237.
5. The word *monomyth* was coined by James Joyce in *Finnegans Wake* (1939: 581). For Campbell, it refers to the idea that all 'myths' follow a single pattern.
6. Campbell 2004 [1968]: 16–18, n. 18.
7. Jung 1938: 64, 122 n. 12.
8. Nietzsche 1996 [1878]: 18.

Campbell's 'insistence on the existence of archetypes' to be the 'most disturbing' aspect of his analysis.[9] In the present study, the focus is on heroism as a theme, not on archetypes.

One possible, while somewhat broad, understanding of the term *hero* would see it as referring to the main character of any given work of literature, art, drama, or film. The endowment of a character with the *hero* title should, however, be treated with care, as not all main characters embody qualities identifiable with heroism. Although such a common equation of *hero* with *protagonist* is a simplification of the hero's role, it does reveal the frequent centrality of the hero character. If the tale being told is the hero's own tale, the hero is inevitably paramount as a character; furthermore, the placing of the hero at the hub of events or the focalised telling of the tale from the hero's point of view can create a clearer emotional focus for the tale's intended audience. If a hero – or, for that matter, any protagonist – is to be a good role model, empathy and identification with them are key. A good way to facilitate such compassion can be through radiating the story out from the hero. Character-centric storytelling is, indeed, as typical of most of the children's literature of the twentieth century as it is of classic folk tales.

The definition of heroism that will be preferred in this investigation will be that which represents the coming together of well-regarded qualities, values, and character traits in one person, making them into a figure revered by a certain group. Antiheroism, on the other hand, will be considered to be the profound lack of heroic qualities displayed by an individual. Pinning down these heroic qualities themselves could prove problematic. After all, every society can value different personal merits, and it only takes a brief look at modern history to realise that one society's enemy, embodying all its fears

---

9. Dundes 2005: 397.

and nightmares, can be another society's hero, fulfilling that society's every hope and dream. Crucially, the selection of which traits are considered heroic is also highly conditioned by hegemonic narratives and power structures in society, a fact that is problematised in *Gummi-Tarzan*, as will be seen below.

## Shifting historical narratives of heroism and morality

In a comparative study of national heroes in Scotland, Norway, and Lithuania, Linas Eriksonas outlined the significant role played by hero figures, such as William Wallace, St Olav, or Vytautas the Great, in reinforcing national identities. Eriksonas argues that the foundation of national heroic traditions took place in the last years of the sixteenth century and at the beginning of the seventeenth century, at a time when humanism and the Reformation were making an impact.[10] Although there are many cases where national and religious narratives of heroism clearly overlap, the national heroic traditions may provide an alternative to, for instance, the Christian heroic tradition of sainthood. With the influence of humanism, many tales lost Christian moralising elements that had gradually been injected into the original texts over the centuries.[11]

The texts to be examined here are both Danish, and Denmark does share with Iceland, Norway, and Sweden a common Norse mythological tradition. If such a tradition is taken to embody deep-seated cultural ideals and aspirations, it might be assumed that these countries share similar historical notions of heroism. Indeed, the sagas already provided a template of sorts for glorification of heroes.[12] In addition to national or

---

10. Eriksonas 2004: 295.
11. Ibid.: 301–302.
12. Ibid.: 303.

regional factors, however, the aspirations of any given society will often vary over time. The morals and ideals of the 1970s, when the two texts under consideration were both written, were particular to that decade, and differed in many respects from principles of the sagas. Some traits may, however, have survived over the centuries, or may even have been resurrected at that time.

In 1840, long before Joseph Campbell first put pen to paper, the Scottish mathematician and historian Thomas Carlyle's collection of six lectures *On Heroes, Hero-Worship and the Heroic in History* was published, which Eriksonas describes as 'the first attempt to come to grips with the heroic in the modern moral-philosophical terms'.[13] In the chapter on 'The Hero as Divinity', Carlyle examines Norse mythology, concluding that its true essence lies in the 'recognition of the divineness of Nature'.[14] While generalising, Carlyle claims that the sincerity of the Scandinavian appreciation of nature is notable:

> I feel that these old Northmen were looking into Nature with open eye and soul: most earnest, honest; childlike, and yet manlike; with a great-hearted simplicity and depth and freshness, in a true, loving, admiring, unfearing way.[15]

Alan Dundes criticised Campbell as 'a throwback to nineteenth-century theories of psychic unity'.[16] Perhaps we see such a notion represented in Carlyle's words here, and this kind of attention towards the natural world is by no means unique to the Scandinavian mythological tradition. Still, this aspect that Carlyle highlighted clearly resonates in the portrayal of nature

---

13. Ibid.: 32.
14. Carlyle 1840: 27.
15. Ibid.: 28.
16. Dundes 2005: 396.

in *Heksefeber*. The character of Hans, to be examined presently, has a relationship with nature that places great emphasis on respect. In return for this respect – especially evident in his veneration of the fjord and his friendship with a fox, not to mention his knowledge of the properties of plants – nature will respect him: '*Du må lære at respektere den [fjorden]. Så vil den også respektere dig.*'[17] ('You must learn to respect it [the fjord]. Then it will also respect you.')[18]

Although this reverence for the natural world is seen as the devil's work by many members of the local community depicted in the book, Andersen portrays such a relationship with nature in a positive light, so while this is an ideal emblematic of the conservationist movement that was expanding in the 1970s, perhaps *Heksefeber* also shows a return in some way to what Carlyle interpreted, rightly or wrongly, as a moral standard of Nordic antiquity. The apparent opposition of these ideals with those of the church, in the setting of the book, effectively demonstrates an alternative moral code no longer based on religious dogma but rather on respect for, if not the beatification of, nature.

## Masculinity, morality, and language

Traditional and stereotypical gender roles are a significant aspect of many myths, legends, and tales. In such tales, as in reality, heroism is certainly not a purely masculine domain. Clarissa Pinkola Estés, for example, has challenged popular misconceptions of the portrayal of women in mythology.[19] Still, bearing in mind the power structures inherent in the definition of heroism,

---

17. Andersen 1974 [1973]: 17.
18. Andersen 1976: 15.
19. Estés 2004: lvi–lviii.

it is perhaps no coincidence that Campbell continually refers to the nameless hero as if 'he' were masculine. Strength is a stereotypical indicator of masculinity, and physical strength is often depicted in mythology as indicative of moral strength.[20] This resonates with the depiction of Hans in *Heksefeber*, who is known as *Store-Hans* ('Big Hans') for his physical presence, but sometimes also as *Kloge-Hans* ('Wise Hans').[21]

The treatment of gender roles in *Gummi-Tarzan* has a substantial impact on the morality of the text, and this is also typical of its era. Kirkegaard confronts stereotypes of masculinity when the protagonist, Ivan Olsen, does not want to live up to his father's ideal of how a 'real man' should behave. Herr Olsen idolises the character first brought to fame as the protagonist of Edgar Rice Burroughs' *Tarzan of the Apes* (1912), but his son pokes fun at the first drawing he is shown of Tarzan, asking why he is sitting in a tree and why he is only wearing a loincloth, as well as suggesting that Tarzan looks a little overweight, notions that enrage Ivan's father.[22]

Ivan Olsen's profound lack of physical strength for most of the narrative marks him out as decidedly antiheroic in a traditional sense. However, in a period when the gender roles of men were being redefined following breakthroughs for the feminist movement, other manifestations were becoming possible. Indeed, the challenge to the patriarchy is not only represented by Ivan but also by a woman: the witch herself.[23] Arguably Ivan's greatest triumph is the wish he comes up with for the witch to satisfy:

---

20. Kirkham and Thumim 1993: 15.
21. Andersen 1974 [1973]: 13; Andersen 1976: 11.
22. Kirkegaard 1975: 33. For more on the origins of the Tarzan character, see Morton 1993: 106–107.
23. Waage 2004: 100.

*Jeg vil ønske mig, at **alle mine ønsker kan gå i opfyldelse**,' råbte Ivan Olsen.*[24]

'I wish for **all my wishes to come true**,' yelled Ivan Olsen.

This instance of brain over brawn shows where Ivan's true strength lies: in original thought rather than in brute force.

The protagonist also struggles to read, and the portrayal of these trials may hint at dyslexia. This is intriguing when considering the intended audience of *Gummi-Tarzan*, who may well be dealing with similar challenges. The subdued tone of the text, while still humorous, rewards readers without patronising them. Other satisfying rewards for the reader come in the form of expressive interjections such as '*arhh*', '*næhh*', '*æhh*', and '*jahh*', which are used to superb effect, and in the extensive use of text within the illustrations. Indeed, the way illustrations are integrated into the narrative makes for a powerful multimodal text.[25] More subtle techniques are also used to engage early readers, such as bold text, and interpunct hyphenation points between elements of compound nouns. Books such as this may indeed be a milestone in the hero's journey of many a child learning to read.

Another of Ivan's heroic features, which could again be interpreted as a product of the time the text was written, is the very fact that he challenges the status quo, questioning both established gender and educational conventions. His extraordinary perceptiveness, objectivity, and nonchalance are also quite unusual attributes for a child, as is his incredible tolerance. Ivan puts up with being bullied both at home and at school, but he does not let that dishearten him. This tolerance and nonchalance when it comes to being bullied are, however,

---

24. Kirkegaard 1975: 70. Emphasis in original.
25. Hennig 2012.

of questionable value to him. Nevertheless, Ivan is certainly a character to be admired.

## The hero's journey in *Heksefeber*

Joseph Campbell's investigation of the monomyth places particular emphasis on its structure. He claims that the hero's adventure, or the hero's journey, follows a standard cyclical pattern in all tales.[26] Although it could be argued that this model is too elaborate because it would be a tall order to include every single one of its multitude of possible narrative situations in one tale – from such incidents as battling a dragon and being swallowed by a whale to a crucifixion or an elixir theft – it is important to bear in mind what Campbell wrote about variations of the monomyth:

> The changes rung on the simple scale of the monomyth defy description. Many tales isolate and greatly enlarge upon one or two of the typical elements of the full cycle […], others string a number of independent cycles into a single series […]. Differing characters or episodes can become fused, or a single element can reduplicate itself and reappear under many changes.[27]

If the idea of these cycles is applied to the texts in question, it becomes clear that the hero's adventure in *Heksefeber* is incomplete. Esben, the young protagonist, flees the scene of his mother's execution in what could be termed a *call to adventure*.[28] This was Campbell's term for the 'first stage of the mythological

---

26. Campbell 2004 [1968]: 227–228.
27. Ibid.: 228.
28. Ibid.: 45–54.

journey'.²⁹ Destiny has placed Esben in this situation. In his failure to prevent his mother from being burned at the stake, he essentially feels challenged by the local society to stand up for the values his mother stood for. His mother's problems all began when she was blamed for the death of a girl with pulmonary tuberculosis she had not been able to heal.³⁰ While his mother may have had an unusual aptitude for healing the sick, Esben knows that this is because she knew how to make use of natural remedies, not due to any evil powers, and that the girl who had died was already too ill to heal.

Esben's encounter with Hans is where his adventure really begins in earnest. Hans helps him to get accustomed to a new way of life and develop both physically and morally, but his training comes to an abrupt end when Hans is taken away by a group of men from the village for the same reason Esben's mother had first been suspected of witchcraft: a dying man was taken to Hans for healing when it was already too late.³¹ In one of the many instances of premonition in this novel, Hans already knew that 'they' would come for him as they came for Esben's mother. Abduction is one of the events that can lead to the *crossing of the first threshold*, where the main act of the hero's adventure begins.³² Here Esben is forced to face the *threshold guardians*, that is to say the men who already took away his mother, 'at the entrance to the zone of magnified power'.³³ Following this brief confrontation, Esben takes flight, and the end of the book thus mirrors the very beginning. Here his trials will begin as he takes on the role of the solitary outsider, as Hans had done before, and the knowledge passed on to him

---

29. Ibid.: 53.
30. Andersen 1974 [1973]: 24–25.
31. Ibid.: 76–77.
32. Campbell 2004 [1968]: 71–82.
33. Ibid.: 71.

from Hans will surely stand him in good stead for the hard times ahead.

As for what form the apex of his adventure may take, the most obvious probability, following Campbell's schema, would seem to be *atonement with the father*.³⁴ It is commonplace in myth and folk tales, as in literature, for the destiny of the protagonist to be inexorably linked to their genetics.

> *Jeg har ikke nogen far. Jeg har i hvert fald aldrig set ham, og mor har aldrig fortalt mig om ham.*³⁵

> I have no father. Anyhow, I've never seen him and Mother has never said anything about him to me.³⁶

Esben clearly does not know who his biological father is, although Hans has been an excellent substitute in that role. Already having known his mother, Esben may need to find out about his father if he is to understand fully who he truly is:

> The problem of the hero going to meet the father is to open his soul beyond terror to such a degree that he will be ripe to understand how the sickening and insane tragedies of this vast and ruthless cosmos are completely validated in the majesty of Being. [...] He beholds the face of the father, understands – and the two are atoned.³⁷

This coming to terms with who he is, 'beholding the face of the father' and realising that face – at least to some degree – to be his own, is essential to an understanding of cruelty. Excluding

---

34. Ibid.: 116–137.
35. Andersen 1974 [1973]: 24.
36. Andersen 1976: 20.
37. Campbell 2004 [1968]: 135.

the possibility that Hans is Esben's biological father, Esben may need to confront his father before being able to triumph. If his father is still alive, maybe he is one of the villagers who stoned Esben's mother on the pyre, which would certainly provide an interesting treatise on the theme of being one's own enemy.

## The hero's journey in *Gummi-Tarzan*

In *Gummi-Tarzan*, the reader is party to a more complete hero's adventure. Ivan Olsen's lack of physical strength means he is sidelined in most social situations: at school, at home, on the football pitch, and on the street where older boys participate in long-distance spitting contests. His *call to adventure* comes when he has a chance encounter with a witch.

An interesting contrast between the two protagonists is the different reactions they have when they first encounter their *mentors*, and how this relates to fear. Fear is a theme common to both texts, with the word *bange* ('afraid, frightened, scared') appearing frequently throughout them. Overcoming or conquering fear is indeed connected to valour, one of the cornerstones of traditional heroism. This is highlighted by Thomas Carlyle, who clearly seems to associate it with masculinity too: 'The first duty for a man is still that of subduing *Fear*.'[38] Esben is at first scared of Hans, although his traumatic recent experiences certainly contributed to his fear, as we later find out that Esben is, in fact, extremely courageous. Ivan, on the other hand, is not scared of the witch at all. This is a break with convention.[39] It may, however, be more a result of his general nonchalance than genuine courage:

---

38. Carlyle 1840: 29. Emphasis in original.
39. Alfarnes 1998: 27.

*Jeg er bange for bukse·vand og næse·blod og al den slags. Men jeg er ikke bange for dig.*[40]

I'm afraid of getting water poured down my pants and nosebleeds and all that stuff. But I'm not afraid of you.

His attitude does nevertheless greatly impress the witch, and it is because of this that she challenges him to come up with a wish. This challenge could be considered the first of the *hero's trials*, if Ivan is to be deemed a hero.[41] After having his wish fulfilled, Ivan proceeds to face other tests: long-distance target spitting, cycling, playing football, and reading an enormous book, all of which he excels in. During his extraordinary day of adventure, Ivan also seeks atonement with his father and confronts him, making him experience what it is like to have a nosebleed after falling from a tree.

Like Esben, Ivan also undergoes a physical transformation, but this development is merely a temporary one; the next day, Ivan's torment continues as if nothing had happened at all. It is unclear whether the events of the previous day were just a dream. Although that would seem the most plausible case, there was still a black mark on the grass where the witch had placed her cauldron, allowing for ambiguity.[42] Whether it was a dream or a supernatural experience, however, matters very little. As the adventure only affected Ivan himself, the ending provides no salvation, no *elixir* for Ivan or for society. This is the greatest deviation from the classic hero's journey: it was all apparently to no avail. Instead of a hero's journey proper, Ivan's adventure is more of an antihero's day off.

In an interview published in the year of his death, Kirkegaard made clear that it was a conscious aim in much

---

40. Kirkegaard 1975: 62.
41. Campbell 2004 [1968]: 89–100.
42. Kirkegaard 1975: 121.

of his writing to react against hero worship and instead to create antiheroes.[43] Still, through its laconic use of irony, the book's anti-authoritarianism points at other kinds of inner strength that may outlast Ivan's extraordinary day.[44] The author himself stated that a consistent aim in his work was to show solidarity with children, whom he described as a '*mindretalsgruppe*' ('minority group').[45] An anti-authoritarian stance can often be seen as heroic regardless of the outcome, and Ivan's rejection of traditional, normative imperatives of masculinity may offer an alternative type of heroic accomplishment in its promotion of a more nuanced understanding of male roles.

## Conclusion

Despite the fact that the hero's adventure in *Heksefeber* is incomplete, it would certainly appear to be leading to a life of heroism for Esben. This is aided by the strong presence of a mentor, whereas the witch in *Gummi-Tarzan* is but a momentary helper for Ivan. If only she were always there to help Ivan, every day would be heroic for him. All the same, Ivan displays several admirable and original attributes, not least his anti-authoritarian sensibilities, that make him into a remarkable modern-day hero-antihero hybrid, in stark contrast to the more traditional or historical hero figure represented by Esben. It must also be remembered that Ivan succeeded in all his tasks, and Campbell considered such trials to be the deciding factor as to whether or not a character qualified as a hero.[46]

---

43. Gormsen 1979: 222.
44. Alfarnes 1998: 28–30.
45. Cited in Gormsen 1979: 231.
46. Campbell with Moyers 1988: 154.

The average complexity of such aspects as narrative, plot structure, tone, and focalisation in children's fiction has long been on the increase, not to mention the more indistinct boundaries between genres.[47] In her work on 'fantastic tales' in Danish children's literature, Anna Karlskov Skyggebjerg has shown how works such as *Gummi-Tarzan* draw on pre-texts to produce what John Stephens and Robyn McCallum call 're-versions'.[48] Skyggebjerg justifiably argues that in Danish children's literature this widespread intertextuality enriches the genre by playfully challenging and upending pre-texts and literary conventions. The examples above support this view with reference to extremely deep-seated cultural conventions embodied in the hero's journey. In particular, it so happens that the structural template of the hero's journey reveals similarities with the journey of an antihero in *Gummi-Tarzan*. By subverting this convention, Ivan Olsen's valiant challenge to more stereotypical ideals of masculinity illuminates how some generally accepted concepts of heroism can be heavily influenced by inherited and outmoded power structures, to the extent that they may directly mirror these structures. In turn, this questions some of the traditionally conceived archetypes discussed by Campbell, showing that they may include internalised socio-cultural notions based on imbalances of power.

## Bibliography

Alfarnes, Oddvin. 1998. 'Når vi ler av *Gummi-Tarzan*'. *Norsklæreren* 1998:1, 24–31.

Andersen, Leif Esper. 1974 [1973]. *Heksefeber*, 2nd edition. Copenhagen: Gyldendal.

---

47. Nikolajeva 1998.
48. Skyggebjerg 2005: 291; Stephens and McCallum 1998.

———. 1976. *Witch Fever*. Joan Tate (trans.). London: Pelham.

Campbell, Joseph. 2004 [1968]. *The Hero with a Thousand Faces*, commemorative edition. Princeton: Princeton University Press.

Campbell, Joseph with Moyers, Bill. 1988. *The Power of Myth*. Betty Sue Flowers (ed.). New York: Anchor.

Carlyle, Thomas. 1840. *On Heroes, Hero-Worship and the Heroic in History*. London: Chapman and Hall.

Dundes, Alan. 2005. 'Folkloristics in the Twenty-First Century'. *Journal of American Folklore* 118:470, 385–408.

Eriksonas, Linas. 2004. *National Heroes and National Identities: Scotland, Norway and Lithuania*. Brussels: Presses interuniversitaires européennes/Peter Lang.

Estés, Clarissa Pinkola. 2004. 'What Does the Soul Want?', introduction to the 2004 commemorative edition of Joseph Campbell, *The Hero with a Thousand Faces*. Princeton: Princeton University Press, xxiii–lxv.

Glistrup, Eva. 1992. 'Fra stilstand til højkonjunktur: Billedbøger og illustrationer 1960–1990'. In Kari Sønsthagen and Lena Eilstrup (eds), *Dansk børnelitteraturhistorie*. Copenhagen: Høst & Søns Forlag, 101–136.

Gormsen, Jakob. 1979. *Elleve nordiske børnebogsforfattere*. Copenhagen: Gyldendal.

Hansen, Gregory. 1997. 'The End of Folklore and the Task of Thinking'. *Folklore Forum* 28:2, 99–101.

Hennig, Åsmund. 2012. 'Multimodal makt og frihet: Personframstillinger i *Gummi-Tarzan* (1975)'. *Barnelitterært forskningstidsskrift/Nordic Journal of ChildLit Aesthetics* 3. DOI: 10.3402/blft.v3i0.20083.

Joyce, James. 1939. *Finnegans Wake*. London: Faber and Faber.

Jung, Carl Gustav. 1938. *Psychology and Religion*. New Haven: Yale University Press.

Kirkegaard, Ole Lund. 1975. *Gummi-Tarzan*. Copenhagen: Gyldendal.

Kirkham, Pat and Thumim, Janet. 1993. 'You Tarzan'. In Pat Kirkham and Janet Thumim (eds), *You Tarzan: Masculinity, Movies and Men*. London: Lawrence & Wishart, 11–26.

Morton, Walt. 1993. 'Tracking the Sign of Tarzan: Trans-Media Representation of a Pop-Culture Icon'. In Pat Kirkham and Janet

Thumim (eds), *You Tarzan: Masculinity, Movies and Men*. London: Lawrence & Wishart, 106–125.

Nietzsche, Friedrich. 1996 [1878]. *Human, All Too Human*, 2nd edition. R.J. Hollingdale (trans.). Cambridge: Cambridge University Press.

Nikolajeva, Maria. 1998. 'Exit Children's Literature?'. *The Lion and the Unicorn* 22:2, 221–236.

Skyggebjerg, Anna Karlskov. 2005. *Den fantastiske fortælling i dansk børnelitteratur 1967–2003*. Frederiksberg: Roskilde Universitetsforlag.

Stephens, John and McCallum, Robyn. 1998. *Retelling Stories, Framing Culture: Traditional Story and Metanarratives in Children's Literature*. New York: Garland.

Waage, Lars Rune. 2004. '"Skidt med Tarzan" – *Gummi-Tarzan* og maskuliniteten'. In Lotte Selsing (ed.), *Feministisk teori, kvinne- og kjønnsforskning i Rogaland*. Stavanger: Arkeologisk museum i Stavanger, 93–102.

# · 16 ·

# On the Right Frequency

## Charlotte Berry

My obsession with Denmark began as a child, with a language-obsessed father sending off regularly to the Danish Tourist Board for travel brochures. We never actually made it to Denmark as a family until I was living there in later years, but I always wondered at the time what Denmark was like. Whilst living in East Anglia, it was occasionally possible to get Scandinavian radio (language unidentified!), but that stopped when we moved over to the Welsh border. Scandinavia seemed very far away in the days before the internet.

    I followed in the family footsteps and did language A levels, and was looking for a new language to go with German at university. Arabic, Spanish, Chinese, and Italian were ruled out immediately – too hot, too far. I looked at the Slavic languages listed in the university course directory in the local library but couldn't imagine going behind the Iron Curtain so soon after it had fallen. So Scandinavia popped up again, prompted by memories of those photographs in the Danish Tourist Board catalogues. Four intriguing countries: Finland, Sweden, Norway, Denmark. Which to choose? Watching ski-jumping on telly had put me off the first three: too mad, too cold. Denmark seemed the ideal compromise; it was a bit nearer everywhere else, and a ferry ride from a few English ports. A flat landscape

– like East Anglia with its big skies. And lashings of Danish pastries and Hans Christian Andersen. Perfect.

At this point, I hadn't met any Danish people (few and far between in Herefordshire, except one house in the neighbouring road which bizarrely had its own flagpole and the Dannebrog flying). I had no clue what the language sounded like. It looked a bit like German, so how hard could it be? So I trekked up the M5/M6 in the summer of 1994 for a university open day, having no idea what to expect and what the Scandinavian department would be like.

In 1994, Scandinavian was still located at 18 Buccleuch Place, and the department occupied a flat on the first floor. It seemed a very cosy place (in fact, '*hyggelig*', as I was to discover later on), and had Danish newspapers available; I had never seen one before. I don't remember meeting any of the staff there, but I do definitely remember meeting Bjarne for the first time as the departmental rep, in one of the David Hume Tower faculty rooms. Bjarne was friendly and reassuring, and emitted a quietly confident enthusiasm in all directions Scandinavian. I was impressed – going to university was a big jump, especially to study a mystery language, but suddenly everything seemed less scary and eminently doable. I met a fellow prospective student who also applied. We met again at a UCL interview but agreed between ourselves that Edinburgh, course and city, seemed much more like it. And we both duly arrived in autumn 1995 to start Danish, amongst other things.

There were thirteen of us in the Danish 1A class. Oddly, three of us had connections with the visually impaired world, and Ida, our lector, couldn't quite believe it: two students with parents who taught Braille, and another who trained guide dogs.

We didn't see that much of Bjarne in first year; we were busy getting to grips with the language. I struggled not to keep putting verbs in subordinate clauses at the end of the sentence

– Ida had quite the Paddington Bear stare for those moments. But we felt very pleased with ourselves when we finished reading our first real book, *Gummi-Tarzan*, and then we moved up to proper literature classes with Bjarne. By this time, we were reduced to a hard core of five students in second year, and we got to know Bjarne very well in those small tutorials; they were such a haven compared to the much larger English Language lectures.

Despite us still struggling with the challenges of Danish pronunciation (I noticed the Scottish students seemed much better at this than the English!), Bjarne's bottomless patience and kindness encouraged me to sign up to go to Copenhagen as an Erasmus student for my third year. Indirectly, this decision meant I found my future career as an archivist during my Erasmus year.

Whilst struggling to keep up with a class on medieval Danish history, the tutor (an archivist from the National Archives) took us to see the stupendous Arnamagnænske Institute and its Icelandic saga manuscripts. I realised that this was a possible career, although it took a few years more to find my way. Again, Bjarne made his input into my future life's direction indirectly, through encouraging me to apply for a scholarship with the Anglo-Danish Society to study history at Aarhus for a semester, and then helping to set me up teaching English at a folk high school nearby through the European Voluntary Service after I graduated. All this gave me the thinking time to sort myself out and to make the transition into professional life as an archivist.

I still kept in touch with the department from a distance, but then moved back to Edinburgh in 2007 for a job and found myself able to consider doing a part-time PhD. Having always regretted not taking Bjarne's fourth year honours course in children's literature, I took that as my focus, and started on a six-year marathon research project. I don't think I'd have taken that bold step if Bjarne hadn't still been ploughing the Danish furrow in the department! Even now, nearly ten years since getting my PhD ready to submit in 2013, I still cannot quite believe I even started it, let alone finished it. Having heard horror stories from an archive colleague about bloodthirsty supervisors aggressively protecting their own research interests and piling on the written work, my relatively stress-free progression through my studies with Bjarne at the helm seemed a bit too good to be true. I loved the research itself but disliked the writing up and analysis phases intensively. Was I doing enough work? Was it good enough for PhD level? Was Bjarne being too kind, too positive? Was he being a rigorous enough critic? Was I going to bomb out at the viva, when it would be revealed that I was a complete fraud?

Happily all ended well – my viva was a joyful opportunity to discuss my research with the external examiner, who had a very similar research focus to mine, and Bjarne sat there throughout oozing serene tranquillity and positive vibes. And I found that I'd joined the (at that time) select ranks of those finishing PhDs in Scandinavian Studies at Edinburgh.

Only very occasionally have my Danish skills been useful to me as an archivist; one career highlight was presenting a paper at an international conference held at Møller-Mærsk in Copenhagen, where I got to meet the Georg Jensen and Lego archivists. What incredible collections they must have! Most recently, whilst working at an Oxford college, I became very possibly somewhat overexcited when taking in and cataloguing an album of Danish-language press cuttings documenting the college cricket XI's tour to Denmark in the 1950s, arranged by the Danish ambassador, who had been a student at Oxford.

My Danish is becoming increasingly creaky these days, and I am too embarrassed to email Bjarne in Danish with all those toe-curling mistakes now, but I still end my messages with *'Bedste Hilsner'* in true Bjarne style, and keep trying to resurrect my language proficiency when time permits. Life as a Danophile is much easier these days online, but there is no substitute for the real thing. I've recently found a Danish neighbour who is kindly letting me practise my bad Danish on her; happily, she also hails from North Jutland and has an accent similarly kind to the ear as Bjarne's. So I feel I am in good hands. And in twenty years working as an archivist, I've never come across any handwriting quite as clear and beautifully crafted as Bjarne's – now this is really a true skill to celebrate in these digital days. So, to Bjarne: *tusind tak* for everything, and especially for being on my wavelength at key life moments!

## · 17 ·

# Rewriting the Homeland – Danish Islands: Real, Imagined, and Between the Lines

## Henk van der Liet

> *Ingen kan forlate en øy, en øy*
> *er et kosmos i et nøtteskall, der stjernene*
> *sover i graset under snøen.*
> *Men det hender at noen forsøker.*
> *Og på en sånn dag*
> *blåser en sakte østavind.*
>
> Roy Jacobsen, *De usynlige* (2013)[1]

## Introduction[2]

A few years ago, I was invited to teach a class in a course entitled 'Islands – Models for our Planet, Metaphors for our World'. I

---

1. 'No one can leave an island, an island is a cosmos in a nutshell where the stars sleep in the grass underneath the snow. But sometimes someone tries. And on such a day, a gentle breeze blows from the east.' Jacobsen 2013: 21. Unless indicated otherwise, all translations are by the author of this essay.
2. Minor parts of this chapter were presented at the conference *The Tower at the End of the World*, held at The Nordic House in Tórshavn, the Faroe Islands on 11–14 May 2017. My warmest thanks go to Bergur Rönne Moberg, Copenhagen University for inviting me.

found the title of the course intriguing, mainly because of the metaphoric juxtaposition of the world with insularity, and thus, I accepted the invitation for the lecture. I also felt honoured, because when I studied the course manual it turned out that the majority of the participants, both the teaching staff as well as the students enrolled in the course, predominantly came from the science faculty and the social sciences, and not from the humanities, my own home base. The fact that I would be teaching in a new disciplinary environment, with colleagues with scholarly expertise other than my own, made it even more attractive for me to teach this class.

The reason why the organisers of the programme invited me in the first place was simply because they knew about my personal interest in islands and they themselves had become aware of the disciplinary hiatus in the curriculum. A wide variety of aspects concerning islands were taken care of in this multidisciplinary programme, but cultural – and notably literary – approaches to islands and 'islandness' were, by and large, absent.[3]

So, there I was, a literary scholar among colleagues from the 'science' faculty, who were familiar with gathered data, doing statistics and anthropological, botanical, or geological fieldwork, while I had to persuade the students to study islands in a radically different manner. Primarily by reading books, watching films, and studying images, I showed them the various iconographies and representations of both real as well as imagined islands, hoping to convince them of the viability and importance of these aesthetic sources to apprehend islands also as metaphors, as frames of reference for a variety of different phenomena – insularity as a tangible and concrete phenomenon

---

3. For additional information on this particular university course, see the review essay by the organisers Norder and Rijsdijk 2016: 673–686.

but also as a cultural denominator in general terms.[4] Last but not least, I tried to make the students aware of the importance of thinking about islands diachronically, i.e. to study islands and island-imagery historically, and – because my main field of expertise is Scandinavia – my prime examples were from the north.

This essay is one of the spinoffs of this course. First it will take a brief look at 'island' and 'insularity' in a historical and literary context, especially pertaining to Denmark. Then it will discuss the 'discovery' of islands as part of a 'new' Danish national identity in the course of the nineteenth century. Next, focus shifts to early-twentieth-century literary expeditions, their spinoff, and, finally, how in our postmodern era these literary explorations of Denmark as an archipelago culminate – or rather implode – into a deeply fascinating minimalist expedition report which, in my opinion, opens new vistas for future island literatures.

## The unknown backyard

In numerous ways, the island as a notion or a concept is a difficult entity to deal with. Islands can be understood as places of isolation and captivity – like prison islands – but they can also be experienced as the quintessence of liberty, and function as exemplary models – as often is the case in utopian island-novels and idealising websites for luxurious holiday resorts at tropical destinations. Furthermore, the word island does not exclusively identify a territory surrounded by water. We can also use the word metaphorically, e.g. when linguists

---

4. For a critical discussion of the scholarly relevance of these different approaches to the field of Island Studies, see Hay 2013: 209–232.

study minority languages, their position in relationship to the dominant majority language can be described as 'a linguistic island'. In modern urban traffic planning it is not uncommon to refer to areas strictly reserved for pedestrians as 'traffic islands', because they intend to offer refuge to the vulnerable pedestrian in urban environments dominated by motorised traffic.[5] Even in contemporary clinical psychology, the island metaphor is utilised as a tool in its self-critical disciplinary discourse, in order to concretise the discrepancy between the clinic as professional space and the outside world.[6]

Thus, the word 'island' is employed for various purposes and with different connotations. And it is not surprising that lots of painters, writers, musicians, and filmmakers are attracted to insularity as an artistic theme, as islands seem to question everyday notions of space, place, and trigger our imagination.[7]

The island as a literary theme – narrowing the topic of this essay down to literature – has a long pedigree, going all the way back to Odysseus, and probably even further back into prehistorical times. And most islands in literature are no pure representations of the idyllic or the utopian but rather combinations of both, mixing utopian as well as dystopian visions of confinement. Islands can also be part of other, far more concrete narratives, e.g. islands that are envisaged as peripheral in relationship to the rest of a particular culture or nation. This

---

5. The phrase 'traffic island' was first recorded from app. 1935, when the increase in motorised traffic made it necessary to separate traffic lanes and participants from each other, especially in urban surroundings. The second paragraph of the European Charter of Pedestrians' Rights, which was adopted in 1988 (European Session Document A 2-0154/88) by the European Parliament, e.g. states that: 'The pedestrian has the right to live in urban or village centres tailored to the needs of human beings and not to the needs of the motor car and to have amenities within walking or cycling distance.'
6. See Desai 2018: 1–25.
7. See e.g. Holm 2000: 329–336; Royle 2014: 102 ff.

has – notably in the colonial era – been the dominant political and cultural discourse. But the reverse can also be observed: islands that seem to represent the very essence – or even stereotype – of a region, nation, or an entire culture. An interesting development in this respect is that the decline of the European colonial empires in the twentieth century went hand in hand with the (re)discovery of their own national 'Hinterland'. Once the colonial enterprise began to dissolve, the 'Motherland' had to be (re)described and charted and sometimes even colonised 'from within', symbolically compensating for loss of overseas territories, power, and prestige.

A significant example of such a radical reorientation – resulting in a shift from a global understanding of the national identity towards a far more introspective alternative self-understanding – happened in Denmark during the nineteenth century. In that case the (re)discovery – or maybe one could even label it the invention – of the then diminished country as a new nation with a subsequently new identity was initiated several times during this era. Before the romantic era, the inventory of the country was inaugurated as a royal enterprise, mainly in order to acquire a more reliable system of taxation of the population, but later the gathering and presenting of information about the nation became a crucial element in the nation-building process itself. After the disastrous loss of Norway as an integral part of the kingdom in 1814, the loss of the southern provinces of Jutland to Germany in 1864, and finally the sale of the Virgin Islands to the US in 1917 mark the implosion of Denmark in the nineteenth century, causing a reboot and redefinition of its national identity, or at least forcing a radical makeover of the prevailing national narrative to take place. In the course of the twentieth century, this process initiated a number of 'internal expeditions' with a clear cultural and literary focus, notably to 'discover', describe, and proliferate knowledge about 'remote' parts of the 'new' nation.

The earliest examples of this interest in 'exotic' folklore mainly dealt with oral traditional culture, and an important role must be assigned to the ethnographic collectors Evald Tang Christensen (1843–1929) and Svend Grundtvig (1824–83).[8] Furthermore, inspired by the ideas of the first Danish art historian N.L. Høyen (1798–1870), numerous painters of the so-called Danish Golden Age also started to prefer local sceneries instead of exotic, mainly Italian, localities and landscapes. As a result, the peninsula of Jutland was 'discovered'[9] and marine painting flourished.[10]

Apart from this cultural reinforcement of the dented Danish national identity, 'real' expeditions to the lesser-charted periphery of the diminished nation also started to pick up, primarily bound for the Arctic, especially Greenland.

## Scandinavia

As most foreigners will know, the Scandinavian countries – as far as their natural conditions are concerned – are quite diverse. Norway is characterised by mountains and magnificent fjords, while in Sweden it is impossible to overlook its many forests and woodlands. Finland, on the other hand, is known for its countless lakes, Denmark for its gentle and hilly landscape, while Iceland stands out because of its rugged volcanic terrain,

---

8. Evald Tang Kristensen (1843–1929) collected innumerable amounts of songs and ballads, especially in Jutland. His work appeared in a range of anthologies a.o. *Jyske Folkeminder I–II* (1871–76), while Svend Grundtvig (1824–83) mainly collected and published traditional Danish fairy tales.
9. Cf. an interesting article on the 'discovery' of Jutland by a number of nineteen-century Danish painters is Oelsner 2019: 278–291. See also Frandsen 1996.
10. A sign of the thematic introspection in the visual arts is the upswing in Danish marine painting in the same period. See Helleland 2021: 11–12.

and the Faroe Islands for their Atlantic weather conditions and rich foliage. Each of these countries has distinct geographical features and different natural characteristics, which lead to a wide variety of landscapes, flora, and fauna. Some of these aspects have received additional attention as particular markers of national identity and thus have become crucial in defining each country's cultural identity.

Although the differences between these countries are enlarged and put forward as quintessential national denominators, we can still speak of Scandinavia in unifying terms, albeit that the name then primarily must be understood as an expression used in the realm of culture (e.g. in Scandinavian design or Scandinavian noir) – instead of a clear geographical entity (just try to draw the borders of Scandinavia). Understood in this way, Scandinavia is formed by common history, linguistic roots, and parallel socio-cultural developments, rather than common geographical features.

But in my opinion there still is another common feature that is part of the fabric that composes Scandinavia – namely the role of insularity in the overall conceptualisation of Scandinavia.[11] Of course, the inhabitants of the Scandinavian countries tend to stress the differences between the various countries of the north, often emphasising their variety, instead of their similarities, in defining their cultural identity. Just think of the uncontested predilection of the Norwegians for hiking, the Swedes for their Vasaloppet, the Finns for their plunge into the icy water after sauna, the Islandic affection for hot springs, and the Faeroese for their traditional whaling event (*'grindadráp'*), while the Danes boast about their beer and *hygg*e. Strangely enough, the notion of insularity does not immediately jump to mind as one of the typical characteristics of Scandinavia. But in my opinion, it should.

---

11. See also Frank 2017: 187; Wærp 2017: 147.

The first thing to do is literally to find out what we have in mind when we talk about islands. We should start by looking through an insular lens and understand islands as part of geographies, which either are real or imaginary, i.e. we must try to find islands that can be found on maps and visited, islands that merely exist in art and literature, and, finally, islands that belong to both worlds. This essay presents a case study, a brief journey into the historiography of islands, with special attention to Scandinavia and in particular Denmark in the twentieth century.

## Landfast or seaborne

In comparison to the rest of Scandinavia, Denmark stands out somewhat bleakish, at least as far as landscape and climate are concerned. Denmark is – no harm intended – extremely unimpressive, as there are no high mountains, no volcanoes nor any spectacular fjords, and the climate is relatively mild. Compared to the rest of Scandinavia, Denmark is, frankly speaking, quite an ordinary place.

Nevertheless, there is at least one striking phenomenon that is characteristic of the Danish landscape, and that to some extent determines the identity of the Danes. This feature may at first glance be overlooked, but it is important, because the Danes do not inhabit one country, but – in a way – a number of small countries or a bunch of 'social biotopes'. After all, according to most sources, the country consists of some 400 islands.[12]

The fact that Denmark is a collection of many different islands also resonates in the third stanza of the Danish national

---

12. According to Wikipedia there are 1,419 Danish islands larger than 100 m², of which 443 have a name and seventy-eight are inhabited. See https://da.wikipedia.org/wiki/Beboede_danske_øer.

anthem, 'Der er et yndigt Land' also known as 'Fædrelands-Sang' (1819), which goes like this:

*Og ædle Qvinder, skiønne Møer,*
*Og Mænd og raske Svende*
*Beboe de Danskes Øer.*

And noble women, beautiful maidens,
and men and brisk swains
inhabit the islands of the Danes.

The author of the text of the Danish national anthem, Adam Oehlenschläger (1779–1850), draws attention to the fact that Denmark comprises a respectable number of islands, i.e. landmasses entirely surrounded by (salt) water.

The sea and the country's insularity has had a huge impact on its history and culture. Before the introduction of modern land-based traffic infrastructures, such as railroads, bridges, motorways, and tunnels, travel by boat was the predominant form of transportation in Denmark. And narratives, like the national anthem, that support and solidify the national self-image, show a clear consciousness of the nation's seaborne identity, e.g. by constantly repeating the myths and iconography of the so-called Viking Age.

This image of the Viking mariner was often contested by a likewise potent counter-mythology rooted in pre-historic farming in Denmark. The framing of Denmark as a country primarily built on agricultural ancestry became the dominant trope in the nineteenth and twentieth century, due to the persuasiveness of archaeologists, literati, and politicians. Especially after the demise of the Danish fleet in the final years of the Napoleonic wars and the lost battles with Germany in 1864, the Danes seemed to prefer introspection and understand themselves as a land-based instead of a seaborne nation connected to the rest of the globe.

One of the few mavericks who opposed this one-sided cultural image is the author Carsten Jensen (1952). Jensen focuses on the maritime history of the island of Ærø in his seminal novel *Vi, de druknede* (2006)[13] as a complaint against the perversion of Danish history by prioritising land over sea.[14]

Long before the age of the internet, the sea was the information superhighway par excellence. In the past, islanders would often be better informed about what was going on in the rest of the world, precisely because the sea was their open source of information and communication. And although sailing always has been a perilous endeavour, it still was faster and less dangerous than most land-bound forms of transportation.

Of course, this has changed radically in the course of the twentieth and twenty-first century, not only in Denmark but globally. One of the consequences of the increase in travel on land – and through the air – combined with the growth of urbanisation and globalisation was the initial depopulation of numerous small islands. Later, as one of the effects of the digital age, the depopulation – at least in part – seems to slow down and in some cases is even reversed. Living on remote and scarcely populated islands has become an increasingly attractive option to newcomers, due to the internet.[15]

---

13. The book also appeared in English translation as *We, the Drowned* (2011).
14. See Frank 2017: 200. Recently Søren Frank published an interesting plea for an ecocritical, 'amphibian' literary approach which deals with Siri Ranva Hjelm Jacobsen's *Havbrevene* (2020), advocating an 'oceanic perspective on planetary and human history' (Frank 2021: 81).
15. Cf. https://danske-smaaoer.dk.

## Mapping the nation

As a result of the Enlightenment and the European colonial enterprise of the eighteenth century, huge amounts of time and energy were dedicated to exploring, prospecting, and mapping the surface of the earth, often motivated by commercial or military interests, or both. The urge to explore, describe, and map the overseas possessions of the nation lead in the case of Denmark in the early eighteenth century e.g. to the description of Greenland by the missionary Hans Egede (1686–1758), *Det gamle Grønlands Nye Perlustration etc.* (1741), while the scholar Árni Magnússon (1663–1730), on a surveying mission to Iceland in the beginning of the eighteenth century (1702–12) not merely described the country but also assembled an impressive collection of medieval manuscripts there, which became his most important and lasting legacy.

As far as the Danish motherland is concerned, one of the richest illustrated descriptions of the country was, in the middle of the eighteenth century, published by the historian and antiquary Erik Pontoppidan (1698–1764) – *Den Danske Atlas eller Konge-Riget Dannemark* [...] *Lands-Beskrivelse* (1763–81) – in no less than seven sturdy tomes.[16] Later, in the nineteenth century, and especially after the separation of Norway in 1814 and the loss of the southern provinces to Germany in 1864,

---

16. The complete title of this work is comprehensive and summarises the contents adequately: *Den danske atlas eller konge-riget Dannemark, med dets naturlige egenskaber, elementer, indbyggere, væxter, dyr og andre affødninger, dets gamle tildragelser og nærværende omstændigheder i alle provintzer, stæder, kirker, slotte og herregaarde. Forestillet ved en udførlig lands-beskrivelse, saa og oplyst med dertil forfærdigede land-kort over enhver provintz, samt ziret med stædernes prospecter, grund-ridser, og andre merkværdige kaaber-stykker.* The first volumes were published by Erich Pontoppidan (1698–1764) while the project was finalised by Hans de Hofman (1763–93).

the re-charting of the country became a crucial project in the nation-building process.[17] As mentioned earlier, Denmark had to reboot and redefine its national identity. From being an intrinsic multilingual, multicultural and multi-ethnic society, the new cultural ideal of the geographically diminished nation state now became increasingly monolingual, monocultural and mono-ethnic. One of the most remarkable steps towards the realisation of this ideal of cultural homogeneity was the sale of the Virgin Islands to the US in 1917.[18]

The sale of the Virgin Islands coincided with a growing Danish interest in the Arctic. A number of expeditions, mainly focusing on Greenland, appropriated Greenland as an integral part of the Danish nation and its cultural self-image. While the tropical parts of the empire were sold off and erased from Danish collective memory, the Arctic part, on the other hand, became increasingly important, notably Greenland, while Iceland and the Faroese attracted far less attention.

Among the most renowned of the expeditions to the Arctic were the so-called Thule expeditions (1912–23), led by the anthropologist, writer, and adventurer Knud Rasmussen (1879–1933), but also other parts of the kingdom of Denmark were 'discovered', described, and amalgamated into a new national narrative under construction.

These expeditions were not primarily undertaken with the explicit objective of colonising or charting the 'lesser known' parts of the country but rather to bring them to the attention of the general public, in order to demonstrate the natural richness

---

17. An example of this tendency is Jens Peter Trap, *Statistisk-topographisk Beskrivelse af Kongeriget Danmark* (1856–59) in five volumes. Since its first appearance, this work has been revised and republished frequently. The latest version, the 6th edition in thirty-four volumes, is produced at present. Cf. http://trapdanmark.dk/om-os/det-nye-trap-danmark.
18. Olsen 2017: 320–347.

and cultural diversity of the nation, despite the loss of territory. Arctic expeditions and travels to Iceland and the Faroese were not merely a matter of putting hidden gems of the kingdom on display, nor purely to exoticise these peripheric parts of the nation, but rather a dual strategy: on the one hand to induce awareness of the uniqueness of the country as a commonwealth, and on the other to domesticise these remote places in order to procreate a sense of unity, i.e. a national identity despite the many dissimilarities with the 'Motherland'.[19]

In the slipstream of these expeditions to the far north, other parts of the nation were also described and brought to the attention of the general public, a process in which literature played a prominent role, thus paving the way for new, twentieth-century national narratives. And just as in the case of the Arctic expeditions, these expeditions to the 'lesser known' parts of the nation, especially the smaller islands, were primarily undertaken with the objective to bring them to the attention of the general public in order to register and preserve the cultural versatility of the country. And it is here that insularity stands out as a cultural resource that could be made productive in the process of rethinking Denmark's national identity.

## Exploring the heartlands

As mentioned earlier, the Danish national anthem speaks of the country's insularity in positive terms, and islands also play a vital role in Danish literary history.[20] Nevertheless, Danish

---

19. See i.a. Jensen 2012; Thisted and Gremaud (eds) 2020.
20. Danish literary history contains numerous islands. To mention just a few: the play *Peder Paars* (1719–20) written by the well-known Dano-Norwegian playwright Ludvig Holberg (1684–1754), which has the island of Anholt as its backdrop. Islands also take centre stage in twentieth-century

literature does not differ from most other European literary traditions – sometimes islands function as metaphors or metonymies signifying isolation, remoteness, or even incarceration. In other instances, islands represent miniature models of the world, mankind, or the universe as a whole.[21]

In the course of the twentieth century, a number of illustrated multi-volume literary expedition reports, primarily dealing with Danish islands, were published. The project I would like to focus on here is the remarkable, massive three-volume work *De danskes Øer*, I–III (1926–28) by the author and Arctic explorer Achton Friis (1871–1939) and the painter Johannes Larsen (1867–1961), a project which exclusively dealt with the country's many small islands.[22] Some years after the publication of these three sturdy tomes, the two authors decided to follow up on the vast success of the first volumes and added another two volumes to the series, *Danmarks store Øer*, I–II (1936–37),

---

Danish literature, such as in the novel *Barbara* (1939) by the Faroese author Jørgen-Frantz Jacobsen (1900–38) and *Løgneren* (1950) by Martin A. Hansen (1909–55), one of the most famous modern existentialist Danish novels situated on a fictitious island (Sandø). More contemporary literary texts dealing with life on Danish islands are *Tilbage til Anholt* (1978) by Vagn Lundbye (1933–2016), *Havside sommer* (1993) by Henning Mortensen (1940–) featuring Fanø, and *Øer* (2016) by Rakel Haslund-Gjerrild (1988–) with Bornholm as backdrop. Other 'insular' authors are: Vibeke Grønfeldt; Thorkild Bjørnvig (both dealing with Samsø); Thorkild Hansen (the historical Danish Virgin Islands); Erik Aalbæk Jensen (Nekselø); Frank Jæger (Langeland); Klaus Rifbjerg (Amager); Dennis Gade Kofod (Bornholm); Carsten Jensen (Ærø), and many more. See also Frandsen 2012: 8–14.

21. The latter is e.g. the case in *Tårnet ved verdens ende* (1976) a collection of short stories by William Heinesen (1900–91), translated into English as *The Tower at the World* (2018). In a way, the near absence of the word island itself in Heinesen's book (where it is only used once) emphasises and explains that in Heinesen's art, insularity is not necessarily connected to physical islands, but rather that it is a quintessential, metaphysical aspect of it.

22. Friis defines an 'island' as a piece of land surrounded by seawater. Cf. Friis 1926: 8.

this time focusing on the country's larger, more densely populated and well-known islands.²³

Achton Friis' and Johannes Larsen's project mirrors in many ways the Arctic explorations, in which Friis himself had been actively involved.²⁴ And the most remarkable feature of *De danskes Øer* is the fact that it does not describe an expedition to an exotic faraway destination. On the contrary, it records parts of the home country, 'discovering' and describing the Danish cultural heartlands, those parts of the country that most citizens hardly new existed, let alone would apprehend as part of their own cultural heritage.²⁵

One of the intriguing aspects of the published 'reports' of the insular expeditions by Friis and Larsen is, of course, the fact that they travelled by boat and, in a way, enacted a 'real' expedition to some remote destination, like performing a reversed Viking exploration. Apart from describing people, traditions, vegetation, wildlife, and weather conditions, the books also offer lots of pictures, drawings, hand-drawn maps, and photographs. Looking at the printed volumes, it is obvious that *De danskes Øer* is meant to be an impressive, monumental, and prestigious work of national importance. One could call the book part of

---

23. Not merely the timing of the additional volumes – in the wake of the Second World War – is remarkable – that is also the case with the metamorphosis of the title of the first series: *Islands of the Danes* (i.e. of the people) were transformed into *Denmark's Islands* (i.e. islands of the nation). The larger islands described in the two volumes are: Funen, Langeland, Seeland, Lolland, Falster, Møn, and Bornholm.
24. E.g. Friis 1987.
25. Achton Friis had in 1906–08 been a member of the polar expedition to the barren north-eastern territory of Greenland, during which among others the leader of the expedition L. Mylius-Erichsen (1872–1907) died. Instead of venturing again to Greenland, Achton Friis was prompted by his colleague-author Jeppe Aakjær (1866–1930) to undertake an expedition in Denmark itself and 'explore and describe' the country's barely known archipelago.

an archive, a recording of a huge amount of social-geographical and historical data, embedded in a textual and visual narrative, in order to preserve a typical historical phenomenon, i.e. the living conditions on Danish islands in the wake of modernity. Hence, *De danskes Øer* clearly has a nostalgic undertone, and in some passages the text even reproduces the racist stereotypes and social-Darwinist misconceptions that were mainstream in early-twentieth-century public discourse.[26]

In the course of the twentieth century, daily life in Denmark changed profoundly, and of course this also happened on the country's islands. Or maybe one should say: especially on the islands, because they were, to some degree, more severely exposed to the onslaught of modernity, due to depopulation and the increasing importance of land-based transportation and communication, favouring the main land over islands and tarmac over waterways. Many island communities disappeared when shops and schools closed, while dwellings and farms were turned into summer cottages for holidaymakers and tourists.

Especially after the Second World War, and after the introduction of the modern welfare society, much of what Friis and Larsen had registered in their monumental *De danskes Øer* in the 1920s had disappeared by then, or was about to fall prey to oblivion. Maybe not so much out of nostalgia but rather because he wanted to preserve information about the folklore and especially the various insular lifestyles, the author Erik Aalbæk Jensen (1923–97) repeated and updated the work that had been done by Friis and Larsen, more than half a century earlier. In the company of his wife Hanne, Aalbæk Jensen

---

26. Also the fact, that the third member of the crew merely is referred to as 'Skipper' and not addressed by his given name, i.e. Christian Andersen, is a sign of the traditional and rock-steady social hierarchy on board the ship. See Houkjær 2006: 13.

visited as many inhabited islands in the Danish archipelago as possible in the 1970s with a tape recorder and a photo camera, eventually to disembogue in the lavishly illustrated eight-volume work *Livet på øerne* (1981–87). In the preface of the first volume, he explains his aims as follows:

> [A]*t fortælle om rejser, der blev gjort, om mennesker, vi traf, og vejr, vi var ude i, alt sammen sanset og oplevet fra fortællerens egen synsvinkel og fortalt videre så subjektivt og personligt, som man nu engang må, hvis man vil gøre sig håb om at nå det, der er fortællingens mål, læserens opmærksomhed.*[27]

> To tell about journeys that were made, people we met, and the weather we were out in, all sensed and experienced from the narrator's own point of view and narrated as subjectively and personally as one is permitted to do, if one hopes to reach the goal of the story, the reader's attention.

Since the 1970s, cultural change has not come to a halt – on the contrary – and the urge to update and revisit the sites that Friis, Larsen, and later Jensen had described and depicted seems to be even more urgent. Since new media technologies for publishing and disseminating information have accelerated, it is hardly surprising that updated versions of earlier works about Danish islands are in tune with new forms of representation.

In 2005, a series of documentary films called *Gensyn med De Danskes Øer* ('Revisiting The Islands of the Danes'), directed by Jørgen Flindt Pedersen (1940–2021), was shown on Danish television. The series clearly aimed at updating the work by Friis and Larsen, but this time on film. And in order to emphasise the close relationship between the two projects and to pay

---

27. Jensen 1981: 12–13.

homage to his predecessors, Flindt Pedersen used the same vessel as Friis and Larsen had done, nearly a century earlier.[28]

Danish islands appear to be an increasingly popular cultural subject. In the first decade of the twenty-first century and the year after Flindt Pedersen's TV series, the journalist Niels Houkjær published *De danske øer* (2006), a richly illustrated and well-documented guide to fifty of the smaller inhabited Danish islands.[29] Although Houkjær in the preface of his book claims that neither Achton Friis' and Johannes Larsen's multi-volume expedition reports nearly a century earlier, nor Aalbæk Jensen's extensive documentation from the 1980s had served as models for his work, this seems to be refuted by the text itself.[30]

The persistence and longevity of the Danish public interest in islands and culturally induced insular expedition reports since the beginning of the twentieth century was recently also demonstrated by two remarkable books by the journalist Christina Vorre, *Forladt* (2017, '*Abandoned*') and *De sidste øboere* (2019, '*The Last Islanders*'). In the introduction to *Forladt*, Vorre acknowledges that she is following in the footsteps of early-twentieth-century explorers and pays tribute to literary (!) adventurers as Ludvig Mylius-Erichsen (1872–1907) and Knud Rasmussen.

In a way, these two books wrap up the project initiated by Achton Friis and Johannes Larsen nearly a century earlier. The very fact that *Forladt* exclusively deals with uninhabited and deserted Danish islands and *De sidste øboere* describes islands that are on the brink of suffering the same fate, does – at least for

---

28. The vessel was called *Rylen* ('*The Sandpiper*'). The series is available here: https://ostfynsmuseer.dk/vare/gensyn-med-de-danskes-oeer-i.
29. Houkjær had previously in 2003 published a likewise richly illustrated and accessibly written cultural guide of *Denmark: Det er Danmark. En lystrejse gennem det danske landskab* ('*This is Denmark: an enjoyable journey through the Danish countryside*').
30. E.g. in the introduction, where Houkjær describes his predecessors, a.o. Friis and Larsen, as well as Aalbæk Jensen. See Houkjær 2006: 12–13.

the time being – bring the process of (re)discovering Denmark as an archipelago of insular narratives to completion.[31] What lies ahead seems to be mere nostalgia: '*en opdagelsesrejse tilbage til det gemte og glemte ørige Danmark*'[32] ('a voyage of discovery back to the hidden and forgotten islands of Denmark').

## Same place, different story

Vorre and Houkjær are not the last authors who try to rediscover and redescribe Danish islands. New media and new forms of literature will add new perspectives and dimensions to the ways in which islands can be approached in an up-to-date manner. A recent and, in my opinion, enticing experiment that meets today's conditions, originates from postmodern artistic philosophy. This approach does not aim at describing islands per se but rather wants to deconstruct the existing discourses on islands and subsequently transforms earlier textual and visual representations of islands into a bricolage or hybrid. This descriptive strategy is not utilised in order to produce new insular narratives but rather to rearrange existing texts and images and present them in new ways. Vorre and Houkjær clearly write in the context of the contemporary tourist industry,[33] catering for a culturally informed readership, while Friis and Larsen, as well as Aalbæk Jensen, had more literary, folkloristic, and, to some extent, political objectives.

---

31. An intriguing issue is whether the title of Vorre's latest book, *De sidste øboere* ('*The Last Islanders*'), which annunciates the end of insular habitation, is substantiated by the present situation and development. Notably the spread of modern forms of digital communication and the recent increase in the acceptance of working from home during the Covid-19 pandemic may well turn out to be game changers in the popularity of living on an island permanently.
32. Vorre 2017: 7.
33. In Danish the ambiguous term '*oplevelsesøkonomi*' is often applied to describe this phenomenon.

Figure 1: The covers of *De Danskes Øer*, Vol I, by Achton Friis and Johannes Larsen (1926) and Sigurd Buch Christensen's remake (2014). Reproduced by permission.

The future of literary explorations of Danish islands has definitely not come to a halt, and the abovementioned postmodern approach has already produced one fascinating but also unobtrusive little book with exactly the same title as the standard work by Achton Friis and Johannes Larsen from the 1920s. In 2014, the young poet and boatbuilder Sigurd Buch Kristensen (1988–) published his *De danskes Øer. Bind 1*. The booklet consists of no more than fifty-eight numbered pages (with quite a few blanks) containing fragmentary notes, some short poems, and a handful of photographic snapshots. Despite the title and the design of the cover of the book (see figure 1), the language and substance differ profoundly from the monumental work of Achton Friis and Johannes Larsen, and the eight volumes by Aalbæk Jensen. Nevertheless, it is obvious that Kristensen intends to engage in a literary dialogue with his predecessors, notably Friis' and Larsen's *De danskes Øer*, and that he is less keen on touristic texts and guidebooks.[34]

Kristensen's miniature book not only deviates radically from Friis and Larsen's work because of the differences in size – fifty-eight against over 400 pages (of the first volume only). Nevertheless, Kristensen wants to write realistically and accurately in his 'expedition report': *'Vi skal dokumentere det hele*, siger jeg, *nu er vi antropologer, opdagelsesrejsende.'* ('We must document everything, *I say,* now we are anthropologists, explorers').[35] At the same time, the author deconstructs, transforms, and 'morphs' Friis' and Larsen's text, and in order to do this he employs a number of literary techniques, such as imitation, copying, ekphrasis, and parody. This can easily be observed by comparing the front covers of the two books – the similarities in layout and typography are striking – and also some of the organisational features of the contents refer back to Friis' and Larsen's original work.

With his own version of *De danskes Øer*, Kristensen follows in the footsteps of his illustrious predecessors, but at the same time he is aware of the necessity of alternative aesthetic approaches, in order to keep clear of the obtrusive touristic discourse. Kristensen is obviously inspired by the American poet and conceptual artist Kenneth Goldsmith's seminal work *Uncreative Writing. Managing Language in the Digital Age* (2011). Goldsmith (1961–) proposes a fundamentally different approach to literature and language and asks questions like: why should a text necessarily have to be new? Is everything that has been written until now really so bad that we really have to do it all over again and add even more text to the existing amount? Are there ways to use the same words and phrases

---

34. Kristensen is well aware of the difficulty to keep away from the touristic 'gaze'. See: Kristensen 2014: 13.
35. Ibid.: 18 (italics as in the original).

again i.e. to 'recycle' them and, at the same time, procreate new meanings? In his own work – especially in his concrete poetry – Goldsmith takes on these challenges, mixing content and form, fusing words and images, copying, pasting and plagiarising in order to create something new from existing linguistic and visual material. Goldsmith and other advocates of this alternative postmodernist literary practice call it *uncreative writing* or *patchwriting*.

Figure 2: Two sample pages from: Friis and Larsen, *De danskes Øer*, Vol I. © Johannes Larsen, *De danskes Øer*, 1926 c/o Pictoright Amsterdam 2022.

Sigurd Buch Kristensen lived most of his life on Ærø, a tiny island off the south-east coast of Funen. And in a sense his version of *De danskes Øer* has all the characteristics of a *sentimental journey*, in which he rekindles memories of his happy childhood on the island. At the same time, Buch Kristensen's book is a narrative about *coming of age*, falling in love, sultry summer evenings, etc. The sober and inobtrusive art of Achton Friis, his skilfully crafted lyrical prose, is subjected to parody and mimicry by Kristensen, and by doing so he also praises and salutes Friis and Larsen's masterpiece, while at the same time producing a radically different and up-to-date vision of what contemporary insular art is capable of.

Notwithstanding the intriguing technique and postmodern approach that Kristensen's *De danskes Øer* contains and reflects on, the question remains regarding what the limits of creativity – or the conscious lack thereof – are. What are the limits of rewriting, reorganising, morphing, copying, and transforming existing texts? How can a recast text be approached critically?

As a mere example of this dilemma, the very first line of Kristensen's book is a quotation from a poem by Paul Celan (1920–70). But the quoted stanza is incomplete, one word is missing, and the question is, of course, whether this is just an unfortunate mistake or whether the omission is motivated artistically.[36] This example demonstrates how difficult it is when generic – and legal – limits are put aside in a creative process, and how readers should deal with the hermeneutic instability this brings about. In the case of the omitted word in Celan's poem, there seems to be no valid artistic argument, apart from careless quoting. On the other hand, according to the collectively written preface to Kristensen's book, the rewriting process may also entail '*mutation, amputation eller at lægge et værk i graven*' ('mutation, amputation or to bury a book completely') of an existing text, which in the end might explain the maltreatment of Celan's poem.[37]

Apart from recycling texts by other writers, such as Johannes V. Jensen's (1873–1950) national romantic poem 'Hvor smiler fager den danske kyst' (1925, 'How beauteous smiles the Danish coast'),[38] Kristensen also applies an amount of autobio-

---

36. The missing word is the word 'stand', first line, second stanza in the poem 'Stimmen', from Celan's collection *Sprachgitter* (1959). See Kristensen 2014: 9.
37. Kristensen 2014: 3.
38. Ibid.: 14. This poem has become a cherished, well-known song in the context of Danish national identity, set to music by the composer Oluf Ring (1884–1946). See Jensen 2006, vol. 2: 194–197.

graphical material, predominantly childhood memories.[39] And, in the entire text, time and space are closely connected and rendered instable, e.g. by mixing present and past tense, and by suddenly jumping from one location to another. And when the narrator refers to his childhood, time and space sometimes seem to become interchangeable: '*Der er ikke andet end barndom i det her landskab*'[40] ('There is only childhood in this landscape'), while in other fragments, time seems to come to a halt: '*Det er to dage tidligere, og vi ankommer til Strynø.*'[41] ('It is two days earlier, and we arrive at Strynø.') According to the terminology of Mikhail Bakhtin (1895–1975), instances like these can be called chronotopes:

> Time becomes, in effect, palpable and visible; the chronotope makes narrative events concrete, makes them take on flesh, causes blood to flow in their veins. [...] And this is so thanks precisely to the special increase in density and concreteness of time markers – the time of human life, of historical time – that occurs within well-delineated special areas.[42]

Kristensen does not always slavishly follow in the footsteps of Achton Friis and Johannes Larsen – he also distances himself from them, e.g. by allowing his girlfriend on board during his 'expedition' and by not celebrating the nature and culture he is confronted with on the islands he visits and 'explores'. Kristensen's rewritten version of *De danskes Øer* contains on the other hand only a few precise descriptions of the natural and cultural surroundings he encounters, and sometimes he even turns to sarcasm, as if everything is lost anyway: '*Et kæmpe træ,*

---

39. See e.g. Kristensen 2014: 15
40. Ibid.
41. Kristensen 2014: 31.
42. Bakhtin 1981: 250.

*er det en bøg? – jeg kan ikke huske det. // Men vinden tager i dets krone, mens vi er der, den kæmpe lunge flimrer, som en blodprop i hjertet flimrer i hjernen på en døende.*' ('A giant tree, is it a beech? – I can't remember. // But the wind wags its crown while we are there, the giant lung flickers like a blood clot in the heart flickers in the brain of someone dying.')[43] The beech tree, the iconic representative of the romantic Danish landscape, changes into a bad omen, announcing death.[44]

Nevertheless, the similarities between Friis and Larsen's monumental project and Kristensen's miniature remake are plentiful, and despite the fact the texts appeared nearly a century apart, they do share the same structural features and a nostalgic, retrospective outlook, and they also agree on criticising the onslaught of modernity with respect to the future of the living conditions on the Danish islands.

Among the common formal characteristics are the already mentioned typographic similarities, but they also share similar captions like 'Intermezzo'. Furthermore, Friis and Kristensen are both keen on registering time, dates, and topographical names meticulously – in Kristensen's case this is an artificial, mock attitude. For Friis, gathering information is motivated by his encyclopaedic objectives, whereas Kristensen uses this type of information in a completely different playful fashion. For Kristensen, naming places implies investing meaning in them and thereby establishing a relationship, an attachment to them.[45] But this relationship is personal and emotional, instead of pragmatic and composed. And when Kristensen refers

---

43. Kristensen 2014: 24.
44. This point is also made by Kamilla Löfström in her newspaper review, see: Löfström 2014.
45. Here I am paraphrasing Tim Cresswell: 'When humans invest meaning in a portion of space and then become attached to it in some way (naming is one such way) it becomes a place'. Cresswell 2015: 16.

sensitively back to older jazz and rock albums,[46] invigorating youth and childhood memories, he at the same time criticises modernity's impact, e.g. through climate change and mass tourism. The sensation of freedom associated with sailing in the archipelago at the southern coast of Funen during summertime, as Kristensen does during his 'expedition', also provokes cynical commentary: '*havet er en motorvej for campister, ikke sejlere, det er til at dø over, så forbandet travlt alle har med at få sig en plads*'[47] ('the sea is a motorway for campers, not yachtsmen, it's a pain in the neck, so damn busy everyone is finding a spot').

In Danish politics as well as literature, insularity has long been associated with negative notions of isolation, backwardness, and imprisonment.[48] But, at the same time, islands can function as a metonymy, as time capsules where culture (presumably) does not change with the same pace as elsewhere, turning islands into refuges from modernity. In my reading of Sigurd Buch Kristensen's *De danskes Øer*, islands – at least in cultural and literary contexts – morph into chronotopes, liminal spaces that literally offer new sensations to the individual reader.[49] Kristensen's bricolage invites us to navigate narrated *insular* spaces which are composed of memories, myths, stories, pictures, and texts made by others and – last but not least – appealing to the senses: the salt of the wind, the roar and whisper of the ocean, the feeling of bare feet touching a warm sandy beach.

---

46. References are made to albums by John Coltrane, *A Love Supreme* (1964), and Neil Young, *Time Fades Away* (1973) – Kristensen 2014: 23.
47. Kristensen 2014: 29, 34.
48. A rather stunning example is the proposal by some Danish politicians to deport refugees to the (deserted) island of Lindholm. See https://www.dr.dk/nyheder/politik/udviste-kriminelle-udlaendinge-sendes-til-oede-oe-i-stege-bugt.
49. See Bakhtin 1981: 84. See for critical approaches i.a.: Liet 1997: 120–128; Andersen 2021: 149–162.

## Lessons learned?

What could the students, mentioned in the introduction of this essay, possibly have learned from my class on islands in a literary, artistic context? In what way can this case study, on insularity as a crucial ingredient in Danish national identity in the twentieth century, be extrapolated and operationalised scholarly?

In the first place, this essay should have demonstrated the importance of literary representations of islands in general. Achton Friis and Johannes Larsen, Erik Aalbæk Jensen, and Sigurd Buch Kristensen are authors who have produced fundamentally different works, notwithstanding the fact that they all engaged with the same geographical subject matter, i.e. islands.

The second lesson learned could be the awareness of how important temporality is in the study of islands. Increasing numbers of islands have been depopulated during the twentieth century, but this trend may well roll back in the near future.

Thirdly, each of the works on Danish islands discussed here can easily become a launching pad for new insular narratives, utilising different media and technologies and thus expanding the artistic possibilities and idioms on offer. Sigurd Buch Kristensen boils more than 400 pages down to less than 10% in an attempt to rewrite Friis and Larsen, merely offering a framework which readers and scholars alike have to deal with and fill in the blank spots themselves.

In a time when virtually all information on islands is available at the tip of a finger, projects like Achton Friis' and Erik Aalbæk Jensen's have simply become obsolete. The results are historically valuable but no longer accurate. The conclusion of this essay may well be that Sigurd Buch Kristensen will turn out to have been the harbinger of a new artistic conversion,[50] just as Friis and Larsen were the forerunners of Aalbæk Jensen and many others. Islands change perpetually and so does their description and, as a consequence, the ways readers and scholars engage with them, and Kristensen takes this elusive – 'floating' – position as the precondition for his work.

## Bibliography

Andersen, Nina Møller. 2021. *Ordet i livet og ordet i kunsten. Bachtins sprogbrugsbegreber.* Copenhagen: U Press.

Bakhtin, M.M. 1981. *The Dialogical Imagination.* Austin: University of Texas Press.

Celan, Paul. 1959. *Sprachgitter.* Frankfurt a.M.: Fischer.

Corbin, Alain. 1994. *The Lure of the Sea. The Discovery of the Seaside in the Western World 1750–1840.* Berkeley and Los Angeles: University of California Press.

Cresswell, Tim. 2015. *Place. An Introduction.* Chichester: Wiley Blackwell.

———. 2019. *Maxwell Street. Writing and Thinking Place.* Chicago and London: Chicago University Press.

Desai, Miraj. 2018. *Travel and Movement in Clinical Psychology.* London: Palgrave Macmillan.

Edmond, Rod. 2006. 'Writing Islands'. In Peter Brown and Michael Irwin (eds), *Literature & Place 1800–2000.* Frankfurt a.M.: Peter Lang, 199–218.

---

50. I just would like to mention Tim Creswell's book *Maxwell Street. Writing and Thinking Place* (2019) as an example of an author (and a scholar) who continues to gather as much information as possible from a wide range of sources, in order to be able to construct a 'comprehensive' narrative of a particular place. In this case he is performing a kind of kaleidoscopic narrative 'excavation', producing a fascinating report that negotiates between various genres, traditions, and styles, and navigates between poetry, storytelling, and scholarly discourse, while at the same time challenging Goldsmith's notion of 'uncreative writing'.

European Parliament. 1988. *The European Charter of Pedestrians' Rights*. European Session Document A 2-0154/88.

Frandsen, Johs. Nørregaard. 2012. 'Øer i dansk litteratur'. In *Reception – tidsskrift for nordisk litteratur* 70: October 2012, 8–14. http://issuu.com/tidsskriftetreception/docs/reception70/145.

Frank, Søren. 2017. 'The seven seas. Maritime modernity in Nordic Literature'. In Steven P. Sondrup et al. (eds), *Nordic Literature: A comparative history. Volume 1: Spatial Nodes*. Comparative History of Literatures in European Languages XXXI, 186–200.

———. 2021. 'Her regerer havet: Siri Jacobsens *Havbrevene* og en amfibisk litteraturvidenskab'. In *Norsk litteraturvitenskapelig tidsskrift* 24:2–2021, 81–98.

Friis, Achton. 1987. *Danmark-ekspeditionen til Grønlands Nordøstkyst 1906–1908*. Copenhagen: Gyldendal.

Friis, Achton and Larsen, Johannes. 1926–1929. *De danskes Øer*. Bind I–III. Copenhagen: Gyldendal.

Goldsmith, Kenneth. 2011. *Uncreative Writing. Managing Language in the Digital Age*. New York: Columbia University Press.

Hansen, Martin A. 1950. *Løgneren*. Copenhagen: Gyldendal.

Hay, Pete. 2013. 'What the Sea Portends: A Reconsideration of Contested Island Tropes'. In *Island Studies Journal* 8:2, 209–232.

Heinesen, William. 1976. *Tårnet ved verdens ende*. Copenhagen: Gyldendal.

Hermann, Iselin C. et al. (eds). 2017. *Her er DK*. Copenhagen: Brøndums forlag.

Holm, Bill. 2000. *Eccentric Islands*. Minneapolis: Milkweed editions.

Houkjær, Niels. 2006. *De danske øer. En lystrejse til Danmarks småøer*. Copenhagen: Gyldendal.

Jacobsen, Roy. 2013. *De usynlige*. Oslo: Cappelen Damm.

Jensen, Erik Aalbæk. 1981–1987. *Livet på øerne*. Vol. I–VIII. Copenhagen: Gyldendal.

Jensen, Johannes V. 2006. *Samlede digte I–II*. Copenhagen: Gyldendal.

Jensen, Lars. 2012. *Danmark. Rigsfællesskab, tropekolonier og den postkoloniale arv*. Copenhagen: Hans Reitzels Forlag.

Kristensen, Sigurd Buch. 2014. *De danskes Øer*. Vol. I. Copenhagen: Arena.

Liet, Henk van der. 1997. *Kontrapunkter. En studie i Poul Vads skønlitterære forfatterskab*. Odense: Odense Universitetsforlag.

Löfström, Kamilla. 2014. 'National u-romantik'. In *Dagbladet Information*, 6 June 2014.

Nicolajsen, Frank and Helleland, Allis. 2021. *Dansk marinemaleri fra Frank Nicolajsens Samling*. Vestjysk Kunst Fond: Lemvig.

Norder, Sietze J. and Rijsdijk, Kenneth F. 2016. 'Interdisciplinary island studies: connecting the social sciences, natural sciences and humanities'. In *Island Studies Journal* 11:2, 673–686.

Olsen, Poul Erik (red.). 2017. *Vestindien. St. Croix, St. Thomas og St. Jan*. (Volume in the unnumbered series: *Danmark og kolonierne*). Copenhagen: Gads Forlag.

Royle, Stephen A. 2014. *Islands. Nature and Culture*. London: Reaktion Books.

Thisted Kirsten and Gremaud, Ann-Sofie N. (eds). 2020. *Denmark and the New North Atlantic. Narratives and Memories in a Former Empire I–II*. Aarhus: Aarhus University Press.

Vorre, Christina. 2017. *Forladt. Fortællinger fra 20 ubeboede danske øer*. Copenhagen: Lindhardt og Ringhof.

———. 2019. *De sidste øboere. Fortællinger fra udkanten af det danske ørige*. Copenhagen: Lindhardt og Ringhof.

Wærp, Lisbeth P. 2017. 'The island in Nordic Literature'. In Steven P. Sondrup et al. (eds), *Nordic Literature: A comparative history. Volume 1: Spatial Nodes*. Comparative History of Literatures in European Languages XXXI, 146–162.

Østergaard, Cecilie Høgsbro. 2019. *Dansk guldalder – Verdenskunst mellem to katastrofer*. Copenhagen and Stockholm: Statens Museum for Kunst and Nationalmuseum Stockholm 2019.

# Our Nordic Neighbours: The Present State of the Danish Community in Scotland

## Ruairidh Tarvet

## Introduction

Scotland and Denmark have a long, shared history of cultural contact, driven initially by Viking and Norse settlers from the eighth to the fifteenth century. Whilst these Viking invasions made a significant and lasting impact on the Scottish language, place-names, cultural practices, and genetic diversity, there has been a revived interest in Scotland's Nordic connections in recent years, sparked in part by debates surrounding the Scottish independence movement and devolution. Rather than contributing directly to the discussion on Scotland's historic ties with Scandinavia, this paper will instead focus on the current Danish community in Scotland, consisting of Danish migrants and students of Danish, as well as the institutions, social organisations, and support structures for Danish language and culture in Scotland. In light of the UK's secession from the European Union on 31 January 2020, this paper will also explore the views of members of this Danish community on issues regarding identity, networking, bureaucracy, and language in Scotland, the UK, and Denmark. The core research questions to be answered as such are as follows:

1. In what ways do Danish culture and language thrive in Scotland?
2. To what extent can there be said to be a 'Danish community' in Scotland?
3. To what extent has this dynamic changed following Brexit?

It is the intention of the author that, rather than presenting a fully representative sample of opinions, the discussion in this paper should provide a snapshot of views pertaining to life in the Danish community in Scotland today. For clarity, the term 'Danish community' shall here encompass both migrants and students, as well as their family and friends in Scotland who actively partake in the expression of Danish language and/or culture in Scotland through social gatherings and/or education.

## Denmark, Danes, and the Danish language in twenty-first-century Scotland

According to data from the UK government's EU settlement scheme, there are around 1,490 Danes living in Scotland.[1] A handful of organisations and institutions are dedicated to the promotion of Danish culture and language in Scotland. The Danish-Scottish Society (and its social media presence Danish-Scottish Network) is the largest social organisation for Danes living in Scotland. Founded in 1986, the society currently has around 200 members and raises funds through membership fees in order to achieve its goal, namely to 'establish a social framework for Danes to meet with Scots and other residents of Scotland who take an interest in Denmark, its language and its culture, as

---

1. UK Government 2021.

well as for Danes to meet each other'.[2] With membership open to Danes and non-Danes alike, the events and activities organised by the society act as a catalyst for cultural contact and exchange.

Alongside traditional Danish celebrations such as Sankt Hans, Mortens Aften, and Fastelavn, the society also hosts regular social events in pubs, cafés and parks for members to gather, discuss life in Denmark and Scotland, and socialise more generally. Moreover, the society operates the Danish School in Scotland, which provides group education in Danish language and culture every second Sunday to children between the ages of five and sixteen. It currently has around eighty members.[3] Whilst most of these classes take place in Edinburgh, classes were held online during the Covid-19 pandemic, which allowed members from elsewhere in Scotland to participate.

An unpublished, informal survey conducted by the Danish-Scottish Society on 100 Danes living in Scotland reveals some detailed insight into the dynamics of the Danish community in Scotland. Although 79% of all respondents live in Scotland permanently, only 42% of all respondents are members of the Danish-Scottish Society, with the location of society events being frequently cited as a hindrance to membership. Around a third of Danes live in the Edinburgh region, with another third in the Glasgow region, and the rest spread out elsewhere in the country. Around half of respondents note that they have Danish friends in Scotland, but whilst 71% of respondents would like to occasionally meet other Danes, only 56% would like to meet other Danes regularly, though 55% of respondents would like the opportunity to speak more Danish.[4]

The Danish-Scottish Society runs a number of social-media pages to promote its activities, foster membership, and

---

2. Danish-Scottish Society 2019.
3. Danish-Scottish Society, *Danish School in Scotland*.
4. Danish-Scottish Society, *Survey on Danish Community in Scotland*.

contribute to its constitutional objectives. In 2020, the society set up the page Danish-Scottish Marketplace on Facebook as a platform on which to trade Danish items, foodstuffs, and gifts in Scotland. Whilst the marketplace itself currently has 251 members,[5] the Scottish market for Danish items is complimented by a handful of Danish shops in Scotland, including Nordic Living by Biehl, BoConcept, and Flying Tiger. In addition to its own, members-only social-media presence Danish-Scottish Society (104 members), the society also administers the Facebook group Danskere i Skotland (518 members) and the page Danish-Scottish Network (959 followers), both of which are open to non-members.

Social media has arguably become the predominant means for Danes and those interested in Denmark to network. It has also filled a gap left behind by the former Danish Cultural Institute. Established at Doune Terrace, Edinburgh in 1956, the Danish Cultural Institute functioned as a hub and venue for Danish music, art, literature, and culture in Edinburgh. Throughout its almost sixty-year history, the Danish Cultural Institute hosted a number of guest artists, politicians, diplomats, and students from Denmark and formed close ties with the Scandinavian Studies section at the University of Edinburgh, hosting annual Danish Christmas dinners with university students and staff. Upon closing in 2015, the then director of the institute, Kim Minke, addressed the role of social media in the closure of the institute, stating:

> [...] improved communications have reduced the need for a physical premises in many European countries, but the cultural differences between some developing nations and Denmark mean an institute is necessary.[6]

---

5. *Danish-Scottish Marketplace* 2022.
6. The Newsroom 2015.

In terms of opportunities for language acquisition, the sole institution in Scotland offering courses in Danish language and culture at undergraduate and postgraduate level is the University of Edinburgh. Founded in 1987, the Scandinavian Studies section currently has six permanent or full-time staff, a handful of honorary fellows and part-time staff, and upwards of 150 students, of whom approximately twenty-five study Danish language and all of whom study aspects of Danish culture and society.

Danish language was first taught in the School of Literatures, Languages and Cultures by Bjarne Thorup Thomsen, who retired in 2021 as the section's longest-serving member of staff. At present, Danish language and culture is taught by a teaching fellow and a teaching and research fellow. In addition to undergraduate and postgraduate tuition, Scandinavian Studies organises a range of public seminars, workshops, conferences, and events relating to Danish (and Scandinavian) culture and society. The University of Edinburgh also hosts the Northern Scholars scheme, which was set up in 1956 in order to '[…] foster co-operation between scholars of the Nordic countries'.[7] The scheme currently welcomes two to three academics per year to give departmental seminars and public lectures at the University of Edinburgh. The Centre for Open Learning at the University of Edinburgh also offers a number of evening courses in Danish language for members of the public. At present, around twenty students are enrolled on Danish language courses at the centre, taking courses at beginner and intermediate level.[8]

---

7. The University of Edinburgh 2022a.
8. The University of Edinburgh 2022b.

## Exploring the Danish community in Scotland: methodology and limitations

In order to obtain the data required to answer the research questions, focus-group research was conducted in two key communities in Scotland with close ties to Danish culture: group 1 consisted of members of the Danish-Scottish Society, whilst group 2 consisted of recent graduates of the University of Edinburgh's MA honours programme in Scandinavian Studies with a language specialism in Danish. Participants in group 1 were recruited through an open invitation on the Facebook page for the Danish-Scottish Society, whilst participants in group 2 were recruited via an email invitation. The groups were invited to participate in a group-specific discussion led by the principle investigator (PI). Full informed consent was obtained from all participants, whereby each participant was informed of the aims, structure, purpose, and outputs of the study, as well as their rights and options regarding data protection, anonymity, and storage. The study was also approved by the University of Edinburgh LLC ethics committee.

The criteria for inclusion in the study varied for each group so as to reflect the overall dynamic of each group's relationship to Denmark. As group 1 consists solely of first-generation Danish migrants, potential participants were invited on the basis that they had been resident in Scotland for at least one year before Brexit (31 January 2020) and one year after Brexit, declared themselves to be active in one or more of the aforementioned Danish organisations/institutions and/or felt part of a Danish community in Scotland. Following recruitment according to this criteria, group 1 gained four participants, plus the PI.

For group 2, which primarily consists of students who have acquired skills in the Danish language and an understanding of Danish culture through undergraduate study, the criteria for inclusion was to have completed an undergraduate degree in Danish language and/or culture in Scotland in the past year and to have been primarily resident in Scotland during that time. Following recruitment according to this criteria, group 2 obtained three participants, plus the PI.

It should be noted that the PI also meets the criteria for inclusion in both groups.

Both group discussions were structured in such a way as to facilitate natural dialogue between participants with minimal prompts from the PI. The role of the PI in these discussions was to steer conversation towards the research questions without following a set script or forcing direct answers. Dialogue between the PI and participants was also encouraged. In the section below, the main discussion points have been highlighted and the overarching conversation streamlined in order to maintain relevance to the research questions. For sake of clarity and conciseness, parts of the discussion that were irrelevant or off-topic have been omitted here but included in the full transcript, which is held by the PI and can be accessed if requested. All names have been pseudonymised, whereby each participant's name has been replaced using a number to represent their group and a letter to represent their name (e.g. 1A).

## Group 1 participant info and discussion

The meeting for group 1 took place in person at a Scandinavian-themed café in Edinburgh on 22 July 2021. In addition to the PI, the group consists of the following members:

- 1A: a Danish woman in her thirties
- 1B: a Danish woman in her twenties

- 1C: a Danish woman in her thirties
- 1D: a Danish man in his forties

Participants were briefed on the research questions, and the PI began by asking whether life as a Dane has become more difficult or easier after Brexit. 1D replied that 'it's kind of been coming at the same time as the Corona crisis so it's hard to distinguish [...]'. All participants agreed with this and began to tell stories of how they had not seen their family in such a long time.

Given the proximity of Brexit to the start of the Covid-19 pandemic, it is clear that not enough time has elapsed to gauge the impact of Brexit on travel between Denmark and Scotland. Nevertheless, 1A noted that Brexit has impacted her connection with Denmark due to new import fees on packages, stating that 'I got my birthday present held up in the customs and had to pay £65 to get it out and it was a sweater. It wasn't that expensive'. The other participants concurred with this notion.

1A then continued, saying that '[...] I feel less welcome in a way [...] not [by] the people, the Scots are lovely as always, it's more like the, sort of, bureaucratic aspect of things'. 1D joined in here, saying that 'the fact that we [...] need to apply for settled status to [...] prove that we are entitled to be here kind of sticks in my craw. I've been living here since 2006 [...] this is my home now and it's not right that the rights that I have taken for granted [...] I need to apply to protect them'. 1C agreed, stating that 'it's a bit weird to have permanent residency and then have to apply for settled status [...] now I've got to justify even staying where I am'.

After sharing a few more personal stories regarding customs charges and travel, the PI asks what the participants feel about the sense of a Danish community in Scotland and whether there is a strong sense of a network. 1C responds, saying:

> [...] I spent eight years in London where there is also like a Danish community but to me it feels very different [...] I personally never really got involved because I was sort of like 'what's the point'? People will be gone soon anyway whereas in Scotland people are here a bit more permanently than they are in London [...] I think it has the potential to be a more lasting community than in London but it requires a lot of effort on the part of people who organise it.

1A replies, stating:

> I've been here for four years but I've just recently sort of discovered the Danish-Scottish community [...] I was aware of it but I never really engaged with it because I sort of had my friends in the beginning from my master's studies and work friends, etc. I kind of wish I had discovered it earlier because, particularly now after, like, the separation from family and friends during Covid and Brexit, it was so nice when we went to the football match together [...] speaking Danish again and I really enjoyed that.

1C notes:

> I lived right next to the Danish Cultural Institute for a while. I used to go in all the time and ask what the next events were [...] it was always very family-focused. People who had married Scottish people. What about the people who are here alone? [...] Eventually they closed down anyway but I tried really for many years to find other Scandinavians and really fell flat [...] the community is a bit fraught.

The PI asks why football was mentioned as a success story for bringing Danes together. 1C replies that it is because we're quietly proud of being Danish. We don't need to talk about it every day […] but when stuff like reaching a semi-final in football happens […] we were there to watch the football but then we could also engage and interact and have a bit of fun and, like, let out a bit of the Danishness and then go back to our daily life.

1B joins in by noting that '[…] it's one of the few times where I'm like, oh, I wish I was with other Danish people […] I'm missing that'.

The participants return to a discussion on how the Danish-Scottish community is too family-focused and suggest that more inclusive events such as Sankt Hans or Melodi Grand Prix would help to build the community network. Nevertheless, the participants noted that many Danes who move abroad do not engage much with other Danes as they are busy with other aspects of their lives abroad. On this issue, 1A says that 'you're so keen on assimilating or sort of becoming part of the place'. 1D replies that 'I was a passive member [of the Danish-Scottish community] for quite a long time and then when my son was born there came a need for it […] I need this Danish community for him to, kind of, develop his connection to the country'.

1A responds that:

[…] it is a great idea to start with like national events or important days to Danes because […] that's when you remember your Danishness and want to seek out other Danes […] I think more people are likely to turn up to Sankt Hans or Mortensaften rather than just a sort of random Wednesday evening at a pub.

## Group 2 participant info and discussion

The meeting for group 2 took place in person online using Zoom on 21 July 2021. In addition to the PI, the group consists of the following members:

- 2A: a female Danish graduate in her twenties from England
- 2B: a female Danish graduate in her twenties from England

2C: a female Danish graduate in her thirties from Scotland
Participants were briefed on the research questions, and the PI began by asking in what ways Danish culture and language thrive in Scotland or at university.

2A begins by pointing out

> it thrives in a commercial sense because even just, you know, a few meters away from the Scandinavian department you've got Söderberg [a Scandinavian-themed café] […] but there are a surprising amount of Scandinavian shops […] that have helped with my understanding of the language and the culture […] I remember being in first year and going into Tiger […] and being like 'oh I can use that word in class' even if it is just something like stationery.

2B joins in by stating that 'products are always, like, slightly a part of it, aren't they?… what you aspire to, like the aesthetic'. 2C replies that 'as the Nordic Noir came into fashion and the whole Scandinavian obsession started in Britain then it became very trendy to speak a Scandinavian language'.

The PI then asks how the students connected with Denmark whilst living in Edinburgh. 2C mentions the Danish Cultural Institute as a key factor, but the other graduates are unable to relate, not having experienced it themselves. 2C undertook an internship at the institute as a student and notes that 'I think it definitely helped me because it made sure that I was speaking Danish, I was there maybe twice a week […] and I got a bit of insight into how it is being in a Danish workplace because it is very different to working in Britain'. 2B says that:

> we have the Scandinavian Society […] at the uni there are quite a lot of Scandinavians, not necessarily Danish, but I did meet quite a lot of them and some of them were actually really sweet and tried to help me, you know, with connections and things on my year abroad […] the Scandinavian department is quite small and feeling connected and able to talk to teachers I guess was a really important part of it […] maybe if it had been a different language department or, like, it had been a bit bigger then it might not have been as easy to feel […] included in a community.

2B continues:

> I will also say that that also prepared me for the teaching style a bit in Denmark because […] in British universities the teaching style is very, like, top down […] when I compare it to experiences other people have had in uni, like, we are a bit more on an equal footing.

2A suggests:

> I think the size of our class helped […] you can't help but start to rely on each other even more in an area where the language isn't spoken particularly widely […] it seems that the Scandinavian department saw us on an equal footing and did everything they could to help us.

2C replies that 'maybe because the department is so open and friendly and welcoming meant that I wasn't prepared for the fact it is not like that [in Denmark] and people are really reserved'.

2B remarks that 'the Scandinavian department [...] they all communicate with each other in their own [Scandinavian] languages [...] Scandinavians in real life don't really do that. They kind of switch to English [...] they don't make the effort.'

The PI then asks whether Brexit has impacted their experience with Denmark and Danish. 2B responds by saying

> [...] that kind of became an icebreaker question that Danes often ask me [...] they would ask me about Brexit and how I felt and it kind of just became an ongoing joke [...] since graduating, Brexit has possibly affected how nervous I feel about trying to move over [to Denmark] and the admin that that is going to take.

2C says that '[...] after Brexit I feel like [...] Scotland is like this little underdog and a lot of people here [in Denmark] support independence [...] it's definitely, like, a talking point [...] and people seem to think that Scotland could be more Nordic'.

2B reflects that '[...] would I, if Brexit had not happened, been a bit more lazy and more passive in terms of moving over? It would have been like "oh, it's not going anywhere [Denmark]" [...] now that it is difficult [...] I need to get it done'.

## Conclusion

Whilst the Danish community in Scotland is relatively small, it is clear that several actors are invested in the promotion of the Danish language and culture. Since the withdrawal of the Danish Cultural Institute, much of this activity has been adopted by interest groups and private citizens keen to maintain a sufficient support network for fellow Danes. In addition to the handful of cultural events annually, education in the Danish language at nursery and university level is a key asset in maintaining Scotland's connection with Scandinavia.

It should nevertheless be emphasised that despite these efforts, the vast majority of Danes in Scotland are not very engaged with the Danish-Scottish Society or the University of Edinburgh, and the responses above suggest that participants do not feel a strong sense of a Danish community. This is not the case for graduates of the university, who generally praise the small and close-knit Scandinavian academic community as a net positive to their personal development and future careers.

The stereotype of Danes as being reserved and difficult to bond with is perhaps reflected in the responses from the focus groups, whereby this cultural facet presents an obstacle to networking. Although it may be the case that Danes in Scotland have sought to assimilate rather than integrate, moments of national importance, such as football championships and national celebrations, present an opportunity for Danes in Scotland to experience and express their Danishness, albeit in small bursts. Without an official physical presence in Scotland, such as a cultural institute or embassy, however, there are few places for Danes and Scots to network and learn about Denmark in a structured or wide-scale manner. As such, it can be assumed that the University of Edinburgh and the Danish-Scottish Society remain the only viable guardians of Danish culture and language in Scotland.

## Bibliography

Danish-Scottish Society. 2019. *Danish Scottish Society Constitution*. https://e9185747-8cca-46e8-a4be-08a228928cf8.filesusr.com/ugd/613a7a_17e68d92193047a48c5b1bf105eacf40.pdf. Accessed 5 July 2021.

———. n.d. *Danish School in Scotland*. https://e9185747-8cca-46e8-a4be-08a228928cf8.filesusr.com/ugd/613a7a_2ee02a4e7c4a4bc8b0a5a6af05b740c4.doc?dn=mission.doc. Accessed 12 September 2022.

———. n.d. *Survey on Danish Community in Scotland*. Unpublished. Copies can be obtained from society chairperson.

*Danish-Scottish Marketplace*. 2022. https://www.facebook.com/groups/526992958032247. Accessed 12 September 2022.

The Newsroom. 2015. 'Denmark culture group's Edinburgh HQ to shut'. In *Edinburgh Evening News*, 12 January. https://www.edinburghnews.scotsman.com/news/denmark-culture-groups-edinburgh-hq-shut-1515719. Accessed 5 July 2021.

The University of Edinburgh. 2022a. *Northern Scholars*. https://www.ed.ac.uk/literatures-languages-cultures/delc/nordic-research/northern-scholars. Accessed 12 September 2022.

———. 2022b. *Danish Courses*. https://www.ed.ac.uk/studying/short-courses/subjects/languages-courses/danish-courses. Accessed 5 July 2021.

UK Government. 2021. *EU Settlement Scheme quarterly statistics tables, March 2021*. https://www.gov.uk/government/statistics/eu-settlement-scheme-quarterly-statistics-march-2021. Accessed 2 August 2021.

# Understanding Scandinavia

· 19 ·

# Small Countries, Media, and Cosmopolitan Thinking

## Dominic Hinde

Copenhagen was hot on 25 June 2016. The night before, thunderstorms had rolled across the city and I had drifted off to sleep on the sofa of a Danish colleague in Amagerbro while watching the results of the referendum on EU membership come in.

The next morning he had got me booked in as a talking head on DR's results show to discuss what it all meant. It wasn't the first time I had worked for DR – I had been freelancing with their European correspondent in Scotland and northern England for the past few years and popped up as an analyst for DR and SR in Sweden.

Standing in the atrium at DR Byen on the south side of Copenhagen, I was struck by the realisation that my route to being there could not have happened without the unique experience I had as an undergrad student at Edinburgh under Bjarne Thorup Thomsen, and his continued support and guidance through my PhD. At a time when universities obsess over graduate trajectories and employment statistics, it was a timely reminder that you can't always plan or quantify what will happen, but when you get there, the path all makes sense.

The Nordic countries are all famously Anglophilic to varying degrees, but it does not always work the other way. Very few news organisations currently have staff correspondents in any of the Nordic countries, with responsibility usually falling under the jurisdiction of Berlin bureaus. As a result, the distinctiveness of the Nordic countries both as a geo-cultural bloc and as individual nations is underrepresented and often oversimplified on the world stage.

During the Second World War and all throughout the Cold War, news from Scandinavia was considered an important part of European coverage, Scandinavia being both a near neighbour and a bulwark against Soviet interests in the North Atlantic and the Baltic. The reorganisation of the world after the 'End of History' in the early 1990s and burgeoning discourses on globalisation led to a reduction in the European capacity of the BBC and others, and a redirection towards Asia, Africa, and what were regarded as important developing economies. Northern Europe was, in the newly unified and harmonious world of the post-communist era, a done deal. In a global news cycle which shifted from reporting on trade deals and international conferences to the real-time happenings of wars, terrorist attacks, and natural disasters, the Nordics simply did not offer the ratings and engagement that British and American broadcasters and newspapers were looking for.

By the mid 2000s, the only English-speaking publication with a dedicated Nordic correspondent was the *Financial Times*, and that was more as a hangover from business reporting on the oil industry (the correspondent was based in Oslo) than from a genuine interest in the cultural and political life of the Nordics. As I found out, this lack of a baseline also had tangible structural effects on the way important stories from the Nordics were reported. Sometimes features would simply be done over the phone from London or Washington, or a camera crew with a pre-agreed idea of the form the story would take would drop in for a few days at a time. Media labour and how it is structured are crucial to issues of representation in international affairs, and the cultural and social knowledge of journalists is vital to achieving a genuinely cosmopolitan field.

This has led to the creation of an incredibly skewed vision of the Nordics in the English-language media in particular. Whereas standing correspondents have more freedom to pitch their own expert ideas and will usually have an allocation of stories to fill multiple slots, the freelance model of foreign reporting that dominates in the Nordics and elsewhere today fundamentally changes interactional and editorial control. Instead of being able to explain to the public why something is important (or just interesting, which can be a question of form as much as newsworthiness), foreign reporting today requires pitching news to editors who may have little concept of what is happening on the ground.

The immigration discourse in Scandinavia is a case in point. Populist right-wing parties in Scandinavia have been successful at making themselves visible in the international media as a legitimate political response to social problems, playing on preconceived notions of the Nordics as being too politically progressive or as having taken immigration 'too far'. The way in which articles are commissioned often asks journalists to prove or disprove these simplistic visions, or to seek out and profile the supposedly concerned citizens behind the movements.

Nowhere was this clearer perhaps than with the international news discourse around 'no-go zones' in Sweden heralded by the Trump presidential campaign in the US. By invoking Sweden as an example of a failed and violent multicultural society in line with the international presentation of the populist right, the race was on to find out the truth about Sweden. In one of the more farcical episodes of American projection, Tim Pool, an independent journalist who had made his name reporting on social movements and gang violence in New York and Chicago, ventured to Malmö with the explicit aim of telling Americans what life was like in the dystopian suburbs of contemporary Scandinavia. All he found were public libraries and an efficient local bus system, and a crime rate lower than Glasgow.

The idea that the clean high-tech society of the modern Nordics and the dystopian and destabilised cityscape are one and the same never makes it to the table, however. DR Byen is a jewel at the centre of an expensive redevelopment of the Copenhagen waterfront, creating an area of high house prices and wealth stretching from the north side down to Amager Strand. This is the flipside of Copenhagen's 'problem' working class and ethnically diverse suburbs, setting up islands of pristine Nordicness that win architecture prizes and attract fawning coverage for sustainable living, surrounded by the spectre of encroaching difference which is not so much alien as an integral part of the new Nordic model.

We don't see any nuance to these perspectives often enough in the Anglophone media, and it is becoming harder and harder to push for cultural knowledge as an end in itself. In the name of globalisation and shifting priorities, the attacks on European cosmopolitan learning within British universities are increasing in severity, with programmes being undermined and minority languages disregarded as a costly indulgence. The existence of modern languages departments – be it Danish, Estonian, Spanish, or Romanian – is critical to fostering cosmopolitanism and its intellectual benefits, and I owe my whole career to the education I was given in Scandinavian Studies in Edinburgh and the opportunities it afforded. The sociologist Ulrich Beck referred to cosmopolitanism and its enemies in the battle for the future of Europe, and it is hard not to see modern foreign languages as being at its front line.

Bjarne Thorup Thomsen had a huge impact on my development as a writer and as a researcher, always embodying the idea that small places had rich and important histories, but moreover that to make sense of them meant using the cosmopolitan gaze and asking the right questions.

## · 20 ·

# The Right Time for a Dane to Cross the North Sea

## Ian Giles

The novel, written by a little-known Danish writer who has refused to be interviewed, has an inhospitable, wintry heroine, a strange title and a sombre blue-black jacket. And although HarperCollins has marketed it as a 'thriller', it is a bleak discourse on the terrors of modern life with long, often scientific descriptions of ice and snow. So why has Peter Høeg's Miss Smilla's Feeling for Snow been near the top of the bestseller lists for three months?[1]

One might imagine that Bjarne Thorup Thomsen was regarded as a role model by the Danish novelist Peter Høeg (1957–), who arguably spent much of his youth following in the footsteps of his compatriot. A couple of years junior to Thomsen, Høeg was also a student of literature at the University of Copenhagen in the early 1980s. Not long after Thomsen had made the move across the North Sea, first to Newcastle and then on to Edinburgh, the young novelist Høeg began to eye a similar trajectory, doubtless

---

1. Gerrard 1995a.

impressed by the opportunities afforded to Danes arriving on British shores.[2]

The cover of the current Vintage Books ebook edition of Høeg's *Miss Smilla's Feeling for Snow* proclaims the book to be 'the original Scandinavian thriller'. Although this claim is somewhat dubious, it was nevertheless groundbreaking in a number of respects. Jakob Stougaard-Nielsen and Claire Thomson identify it as the sole example of a Danish crime fiction international bestseller,[3] and it is arguably the most significant Danish book transmitted to Britain in the last century in terms of impact upon reception.[4] Additionally, the success of *Smilla* in Britain in the early 1990s represents the decline of genre boundaries in British literary circles, as described by Clive Bloom.[5] Much as Thomsen helped to craft a new hub of Scandinavian research and teaching in Edinburgh over the course of a fruitful career, so Høeg leveraged genre hybridity to secure his place in the British literary canon of the late twentieth century. This chapter explores in further detail how the latter went about transforming his financial and literary fortunes.

---

2. The British and Irish isles have long been lands of fortune for Danish visitors, and it should come as no surprise that both Thomsen and Høeg opted to emulate their forbears a millennium earlier in crossing the North Sea. Indeed, the departure of Thomsen's renowned footballing prowess from Danish soil was such a paradigm-changing moment that another young Dane who (may have) looked up to Thomsen, one Peter Schmeichel, opted to accept a transfer from Brøndby to Manchester United in 1991 so that he too might benefit from all that the UK had to offer to a young Dane.
3. Thomson and Stougaard-Nielsen 2017: 240.
4. See Giles 2018 for a detailed account of this.
5. Bloom 2008: 10.

## Høeg and *Smilla*

### About Peter Høeg

Peter Høeg has been a presence on the Danish literary scene since the late 1980s, writing a range of novels in different styles. In particular, he is known for being reluctant to be in the public eye, and has been portrayed over the decades in equal measures as a literary great and as an overrated eccentric.[6] The story of how Høeg came to be published by the small press Rosinante, run by the late Merete Ries – former publisher at Gyldendal – is one that has been repeated regularly in both the press and scholarship over subsequent years.[7]

Høeg's debut novel *Forestilling om det tyvende århundrede* ('*The History of Danish Dreams*') was published in August 1988, and its saga-like style drew immediate attention. It was a front-page sensation in the Danish press, with parallels being drawn to H.C. Andersen, Blixen, and Kierkegaard.[8] It won one of Denmark's leading literary prizes, Weekendavisens litteraturpris, in its year of publication.[9] This set it on a path to relative success for a work by a literary newcomer, being reprinted eight times before enjoying a print run of 30,000 in 1991 when it was added to a book-club list.[10] A subsequent collection of short stories, *Fortællinger om natten* ('*Tales of the Night*'), was also

---

6. For a thorough introduction to Høeg's biography and literature, see Høg 2011.
7. In something of a publishing fairy tale, Høeg, an intense young man, arrived at the home of Ries by bicycle to request that she read his manuscript. Perhaps the best account is provided by Ries herself in Ries 1998.
8. Ries 1998.
9. 'Weekendavisens litteraturpris' 2014. Høeg's award-winning credentials continued. He received the Golden Laurel in 1993 for *De måske egnede* ('*Borderliners*').
10. Ringgaard 2006.

received positively. This led to limited success for Høeg with translations into other Scandinavian languages and German. By the early 1990s, Høeg enjoyed a position within the Danish literary establishment as an entrenched newcomer who was unlikely to be dropped by his publishers or the reading public, setting the scene for continued literary experimentation.

## *The publication and reception of* Smilla *in Denmark*

Rosinante published Høeg's third book in April 1992 with the Danish title *Frøken Smillas fornemmelse for sne*.[11] The novel received rapturous press reviews upon release. Jens Kistrup said that 'the novel's Danish virtuoso had done it again' while Søren Vinterberg congratulated Høeg on successfully taking on the thriller genre and succeeding.[12]

The impact on Rosinante was tremendous, transforming the commercial prospects of the publisher from a house with literary prestige but serious liquidity issues into a publishing commodity that eventually attracted the attention of Gyldendal.[13] This impact was not instantaneous, however. In 1992, the Danish edition of *Smilla* sold just 10,000 copies, one tenth of other bestsellers in the Danish market at the time.[14] Carsten Andersen noted that it was the success of *Smilla* in

---

11. *Smilla* draws on the genres of crime fiction, thriller and science fiction, and the theme of postcolonialism to tell the story of its half-Greenlandic protagonist, Smilla. As a result of investigating the death of a child in her Copenhagen block of flats, she ends up entangled in a complex web of intrigue that takes her to sea and to the fictional island of Gela Alta off Greenland.
12. Kistrup 1992; Vinterberg 1992. Other equally positive Danish press reviews include Bredal 1992; Bukdahl 1992; Schou 1992; Wiemer 1992. Beyond newspaper reviews, the book was clearly appreciated for its crime-fiction credentials, being nominated as Denmark's entry for the 1993 Glass Key award, and winning this prize.
13. Høeg precipitated a boom and bust effect on Rosinante. See Andersen 1996; Andersen 2002.
14. Andersen 2006.

the anglophone world that kickstarted mass sales in Høeg's native Denmark. The widespread critical positivity was noted in a brief article in *The Guardian* in 1992.[15]

*English-language publication details*
Høeg's foreign rights were marketed by Rosinante directly. While some foreign-rights sales had been achieved, there had been little success in attracting the attention of the anglophone market for Høeg's previous works: 'the suggestion that they should consider buying from one a novel by an unknown Dane about Danish dreams resulted in blank faces'.[16] This reflects a variety of issues, not least the difficulty of selling as a small publisher in a global market, alongside the slow pace of literary exports from Denmark in the 1980s.[17]

World English rights to *Smilla* were bought by American publisher Farrar, Straus & Giroux (FSG) before publication in Denmark, with UK rights sublicensed to Harvill Press.[18] Ries attributes this to FSG's Danish editor Elisabeth Dyssegaard, although it should be noted that there is more to the backstory of the English-language rights than Ries' account would suggest.[19]

---

15. 'Hit List: Denmark' 1992. The article outlines *Smilla*'s position on the Danish bestseller lists, and reflects on other contemporary Danish trends. Interestingly no suggestion is made that the book may be translated into English.
16. Ries 1998: 36–37.
17. This slow pace is clear to see in hindsight. For instance, Ellen Kythor opts to use 1990 as the start date for the corpus data used in Kythor 2018.
18. Ries 1998: 37.
19. MacLehose initially believed he had secured UK rights to *Smilla* on behalf of Harvill, only to find that FSG had acquired World English rights, due to a mix-up at Rosinante. Subsequently, MacLehose reached a gentleman's agreement with FSG's Roger Straus to acquire UK rights. For full details of the acquisition of *Smilla*, see Kythor 2019: 158–159. Furthermore, the context of the British acquisition is further muddied by a suggestion that an EU pilot project for funding the translation of European literature had provided support for the translation of Høeg to English, which undoubtedly would have

Harvill published its edition on 6 September 1993.[20]

## Marketing

Unusually for a translated novel at the time, a thorough marketing strategy was adopted for Smilla. Reflecting on Høeg's international success in 1998, Ries concentrated on the American transmission, noting that FSG's editor Elisabeth Dyssegaard had been championing the novel in isolation until a draft translation was available, at which point the publisher's marketing team realised they might have a bestseller on their hands.[21] In Britain, there was a sophisticated approach to selling copies of Smilla that began long before publication, and sought to engage not just readers but also booksellers.

According to Steven Williams, publicist for *Smilla*, the ground had been prepared with literary editors and booksellers markedly far in advance for a translated book of this kind.[22] In particular, there was a focus on securing prominent positions for the book in major bookshops such as Waterstones, while also ensuring consistent word-of-mouth recommendations from booksellers to customers.[23] Booksellers were engaged through the use of promotional gimmicks such as a *Smilla*-themed

---

sweetened the deal for Harvill. See Tucker 1995.

20. It is worth noting that *Smilla* represented a genuine instance of a British literary discovery of a Scandinavian author ahead of other key markets. The English translation was one of the first translations of *Smilla* to appear, with the vast majority of foreign translations appearing in the period 1994–96. Even German, in which Høeg's *The History of Danish Dreams* was published in 1992, was outflanked by English.

21. Ries 1998: 37.

22. Kythor 2019: 207. MacLehose reportedly decided that *Smilla* was to be promoted at the top of Harvill's list for autumn 1993, more intensely than any other book they were releasing. See Pihl 1996: 111.

23. Specially designed stands for copies of *Smilla* were provided to booksellers, and the novel was Waterstones' book of the month in December 1993. See Pihl 1996: 107–110.

jigsaw puzzle sent en masse to bookshops in Britain, which was carried through to the marketing directed at consumers.[24]

Notably, Høeg was extensively involved in the British launch of *Smilla*. Tina Pihl observes that Høeg gave four different radio interviews, while also being interviewed by two British newspapers ahead of the book's release.[25] He also made personal appearances for the book launch in London. The newspaper articles focused heavily on Høeg as an eccentric, covering extensively his past as an actor, dancer, and fencer, while glossing over his literary success.[26]

### *Role of the translator*

FSG commissioned Tiina Nunnally to translate *Smilla* on the basis of a strong translation of another book, Mette Newth's *The Abduction*, translated together with her husband Steven Murray in 1989.[27] Nunnally's translation, which was published by FSG, went on to win the Lewis Galantière Award from the American Translators Association.[28] Høeg, however, was unhappy with the translation. Nunnally suggests that it was Høeg's unfamiliarity with English and nervousness due to the stakes involved in publishing in English that were the cause of his disappointment.[29] Høeg, in turn, stated that he had misgivings in relation to Nunnally's translation, feeling that it was not only error-strewn but also normalised *Smilla* when

---

24. Pihl 1996: 111.
25. Ibid.: 108–112.
26. For example, see Binding 1993.
27. Gwinn 2001.
28. An award bestowed biennially on a book-length literary translation into English from any language except for German, and published in the US; it is awarded directly to the translator for their translation effort. For further details see Feuerle 2014.
29. 'He went from a market of 5 million people to the rest of the world'. See Gwinn 2001.

he preferred what could be described as a quirkier approach.³⁰ Høeg reportedly sent a forty-page letter to FSG with corrections and suggestions, but found that many of these were ignored. When Harvill sent the translation to the author anew, MacLehose reports that Høeg effectively rewrote the novel in the margins.³¹

Despite Harvill sharing the heavily revised translation with FSG, the American publisher opted to stick with its own version, and Nunnally refused to approve the British version. According to MacLehose, the British edition is a 'much more lively, visually exact text' as desired by the author.³² Nunnally describes it as 'rife with grammatical errors and strangely contorted sentences'.³³ Høeg was unaware that he was in a position to veto the American translation but stated in 1996 that he wished he had done so.³⁴ The range of narratives about this situation tend to overlook the role played personally by MacLehose at Harvill, but given the length of the British editorial process, MacLehose's involvement must have been extensive.³⁵

The outcome was two different English-language translations, one British, one American, derived from Nunnally's work, which were published simultaneously on each side of the Atlantic. Nunnally requested her name be removed from the Harvill edition in the UK on the understanding that it appear without a translator credit, but it was instead published under the pseudonym of 'F. David'.³⁶ Høeg reportedly chose

---

30. Follin 1997: 35.
31. Gardner 2010; Kythor 2019: 319.
32. Gardner 2010.
33. Follin 1997: Letter inserted after page 34.
34. Ibid.: 36.
35. This is borne out by observations on the Britishisation of Mankell novels by MacLehose in Venuti 2008: 157.
36. Follin 1997: Letter inserted after page 34.

to withdraw from participating in work on subsequent translations as a result of the latent hostility of the situation with Nunnally.[37] Furthermore, a number of comparative academic studies compare the two translations,[38] while the subject is often discussed by *Smilla*'s British publisher, MacLehose.[39]

## The reception of *Smilla*

### Critical reception

Writing some years after publication, Bloom described *Smilla* as a surprise bestseller, noting that the 'complexity of the plotting, nature of the thematic concerns and seriousness of purpose may make *Smilla* one of many bestsellers bought but never fully read'.[40] Nevertheless, the book was widely reviewed upon release, albeit mostly in the broadsheets, and largely received by critics in positive terms.[41]

Many reviewers chose to focus on the literary quality of *Smilla*. An anonymous review in the *Financial Times* noted that '[i]t's a novel, of course, not a "thriller" – but that has to be said of all good thrillers, because the word, so inappropriate to the boring bulk of them, devalues the exceptions'.[42] Geraldine Brennan, writing in *The Observer*, took a similar line in her

---

37. Ibid.: 34–35. Indeed, speaking in 2017, Høeg's description of his involvement with his current English-language translator, Martin Aitken, is the complete opposite of his involvement with the translation of *Smilla* in the 1990s. See Giles 2017.
38. Satterlee 1996; Follin 1997; Thomson 1997.
39. MacLehose 2004; Gardner 2010; Kythor 2019.
40. Bloom 2008: 305.
41. Pihl notes this was far in excess of what Danish or other translated books tended to receive in the British press during this period. See Pihl 1996: 109.
42. 'Books – Thrills at Turn of Leaf' 1993.

review, describing *Smilla* as 'a riveting psychological novel'.[43] Even a brief but positive review published in *The Mail on Sunday* sought to establish Høeg's literary credentials: 'Hoeg [sic] is a masterful writer, using a thriller-like plot as a means of investigating other, more profound matters, like the experience of foreignness or the longing that is nostalgia.'[44]

Beyond straightforward literary quality, more than one reviewer was attuned to the hybridity of *Smilla*. Writing in *TLS*, Jim McCue clearly found pleasure in Høeg's '[obliviousness] to the dangers to his narrative [...] he writes like an escapologist' as well as in many of the jokes that are added to the prose at the most unexpected of moments.[45] Clive Sinclair, writing in *The Independent on Sunday*, found the novel's ending strongly reminiscent of Shelley and Herge.[46] Marcel Berlins, writing for *The Sunday Times*, was particularly impressed by Høeg's achievement in taking ice beyond the work of writers such as Martin Cruz Smith and Alistair MacLean and making it, along with snow, an essential character in the book, representing the moods and actions of Smilla.[47] Berlins' argument was that while the book is 'a good straight thriller: a tight, unusual plot with politico-ecological overtones, lots of tough action, multiple twists and a shocking, unforeseeable climax', its strength lay in the work that Høeg had done beyond those key elements of any thriller. Writing in *New Statesman and Society*, John Williams argued that *Smilla* demonstrated the elasticity of the contemporary crime novel.[48] He joked that the plot came straight from a Michael Crichton science-fiction thriller.

---

43. Brennan 1993.
44. Trelawney 1993.
45. McCue 1993.
46. Sinclair 1993.
47. Berlins 1993.
48. Williams 1993.

There was also a tendency for predominantly male reviewers to be enchanted by the protagonist, Smilla. This was found in the *Financial Times*' review, while literary translator Shaun Whiteside's review for *The Guardian* lauded the first half of the novel: 'the beguiling build-up is slow, strange, and often very funny, with plenty of quirky detail', and emphasised that the strength of the novel at this stage lies in the humanity of Smilla's journey of discovery as she finds out more about the child Isiah, in tandem with reflecting upon her own relationship with her mother.[49] Ultimately, Whiteside reflected that he would have happily met Smilla under other circumstances. Sinclair commented: 'I look forward to seeing Sigourney Weaver as Smilla Jaspersen.'[50]

In terms of the presence of Greenland throughout the novel, and the postcolonial dimension to the novel, the British critical response was muted. When that aspect was raised, it was with a degree of scepticism. Sinclair highlighted the linguistic determinism of the novel in introducing the reader to the extensive Greenlandic vocabulary for snow, while remaining unconvinced about Høeg's empathy for the Greenlanders. Sinclair suggested that 'when all is said and done […] he is more influenced by American movies than by Inuit culture […] indeed, the book really comes to life in the numerous passages which describe the shedding of blood, not the falling of snow'. *The Guardian*'s Whiteside merely felt the novel offered unusual insight into Greenland. John Williams appeared not to read the novel as a postcolonial text as such but reflected that Høeg had successfully transformed what is typically an empty wilderness in literature, Greenland, into a place where people live. Critics like Berlins had remarkably little to say about the Greenlandic

---

49. Whiteside 1993.
50. Sinclair 1993.

or postcolonial elements of the novel altogether. The picture is one of blithe disinterest in the topic in book-reviewing circles.

Not all reviews were wholly positive. *The Herald*'s Alan Chadwick appeared to damn *Smilla* with faint, or perhaps non-specific, praise, finding it 'chilling', and noting that Høeg is 'probably the best thriller writer in Denmark'.[51] Other reviewers, in particular the *Financial Times* and Whiteside, had been underwhelmed by the quality of the second half of the novel.

Paul Binding's review in *The Independent* provides excellent insight into the cumulative critical response to *Smilla*.

> *Miss Smilla's Feeling for Snow* is, on one level, both a whodunnit and a thriller – ingeniously, elaborately and satisfyingly plotted and with a breathless narrative pace. It is extremely hard to put this long novel down and the excitement it engenders spills over into your time away from it. But this is only one of its attributes; it is also a novel of a riven society, of the relations between Europe and an under-considered part of the world, of science versus the atavistic, of humankind versus the terrifying vastness and power of Nature.[52]

The majority of critics were positive, highlighting the inherent readability of the book due to its thriller and crime-fiction tropes, alongside the more highbrow literary qualities of the novel. While there were some nods to Høeg's postcolonial approach, the majority of reflections upon Greenland were largely related to setting and snow, revelling in the depictions of the exotic north.

---

51. Chadwick 1993.
52. Binding 1993.

## Popular reception

> When Roger Straus and I first published Peter Høeg, we thought we were doing something of a favour for Danish literature, and then *Miss Smilla* abruptly sold a million copies in both England and America.[53] (Christopher MacLehose)

Tracking the undeniable sales success of *Smilla* in the years immediately after release is something of a challenge given the limitations of Nielsen BookScan, which only tracks British sales from 1998 onwards. Bloom laments the absence of a coherent bestseller list during the 1990s and notes that they were often incomplete. As an example, he remarks that while *Smilla* did not feature on the bestseller list for 1995, the book had sold 400,000 copies in the space of two years.[54] Consequently, we are left with the word of *Smilla*'s publisher, which is not necessarily always wholly accurate.[55]

We can dig deeper into these earlier years through consulting the bestseller charts, even if they are deficient, alongside other fragmentary information available to the researcher. Most pertinently, Pihl notes that the first print run of *Smilla*, totalling 10,000 copies, sold out quickly, and that three months after release, a total of 21,000 copies had been sold.[56] However,

---

53. Hitchens 2011: 19. In the early 2000s, Høeg was the all-time bestselling author in translation in the US. See Wirtén 2004: 42.
54. Bloom 2008: 99.
55. The figure of one million has been used rhetorically by MacLehose, and others, for many years, including in conversation with this author. Given that at the time there was an interest in driving hype through high sales figures, and subsequently in building the story of a bestseller, the publisher evidently has a vested interest in sharing this figure. More pertinently, publisher sales figures reflect how many copies it sells to retailers, not how many copies are bought by consumers.
56. Pihl 1996: 113. This three-month period cited by Pihl would have covered the majority of the run into Christmas 1993, one of the most

the spread of these sales over what may have been multiple editions adds to the confusion: while most newspaper reviews in September 1993 reference a hardback edition selling for £15.99, a paperback issue, also published by Harvill, entered the *Observer*/Waterstones bestseller charts in December 1993.[57] It rose as high as number five,[58] before falling to number ten by mid-January 1994.[59]

A Flamingo paperback edition published in October 1994 at a reduced price of £5.99 appeared to have some impact, with the book placed at number one in the bestseller list following a fortnight on sale.[60] It continued to remain in the top ten, moving up and down, before returning to number one in the run-up to Christmas 1994.[61] It is, however, of note that in a compilation of the top-rated books by a spread of publications at the end of 1994, *Smilla* had not made the cut as a regularly selected top book to buy for Christmas – despite being a regular fixture in the bestseller list during the run-up to Christmas.[62]

A major publishing event in 1995 was the collapse of the NBA.[63] Those who had argued in favour of keeping it believed that its loss would lead to a narrowing of the market, a cut in titles published accompanied by price rises on less popular titles, and shorter print runs. The converse argument was that much of the 'rubbish' published with the support of the NBA

---

important times of year in trade bookselling.
57. '*Observer*/Waterstones Best-Seller List' 1993.
58. Ibid.
59. '*Observer*/Waterstones Best-Seller List' 1994a.
60. '*Observer*/Waterstones Best-Seller List' 1994b.
61. '*Observer*/Waterstones Best-Seller List' 1994a.
62. 'Top of the Tops' 1994.
63. The NBA was an agreement between British publishers and booksellers that set the price paid by British customers for books. It collapsed following the withdrawal of publisher Hodder Headline from the agreement and the ensuing domino effect as all other major publishers followed.

would no longer reach the market and that expenditure on books would increase.[64] The end of the NBA had a significant impact on the literary market, permitting true mass production of books for the very first time. This was true in the case of *Smilla*, with the Flamingo edition ending 1995 at the top of the year's bestselling paperbacks list.[65] *The Guardian* even noted that the continued success of *Smilla* throughout 1995 was highly unusual in publishing terms.[66] It examined a number of changes in the publishing industry that had had an impact on sales trends. Apart from the collapse of the NBA, airport sales were said to make up a large proportion of receipts.

By early 1996, *Smilla* had spent a full year in the paperback bestseller chart.[67] The novel benefitted from another repackage in 1996 with the establishment of the Panther paperback list, intended to mark the fiftieth anniversary of Harvill Press, but from this point onwards, sales began to slow down. The main paperback edition of *Smilla*, which continues to be published under the same ISBN, even if jacket designs have varied somewhat, was published on 1 April 1996. Sales figures for this in the first two years of publication are unavailable, but since 1998, 37,494 copies have been sold in the UK.[68] We have Bloom's assertion that *Smilla* sold 400,000 copies in 1994–95. He also notes that it sold 140,000 copies in 1995 – two years after its initial release.[69] The origins of the oft-repeated statement that the novel sold one million copies in the UK are hard to

---

64. Macdonald 1994. A good overview of the decline of the NBA is provided by Jordison 2010.
65. 'Best Sellers of 1995' 1995.
66. 'Titans and Terrors in a Troubled Industry' 1996.
67. 'Chart Watch' 1996.
68. As of 15 July 2017. This two-year gap is significant, however, as the film adaptation was released in 1997 and would presumably have had an impact on sales in that year.
69. Bloom 2008: 305.

trace, but by the turn of the millennium, it was being stated as fact.[70]

Comparing the limited sales figures to hand for *Smilla* is challenging. Ongoing sales of *Smilla* since 1998, covered by Nielsen, are comparable to those experienced by titles like *Roseanna* by Sjöwall and Wahlöö, while the estimated figures for the first few years of sales are obviously significant but pale when compared to a modern megaseller such as Stieg Larsson. Nevertheless, if the figure of one million is taken at face value, it means that it means that *Smilla* sold more copies than books by present-day bestselling authors such as J.K. Rowling's crime-writing pseudonym Robert Galbraith.[71]

In 1996, MacLehose led a management buyout of Harvill from HarperCollins, making Harvill independent. Høeg proactively ensured that he remained with MacLehose and Harvill, rather than parent company HarperCollins, suggesting a strong relationship with his British publisher.[72] However, the commercial sensitivity of this decision can be seen in the repercussions that followed. HarperCollins reportedly dispatched a private investigator to Copenhagen to track down Høeg and offer him a lump sum of £50,000 to stay with them – to little effect.[73] In 1997, matters became more fraught, with HarperCollins issuing a high court writ against Harvill with a view to retrieving the profitable author Høeg and *Smilla*.[74] While the matter appears to have been settled, this degree of animosity indicates the commercial value of Høeg to his British publisher.

---

70. Jaggi 2000.
71. Galbraith having sold 900,883 books across three titles as of 15 July 2017. All Nielsen BookScan data cited by the author accessed during 2017.
72. France 1996.
73. Andersen 1996.
74. 'Snow Joke for Smilla' 1997.

Sales of *Smilla* over the first three or four years after publication were evidently remarkable, all the more so given the relative lack of interest in Scandinavian literature at the time; beyond the book itself capturing the imaginations of reviewers and readers, the marketing initiatives adopted by Harvill must also have been effective. This was evidently combined with canny use of affordable paperback editions, healthy airport sales, and conceivably the additional commercial edge provided by the collapse of the NBA.

## Heirs to Høeg

### *Høeg on British shores*

Most notably, beyond the positive critical reception and sales success, *Smilla* was an award winner, receiving the Fiction Silver Dagger from the CWA in 1994.[75] However, *Smilla*, and to some degree Høeg himself, were adopted into the British literary canon at a time which saw the number of Scandinavian authors being imported to Britain increase. *Smilla* was broadcast as Radio 4's *Book at Bedtime* in 1996, situating it firmly in the heart of the British literary establishment, while a big-budget film adaptation starring a predominantly British and Irish cast further solidified this sense, even if the film itself disappointed.[76] In terms of popular culture, it appears that Høeg's work generated widespread recognition of the multiple Inuit words for snow, with a multitude of articles published in the

---

[75]. See 'The CWA Gold Dagger'. The novel was also an award winner in the US, where it was a finalist for the Edgar Award for Best Mystery Novel, while translator Nunnally won the 1994 Lewis Galantière Translation Award for her involvement.

[76]. 'A Bond Movie on Ice' 1997. Reviewers appeared to find multiple plot changes in the film problematic.

press in the subsequent decade mentioning different types of snow in the same breath as Høeg. In many respects, the novel also became a reference point for the early to mid-nineties, being cited over a decade later in print journalism on multiple occasions each year.

The success of *Smilla* led to the rapid acquisition and translation of Høeg's other works, with four books appearing over a period of three years from 1995.[77] *Borderliners,* published in 1995, was generally found to be wanting by critics. John Bradley found the book frustrating on a number of levels, most notably complaining that Høeg was questioning the intelligence of the reader through his prose.[78] *The History of Danish Dreams* (1996) briefly managed to reach the bestseller top ten,[79] though *The Observer* described it as 'a young man's ramble', overly reliant on a debased form of magic realism,[80] while 1997's *Tales of the Night* did little better with the critics.[81] The worst criticism was reserved for *The Woman and the Ape*, published at the end of 1996, which was met with incredulity over the fact that its author could also have written *Smilla*. Emma Tennant suggested that it was likely to win the Bad Sex Prize, while noting that 'the characterisation and the plot are difficult to follow; the book is frequently incomprehensible'.[82]

Following the 1997 publication of *Tales of the Night*, Høeg entered a decade-long hiatus before returning in 2007. All three

---

77. Høeg 1995; Høeg 1996a; Høeg 1996b; Høeg 1997. These novels were all translated by Barbara Haveland, who reportedly enjoyed a far more positive relationship with the author than her predecessor. See Cunningham 1997.
78. Bradley 1995.
79. 'Best Sellers' 1996.
80. 'Remains of the Dane' 1995. Laura Cumming found the protagonist to be inept and distinctly less likeable than Smilla. See Cumming 1996.
81. For a typical disappointed reviewer, see Knight 1997.
82. Tennant 1996.

of Høeg's novels written this century have been published in English translation.[83] *The Quiet Girl*, published in 2007, was received well in critical terms, with the suggestion that it was a welcome return by Høeg to the literary scene,[84] though *The Elephant Keepers' Children* (2012) was met with a somewhat more lukewarm response.[85] *The Susan Effect*, published in 2017, met with more positivity, although reviews tended towards drawing strong connections between the new novel and *Smilla*. Forshaw harked back to the original and saw *Susan* as a near cousin, while *The Economist* stated that Høeg 'reverts to the Smilla model'.[86] Høeg's two bursts of literary activity in Britain, one over the past decade, and the preceding spell in the 1990s, have all fallen into the shadow of the critical and commercial success enjoyed by *Smilla*.

## *The hunt for other Scandinavian Høegs*

> The fulsome acclaim granted to Peter Høeg's *Miss Smilla's Feeling for Snow* […] was a clarion call to British readers that there was (in the words of Shakespeare's Coriolanus) 'a world elsewhere'.[87]

The race was on to find other equivalent Scandinavian authors to import to the UK. The focus of every British publisher at the 1995 Frankfurt Book Fair was to find the next Scandinavian hit,[88] while Ries noted that every publisher wanted to buy the

---

83. Høeg 2007; Høeg 2012; Høeg 2017.
84. Lawson 2007. 12,865 copies have been sold in the UK as of 15 July 2017.
85. Moss 2012. Only 2,234 copies have been sold in the UK as of 15 July 2017.
86. Forshaw 2017; 'Peter Hoeg's New Novel Is a High-Concept Thriller' 2017.
87. Forshaw 2012: 5.
88. 'Happiness Is A' 1995.

translation rights of a book by any foreign author, so long as they were Høeg.[89] Ries cites the impact of Høeg, in direct parallel with the success of writers such as Jostein Gaarder and Kerstin Ekman, as the reason why Danish and other Nordic writers suddenly became interesting to rights-acquisition departments around the world.[90]

The outcome in this pursuit of other Høegs saw some Scandinavian writers fare better than others in the British literary market. Reviewing Herbjørg Wassmo's *Dina's Book* in 1996, Sam Taylor complained that *Smilla* had 'ploughed a path for lesser compatriots' before going on to say that 'Wassmo writes like Gabriel Garcia Marquez [sic] with a learning impediment'.[91] Pernille Rygg's 1997 debut, *The Butterfly Effect*, found itself subject to similar comparisons with *Smilla*. For instance, Amanda Craig of *The Times* found Rygg's efforts in a post-*Smilla* era to be predictable and 'no great challenge to anything but your patience'.[92]

While Wassmo and Rygg failed to engage British critics as they experimented with what was perceived to be *Smilla*-esque hybridity, writers such as Ekman, toying with the crime genre in a fashion similar to Høeg, enjoyed greater traction in the UK. Her first English translation, published in 1995, was *Blackwater*, which sold 16,000 copies during its launch year despite little-to-no press attention.[93] Reviewers were generally impressed, as with Høeg, by the literary quality of Ekman's work alongside the hints of genre fiction.[94] Binding went so far as to describe it as the

---

89. Ries 1998.
90. Ibid.
91. Taylor 1996.
92. Craig 1997.
93. Feay 1996.
94. O'Sullivan 1995.

most important Swedish novel in Britain of the 1990s.[95] Despite all these factors, Ekman's British publisher in the mid-1990s, Chatto & Windus, appears to have missed an opportunity to capitalise on her as the next Høeg-esque bestseller.

The other major Scandinavian bestseller of the 1990s in Britain was found in the form of a novel almost wholly unlike *Smilla* – Gaarder's *Sophie's World*. The critical response upon publication in 1995 was typically impressed by the philosophical dimension of the book but tended to question whether it was a true novel.[96] By 1998, *Sophie's World* had sold over half a million copies and spent eighty-three weeks on the bestseller list.[97] Gaarder, however, was not another Høeg. Yet, it is evident that the success enjoyed by Harvill Press with a Scandinavian author meant that other publishers were also inclined to consider their options for importing Scandinavian literature in a way they had not done before. In many ways, the success of Høeg and Gaarder with UK readers foreshadowed the diversity of Scandinavian literature that was to arrive on British shores in the two subsequent decades.

## Transatlantic weather books

A further trend that can be identified in the years after *Smilla* is a wave of other novels being published, largely produced in English, that critics began to classify as belonging in the same category as Høeg's novel. These works can be described

---

95. Binding 1998.
96. See, for example, May 1995.
97. Thackray 1998. The book had reportedly sold 50,000 copies in the UK in its first three months on sale, and ended 1995 at number two in the hardback bestseller list. See 'Best Sellers of 1995' 1995; Lyall 1995. The paperback edition, also published in 1995, managed to sell in excess of 160,000 copies before the turn of the year. See Ritchie 1996.

as 'transatlantic weather books'. Prominent examples of these books include David Guterson's *Snow Falling on Cedars*, Annie Proulx's *The Shipping News*, and even Sebastian Faulks' *Birdsong*. Writing in 1996, just over two years after *Smilla* was published, Catherine Bennett described a new genre of 'weather-books' which had been established by Høeg, stating that the genre label had become so established in publishing that a publisher had 'boasted recently of buying "next year's snow book"'.[98] Jason Hazeley chose to focus on snow in particular, describing it as the 'Fargo Factor', a reference to the 1996 film *Fargo*.[99]

The categorisation of these novels typically manifested itself through reviews in the press. For example, in the case of Guterson's *Snow Falling on Cedars*, reviewers were quick to draw connections between Høeg and Guterson, as well as Proulx.[100] Guterson enjoyed success far beyond that expected of a debut writer in much the same fashion as Høeg, with his book selling around 11,000 copies in hardback.[101] As well as the similarity in title, and the parallels drawn between Guterson's plot and Høeg's, it is of note that the marketing of the book actively sought to place the novel into the category of 'Nordic thriller', despite its American origin.[102] Guterson told Suzi Feay that he had not read Høeg's work but said 'we're all just telling the same stories for a new generation. Nobody has any new ideas.'

This author takes the view that Bennett's 'weather-book' best reflects the variety of the books in this sub-genre, but that it could be better described as transatlantic to demonstrate that

---

98. Bennett 1996.
99. Hazeley 1997.
100. Gerrard 1995b. Indeed, it was later suggested by Gerrard that a natural response to finishing *Smilla* was to read Guterson's novel. See Gerrard 1995c.
101. Feay 1996.
102. Ibid. In fact, Guterson's novel takes place in a Japanese community in the Pacific Northwest of the US.

it is not solely a European or North American trend. Other than the focus on grey, weather-driven settings, and in many cases snow, the other trait of these novels is the use of hybridity in the shape of quality literary credentials to present books as elite literature, while making use of genre fiction tendencies to make the books appealing to a wider cross-section of readers.

## Trends and hybridity: *Smilla* in Britain

In *Smilla*, we have a single novel lauded by critics as both literary and readable, exotic and yet somehow familiar. The positivity of reviewers is matched by book buyers, who happily turned the book into the bestselling Scandinavian novel of the decade, and regardless of glib comments that few manage to complete the book, many of the central themes have been adopted into British popular culture. The impact of this one book was also remarkable, with a notable Høeg-inspired flurry of Scandinavian translations commissioned in the years that followed *Smilla*'s arrival in Britain, as well as the emergence of other, less Høeg-esque Scandinavian writers and the establishment of a transatlantic weather-book sub-genre. What follows is an analysis of why this happened, along with an appraisal of the position of *Smilla* and Høeg in the British literary sphere.

### *Response to contemporary trends*

In literary terms, Britain in the 1990s was characterised by diversity:

> examples of novels can be identified that address issues of provincialism and globalisation, multiculturalism and specific national and regional identities, experimentation and a reengagement with a realist tradition, as well as renewed and

reinvigorated interest in a range of differing and overlapping identities: nation, gender, class, ethnicity, sexuality, and even the post-human.[103]

It was a decade of healthy literary production as writers and readers sought to engage with their identities on a number of levels.

*Smilla*'s reception, in particular, with both reviewers and readers is a reflection of the prevailing literary trends in the early 1990s in Britain. Literature of the decade, a *fin de siècle*, was characterised by reflection on the past century, as well as ambivalence about the future.[104] Uncertainty surrounding a rapidly changing, technologising society concerned about the looming millennial shift was accentuated by the dissolution of the Soviet Union, which had for so long provided a straightforward paradigm to many of us versus them. In this wavering light lay fertile ground for *Smilla* to make an impact on British readers, as a novel that reflected the grey areas of society and the places where fact and fiction were easily confused.

Bloom noted that waves of immigration from the 1940s to the 1970s were being reflected upon through second- and-third-generation immigrant literature in the 1990s.[105] Høeg's examination of the postcolonial relationship between Denmark and Greenland, most astutely identified by reviewers such as Binding, and also hinted at by Sinclair and Whiteside, was obviously one that spoke strongly to British readers of the early 1990s. In addition to exploring the experience of non-white immigrants in Britain, Bloom also identifies a trend towards 'ethnically inflected novels' that specifically aim to give white readers a greater understanding of other

---

103. Bentley 2005b: 1.
104. Ibid.: 2.
105. Bloom 2008: 129.

cultures. While Bloom cites authors such as Alexander McCall Smith, Kazuo Ishiguro, and Khaled Hosseini in this regard,[106] the designation is obviously applicable to *Smilla* – a novel about a non-European outsider in Copenhagen, with the remote and unfamiliar setting of Greenland.

Sara Danius argued that the greatest strength of *Smilla* was its contemporary quality, which is imbued with postmodern uncertainty and postcolonial ambivalence.[107] This contemporary quality in the British setting, and the novel's adhesion to British literary currents of the early 1990s, obviously allowed *Smilla* to take up a more central position in the literary polysystem than is typically afforded to translated books.

### *Bestseller by hybridity*

*Smilla*'s successful arrival in Britain was not solely the result of conformance with contemporary literary trends. It went further, by being at the forefront of literary developments in the early 1990s. Figures such as Bill Buford, editor of *Granta*, had pronounced the death of the English novel by the 1980s, suggesting novels had become an essentially middle-class and whining monologue, no more than a 'longish piece of writing with something wrong with it'.[108] Yet Pamela Bickley notes that the 1990s marked the arrival of a diverse range of new literary forms, revitalising the novel in the process.[109] *Smilla* certainly fits into this category.

Høeg's representation of postcolonial issues and pre-millennial uncertainty was presented innovatively, making use of genre hybridity. His use of less prestigious genre forms such as the thriller, and to some extent also science fiction, meant that

---

106. Ibid.: 15–16.
107. Danius 1994.
108. Quoted in Bickley 2008: 10.
109. Ibid.: 11.

*Smilla* was not only more appealing to a wider audience but also at the heart of the revitalisation of the novel in Britain at the time. Ola Larsmo argued that in *Smilla*, Høeg had taken on a genre and twisted it, managing to exploit the clichés of that genre but to his own end.[110] The use of genre no longer automatically set a novel apart as being lowbrow as it might once have done, and indeed became a point of strength for the fickle commentariat when they considered it had been done well. Bo Tao Michaëlis argued that the way in which Høeg not only took into consideration issues understood in the anglophone sphere but also presented them through the use of the thriller genre made *Smilla* ripe for export from Denmark, comparing Høeg to authors such as John Le Carré and Alistair MacLean.[111] This kind of hybridity has worked well over past decades, and *Smilla* took advantage of the growing British predisposition towards books of this ilk.

Mark Morris went a step further in his classification of *Smilla*.[112] He argued that it, along with other titles in the 'transatlantic weather book' sub-genre, was a big bourgeois hit. This was on the grounds of hybridity actualised through these works being sufficiently literary to appear clever to readers, while actually remaining accessible to those readers who did not read widely. *Smilla* was a fresh addition to the literary scene, and one that appealed to a broad cross-section of readers of both popular and elite literature.

## *Tell the people what they want*

While the conformance of *Smilla* to prevailing literary trends paired with its innovative use of hybridity appealed to British readers and reviewers of the early 1990s, this did not occur

---

110. Larsmo 1995: 17.
111. Michaëlis 2005: 148.
112. Morris 2002.

in isolation. The extensive marketing campaign run by Harvill was clearly a significant contributory factor to the reception, popular and critical, of the novel.

Joanna Pitman strongly suggests that the popular success of novels such as *Smilla* was contingent on word-of-mouth recommendations and an apparent faith in 'solid' plots that are easy to follow.[113] There is certainly truth in this observation, but it assumes that the initial recommendations stemmed from straightforward enthusiastic readers passing on tips. In practice, as has been established, Harvill had run a comprehensive campaign to target reviewers and booksellers prior to release, in addition to an advertising campaign run after publication. As can be seen from the range of newspaper articles discussing its success during subsequent years, Harvill were also highly effective at continuing to drive mentions of *Smilla* and accompanying hype. Word-of-mouth recommendations clearly had an impact, but it was only possible for them to do so through a concerted effort to tell people to make those recommendations.

British readers were also provided with an author with whom they could engage beyond the book. As noted, Høeg was involved in the launch of *Smilla,* and press coverage of him served to highlight his consumable eccentricity. Høeg also conveyed a certain degree of mystique: it has been widely reported that he dislikes publicity work.[114] Despite this, Høeg has been interviewed semi-regularly for all of his books' publications in Britain, and has made public appearances at bookshops and literary festivals over the course of the past two decades.

The widespread popular impact of *Smilla* in the early years is down to an intelligent and driven marketing strategy that ensured that patrons of literature, whether reviewers or

---

113. Pitman 1997.
114. O'Neill 1995. Høeg reportedly 'feels at odds with twentieth-century society, unable to move at the pace of modern life'.

gatekeepers, as well as consumers, were fully enthused by the book on offer. In terms of Scandinavian books in translation, this arguably represents the first successful attempt to create a bestseller, by engaging with readers and reviewers on their terms and providing the literary polysystem with a product that fulfilled many contemporary requirements.

## *Transatlantic weather books and the exotic north*

Robin Hunt observed that many books in the early nineties, especially thrillers, used settings that were 'remote, high and cold'.[115] While literature has arguably always acted as a conduit for escapism, the desire of writers to take their readers to places they have never been or imagined seems to have been particularly common during the 1990s, reflecting the increasing uncertainty in a post-Cold War, pre-millennial world. This might be thought of as the 'Fargo Factor', as mentioned earlier, or indeed part of a longer running trend for snow and ice to feature in certain genres.[116] However, the identification of a transatlantic weather book sub-genre common in the 1990s helps to trace the way in which *Smilla* successfully integrated itself into the British literary polysystem. In particular, this sub-genre clearly interfaced well with existing British notions of an exoticised north, especially amongst the literary elite responsible for publishing, reviewing, and recommending books such as *Smilla* to the reading public.

An excellent example of this type of interaction is found in Jane Jakeman, who was quick to draw connections between authors such as Høeg and Ekman and the Norse sagas, while also alluding to the enduring and strong appeal of snow-laden Nordic writing to specifically British readers.[117] Harry Bingham,

---
115. Hunt 1996.
116. Hazeley 1997.
117. Jakeman 1997.

meanwhile, noted that the Danish-Greenlandic element of the novel meant it was easy to portray it as an exciting novelty.[118]

The connection between transatlantic weather books is hinted at by Nicci Gerrard, who noted that *Smilla* was not the only work of the early 1990s in a northern setting to catch the British imagination, citing Proulx and Gaarder too.[119] Her thesis was that the protagonists' desperation in *Smilla* and *The Shipping News* to escape harsh urban landscapes reflected British pre-millennial fears. Drawing a direct connection between Britain and Scandinavia, Gerrard concluded 'the British are a puritanical race – we associate pleasure with fecklessness and sin; a life that is easy must be wrong. Life is not easy in the northern countries'. Thorpe went further, describing the sub-genre as 'northern-oriented fiction' reliant on 'ice-storms, stalling conversations, brooding depression and low temperatures'.[120] In both playing upon the tropes of the transatlantic weather book sub-genre and tugging on the 'borealist' heartstrings of British critics, *Smilla* effectively added a further layer of hybridity that gave it appeal to UK readers and facilitated a smooth passage to the centre of the literary polysystem.

Finally, the presumption of exceptionalism in the case of the British-Scandinavian literary relationship is also worth noting in this regard. Kristine Anderson has observed that there has been a tendency for Danish writers translated to English to be categorised amongst English-speaking writers, rather than as translated authors. She cites Brandes and Andersen, and speculates that the natural progression is for Høeg's work to become part of the canon of a British 'female detective genre' rather than being categorised as foreign fiction.[121] This is ultimately

---

118. Bingham 2006.
119. Gerrard 1995a.
120. Thorpe 2002.
121. Anderson 2000: 335.

a borealist perspective, drawing on the sense that Britain and Scandinavia's shared heritage means that a Danish novel can be considered as part of Britain's domestic literary canon.

## The position of *Smilla* and Høeg in Britain

Overall, the public response to *Smilla* was remarkable, particularly given that it was a translated novel from a small source market. However, the novel clearly responded to a number of prevailing literary themes and was almost universally appreciated by critics on various levels as a diverse, pacey thriller and a complex postcolonial novel. The changes to the British book market that occurred in parallel with the publication of the various early editions of *Smilla* are likely to have aided its continued success – a popular, critically acclaimed book was available in mass-produced form in a wider number of retail outlets than ever before, and competitively priced. Given these elements, it is hardly surprising that the response from the buying and reading public was positive.

*Smilla* acted as a tonic to the British literary scene, reinvigorating the thriller, crime fiction, and science fiction genres, while also highlighting the role to be played by hybrid literature in drawing in new, larger audiences. Discussing the role of thrillers in contemporary literature in 1995, Gerrard remarked that *Smilla* had 'made whodunits chic and sexy and unfamiliar again',[122] while highlighting the increasing prevalence of 'serious' writers, such as Høeg, turning to genre fiction to make a living. Ultimately, the contemporariness of *Smilla* resonated with British readers and allowed the book and its author be integrated into the native literary canon of the 1990s.

---

122. Gerrard 1995c.

While Høeg's star has waned in the years that have followed, *Smilla* remains a presence on the British literary scene. To some extent, it seemed as if Høeg had pitched the perfect British novel at the British market at the right moment in time. His conformity with the British literary zeitgeist and his sophisticated use of genre hybridity allowed him to appeal to popular and elite audiences alike. Just as Bjarne Thorup Thomsen had himself found, it was the right time for a Dane to cross the North Sea.

## Bibliography

'A Bond Movie on Ice'. 1997. *The Guardian*. 31 October.

Andersen, Carsten. 2002. 'Selv et eventyr kan slutte skidt'. *Politiken*. http://politiken.dk/kultur/boger/art4931216/Selv-et-eventyr-kan-slutte-skidt. Accessed 5 December 2017.

———. 2006. 'En Høeg klar til landing'. *Politiken*, Accessed 30/11/2017. http://politiken.dk/kultur/boger/art4858963/En-Høeg-klar-til-landing.

Andersen, Jens. 1996. 'Fornemmelsen for bøger'. *Berlingske Tidende*. 24 March.

Anderson, Kristine. 2000. 'Danish: Literary Translation into English'. In Olive Classe (ed.), *Encyclopedia of Literary Translation into English*. London: Fitzroy Dearborn, 333–335.

Bennett, Catherine. 1996. 'Weather Is Nobler in the Mind'. *The Guardian*. 2 January.

Bentley, Nick (ed.). 2005a. *British Fiction of the 1990s.* London: Routledge.

Berlins, Marcel. 1993. 'The Snow Queen'. *The Sunday Times*. 5 September.

'Best Sellers of 1995'. 1995. *The Observer*. 24 December.

'Best Sellers'. 1996. *The Observer*. 21 January.

Bickley, Pamela. 2008. *Contemporary Fiction: The Novel since 1990*. Cambridge: Cambridge University Press: Cambridge.

Binding, Paul. 1993. 'Dreaming About Footsteps in the Snow'. *The Independent*. 28 August.

———. 1998. 'Five Hundred Years of Solicitude for the Troll of Skule Forest'. *The Independent*. 15 November.

Bingham, Harry. 2006. 'Strong Language: Why Are British Writers So Incredibly Popular?'. *Financial Times*. 7 January.

Bloom, Clive. 2008. *Bestsellers: Popular Fiction since 1900*. Basingstoke: Palgrave Macmillan.

'Books – Thrills at Turn of Leaf'. 1993. *Financial Times*. 4 September.

Bradley, John R. 1995. 'Time and Time Again'. *The Times Literary Supplement* 4802.

Bredal, Bjørn. 1992. 'Peter Høegs fornemmelse for is'. *Weekendavisen*. 24 April.

Brennan, Geraldine. 1993. 'Sex, Snow and Ineffectuality'. *The Observer*. 12 September.

Bukdahl, Lars. 1992. 'Romanen med de rigtige meninger'. *Kristeligt dagblad*. 24 April.

Chadwick, Alan. 1993. 'Peter Hoeg: Miss Smilla's Feeling for Snow'. *The Herald*. 11 September.

'Chart Watch'. 1996. *The Times*. 10 February.

Craig, Amanda. 1997. 'Miss Igi's Feeling for Woe'. *The Times*. 29 March.

Cumming, Laura. 1996. 'When a Dane Dreams'. *The Guardian*. 5 January.

Danius, Sara. 1994. 'Fröken Smilla skakar om'. *Dagens Nyheter*. https://www.dn.se/arkiv/kultur/froken-smilla-skakar-om. Accessed 5 December 2017.

Ekman, Kerstin. 1995. *Blackwater*. Joan Tate (trans.). London: Chatto & Windus.

*Fargo*. 1996. Film. Directed by Ethan Coen and Joel Coen, US: Gramercy Pictures.

Faulks, Sebastian. 1994. *Birdsong*. London: Vintage.

Feay, Suzi. 1996. 'The Snowbiz Phenomenon'. *The Independent On Sunday*. 21 January.

Feuerle, Lois. 2014. 'Honors and Awards'. American Translators Association. http://www.atanet.org/aboutus/honorsandawards_lewis.php. Accessed 20 May 2014.

Follin, Lotte. 1997. 'Peter Høeg's Smilla, Sense or Feeling, a Comparative Study of the Two English Versions of *Frøken Smillas Fornemmelse for Sne*'. Speciale. University of Copenhagen.

Forshaw, Barry. 2012. *Death in a Cold Climate: A Guide to Scandinavian Crime Fiction*. Basingstoke: Palgrave Macmillan.

———. 2017. 'The Best Recent Thrillers – Review Roundup'. *The Guardian*. 15 September. https://www.theguardian.com/books/2017/sep/15/thrillers-fiction-roundup-review-peter-hoeg-fred-vargas. Accessed 23 October 2017.

France, Miranda. 1996. 'A Battle of Words'. *The Scotsman*. 19 March.

Gaarder, Jostein. 1995. *Sophie's World: A Novel About the History of Philosophy*. Paulette Møller (trans.). London: Phoenix.

Gardner, Anthony. 2010. 'Christopher Machelose: The Champion of Translated Fiction Who Struck It Rich with Stieg Larsson'. http://www.anthonygardner.co.uk/interviews/christopher_maclehose.html. Accessed 7 May 2014.

Gerrard, Nicci. 1995a. 'Love for a Cold Climate'. *The Observer*. 1 January.

———.1995b. 'Hot Ice Captures the Mood of the Moment'. *The Observer*. 29 January.

———. 1995c. 'Thrillers'. *The Observer*. 26 November.

Giles, Ann. 2017. 'Thrilling Fiction'. Bookwitch. https://bookwitch.wordpress.com/2017/08/20/thrilling-fiction. Accessed 30 November 2017.

Giles, Ian. 2018. 'Tracing the Transmission of Scandinavian Literature to the UK: 1917–2017'. PhD thesis. University of Edinburgh.

Guterson, David. 1994. *Snow Falling on Cedars*. London: Bloomsbury.

Gwinn, Mary Ann. 2001. 'Finding the Right Words'. *The Seattle Times*. http://seattletimes.com/pacificnw/2001/0909/people.html. Accessed 8 May 2014.

'Happiness Is A'. 1995. *The Guardian*. 20 October.

Hazeley, Jason. 1997. 'Snow Business'. *The Times*. 21 June.

Hitchens, Christopher. 2011. 'The Author Who Played with Fire'. In Dan Burstein et al. (eds), *Secrets of the Tattooed Girl: The Unauthorised Guide to the Stieg Larsson Trilogy*. London: Weidenfeld & Nicolson, 15–20.

'Hit List: Denmark'. 1992. *The Guardian*. 3 July 1992.

Høeg, Peter. 1988. *Forestilling om det tyvende* århundrede. Copenhagen: Rosinante.

———. 1990. *Fortællinger om natten*. Copenhagen: Rosinante.

———. 1992a. *Frøken Smillas fornemmelse for sne*. Copenhagen: Rosinante.

———. 1992b. *Vorstellung vom zwanzigsten Jahrhundert*. Monika Wesemann (trans.). Munich: Hanser.

———. 1993a. *De måske egnede*. Copenhagen: Rosinante.

———. 1993b. *Miss Smilla's Feeling for Snow*. F. David (trans.). London: Harvill Press.

———. 1993c. *Smilla's Sense of Snow*. Tiina Nunnally (trans.). New York: Farrar, Straus & Giroux.

———. 1994. *Miss Smilla's Feeling for Snow*. F. David (trans.). London: Flamingo.

———. 1995. *Borderliners*. Barbara Haveland (trans.). London: Harvill Press.

———. 1996a. *The History of Danish Dreams*. Barbara Haveland (trans.). London: Harvill Press.

———. 1996b. *The Woman and the Ape*. Barbara Haveland (trans.). London: Harvill Press.

———. 1997. *Tales of the Night*. Barbara Haveland (trans.). London: Harvill Press.

———. 2007. *The Quiet Girl*. Nadia Christensen (trans.). London: Harvill Secker).

———. 2012. *The Elephant Keepers' Children*. Martin Aitken (trans.). London: Harvill Secker.

———. 2014. *Miss Smilla's Feeling for Snow*. F. David (trans.). London: Vintage Digital, e-book.

———. 2017. *The Susan Effect*. Martin Aitken (trans.). London: Harvill Secker.

Høg, Pia Andersen. 2011. 'Peter Høeg'. DBC. https://forfatterweb.dk/oversigt/hoeeg-peter. Accessed 30 November 2017.

Hunt, Robin. 1996. 'Gone but Not Forgotten'. *The Guardian*. 10 September.

Jaggi, Maya. 2000. 'The Universal Language of Literature'. *The Guardian*. 15 September.

Jakeman, Jane. 1997. 'Books – More Snow Falling on Readers'. *The Independent*. 15 November.

Kistrup, Jens. 1992. 'Romanens danske virtuos gør det igen'. *Berlingske Tidende*. 24 April.

Knight, Stephen. 1997. 'In Tales within Tales'. *The Times Literary Supplement* 4937.

Kythor, Ellen. 2018. 'Corpus Danish-English Literature in the UK 1990–2015'. Unpublished working paper. University College London.

———. 2019. 'An "Un-businesslike-business": Publishing Danish Literature in Translation in the UK 1990–2015'. PhD thesis. University College London.

Larsmo, Ola. 1995. 'Den sanna förställningen: Peter Høegs pastischer och allegorier'. *Bonniers Litterära Magasin* 64:1, 16–18.

Lawson, Mark. 2007. 'An Unearthly Resonance'. *The Guardian*. 3 November. https://www.theguardian.com/books/2007/nov/03/featuresreviews.guardianreview11. Accessed 6 December 2017.

Macdonald, Marianne. 1994. 'Collapse of Net Book Agreement "within Months"'. *The Independent*. 26 December. http://www.independent.co.uk/news/uk/collapse-of-net-book-agreement-within-months-collapse-1388530.html. Accessed 20 May 2014.

MacLehose, Christopher. 2004. 'A Publisher's Vision'. *EnterText* 4:3, 103–116.

May, Derwent. 1995. 'The Primer of Life'. *The Times*, 12 January.

McCue, Jim. 1993. 'Arctic Nights'. *The Times Literary Supplement* 4720.

Michaëlis, Bo Tao. 2005. 'Frøken Smillas fornemmelse for sammensværgelser. På sporet af *Frøken Smillas fornemmelse for sne* som noget eller meget af en thriller'. In Agnete Bay Harsberg and Lilian Munk (eds), *Abens poetik: portræt af Peter Høegs forfatterskab*. Copenhagen: Forlaget Spring, 145–149.

Morris, Mark. 2002. 'In the Beginning Was the Word'. *The Observer*. 10 February.

Moss, Sarah. 2012. 'The Elephant Keepers' Children by Peter Høeg – Review'. *The Guardian*. 5 October. https://www.theguardian.com/books/2012/oct/05/elephant-keepers-children-hoeg-review. Accessed 6 December 2017.

'*Observer*/Waterstones Best-Seller List'. 1993. *The Observer*. 19 December.

'*Observer*/Waterstones Best-Seller List'. 1994a. *The Observer*. 16 January.

'*Observer*/Waterstones Best-Seller List'. 1994b. *The Observer*. 23 October.

O'Neill, Helen. 1995. 'A Feeling for Silence'. *The Observer*. 2 April.

O'Sullivan, Charlotte. 1995. 'Hippies Go Military'. *The Observer*. 23 April.

Pihl, Tina. 1996. 'The Publishing of Translated Fiction and the Cultural Funding System in Britain and Denmark. A Cross-Cultural Study and Assessment'. PhD thesis. University of North London.

Pitman, Joanna. 1997. 'Word of Mouth'. *The Times*. 15 November.

Proulx, Annie. 1993. *The Shipping News*. London: Fourth Estate.

'Remains of the Dane'. 1995. *The Observer*. 24 December.

Ries, Merete. 1998. 'The Smilla Principle'. *Danish Literary Magazine* 13, 36–83.

Ringgaard, Anne. 2006. 'Høeg over Høeg'. *Politiken*. 7 March. http://politiken.dk/kultur/boger/ECE145412/hoeeg-over-hoeeg. Accessed 20 May 2014.

Ritchie, Harry. 1996. 'How to Write a Million-Seller'. *The Times*. 3 February.

Rygg, Pernille. 1997. *The Butterfly Effect*. Joan Tate (trans.). London: Harvill Press.

Satterlee, Thom. 1996. 'A Case for Smilla'. *Translation Review* 50:1, 13–17.

Schou, Søren. 1992. 'Spor i sneen'. *Information*. 24 April.

Sinclair, Clive. 1993. 'The Agenbite of Inuit; "Miss Smilla's Feeling for Snow" – Peter Hoeg; Trs F Martin'. *The Independent on Sunday*. 10 October.

'Snow Joke for Smilla'. 1997. *The Evening Standard*. 12 December.

Taylor, Sam. 1996. 'Turkey Shøøt: Dina's Book'. *The Observer*. 17 March.

Tennant, Emma. 1996. 'Miss Madelene's Feeling for Primates'. *The Observer*. 22 December.

Thackray, Rachelle. 1998. 'The 50 Best Selling Books of the 1990s'. *The Independent*. 26 September.

'The CWA Gold Dagger'. The Crime Writers' Association. http://www.thecwa.co.uk/daggers/gold.html. Accessed 8 May 2014.

Thomson, C. Claire and Stougaard-Nielsen, Jakob. 2017. '"A Faithful, Attentive, Tireless Following": Cultural Mobility, Crime Fiction and Television Drama'. In Dan Ringgaard and Mads Rosendahl Thomsen (eds), *Danish Literature as World Literature*. London: Bloomsbury Academic, 235–266.

Thorpe, Vanessa. 2002. 'Surprise, Surprise – It's Still Grim up North'. *The Observer*. 4 August.

'Titans and Terrors in a Troubled Industry'. 1996. *The Guardian*. 19 January.

'Top of the Tops'. 1994. *The Observer*. 18 December.

Trelawney, Nicholas. 1993. 'Mysteries of Life'. *Mail on Sunday*. 5 September.

Tucker, Emma. 1995. 'UK Closes the Book on EU Translation'. *Financial Times*. 20 October.

Venuti, Lawrence. 2008. *The Translator's Invisibility: A History of Translation*. Abingdon: Routledge.

Vinterberg, Søren. 1992. 'Peter Høegs fornemmelse for kølig passion'. *Politiken*. 24 April.

Wassmo, Herbjørg. 1996. *Dina's Book*. Nadia Christensen (trans.). London: Black Swan.

'Weekendavisens litteraturpris'. 2014. *Weekendavisen*. http://www.weekendavisen.dk/litteraturpriser. Accessed 20 May 2014.

Whiteside, Shaun. 1993. 'Prints in the Snow'. *The Guardian*. 5 October.

Wiemer, Liselotte. 1992. 'Rejse på liv og død'. *Det fri aktuelt*. 24 April.

Williams, John. 1993. 'Fire and Ice'. *New Statesman and Society* 6, 268.

Wirtén, Eva Hemmungs. 2004. *No Trespassing: Authorship, Intellectual Property Rights, and the Boundaries of Globalization*. Toronto: University of Toronto Press.

· 21 ·

# Bjarne's Quiet Wisdom

## Julie Larsen

I was never really sure whether it was English or Danish Bjarne spoke when you knocked on his door and he replied with a prolonged 'o' as in 'Cooooome in!' or 'Kooooom ind!' – they would have sounded more or less the same, and maybe that was the point, since you would not have been visible to Bjarne yet, and so he would not know whether there was a Danish speaker or a non-Danish speaker knocking. What I do know, though, is that I always felt comfortable knocking on Bjarne's door. He would always find time for a conversation, long or short.

I especially took advantage of Bjarne's hospitality in my first year as a Teaching Fellow in Danish at the University of Edinburgh. As the only senior Danish speaker in the section, Bjarne would be my mentor. This was wonderful, because speaking to a fellow Dane so far from home felt a bit like… home. I spent many half hours in the chair opposite Bjarne's desk, asking too many questions, yet always getting sound advice and thoughtful comments in return. However, the most useful and kind feedback I received from Bjarne was when he observed my class as part of my process of becoming a fellow of the HEA. It felt a bit daunting, having to be observed by someone more experienced. We academics can also feel very protective about the space that is our classroom. Nevertheless,

I would argue that observation can be both a useful and a supportive experience for both parties.

In this case, after my observation, Bjarne's feedback was extremely thorough. The feedback included what went well in that particular class, and so, certainly, I could pat myself on the back for a well prepared and executed class. But what really struck me was how Bjarne had paid attention to all the little details in my teaching, the ones that you cannot prepare yourself for or 'wing' in a class: the components that make you a teacher. Bjarne's comments made me feel very supported in my general approach to learning and teaching. They also emphasised that a teacher does not have to be an entertainer, or be extremely extroverted, to be good. You can be quiet, while leading wisely. This very manner is part of Bjarne's legacy, and I am very grateful to have worked with him. I am grateful to him for taking time for our conversations and for his influence on my own academic practice.

· 22 ·

# Anger and Hypocrisy in Vigdis Hjorth's *Et norsk hus* – Is Alma Complicit?

## Anja Tröger

Alma, the protagonist in Vigdis Hjorth's 2014 novel *Et norsk hus*, is a textile artist and makes tapestries. After the successful completion of two commissions and a TV show featuring her work, she receives a phone call, inviting her to create a tapestry as part of an exhibition accompanying the bicentennial celebration of Norwegian independence. This is her most prestigious commission to date, she is offered a fee that far exceeds her expectations, and she is asked to engage with the development of democracy in Norway, but apart from that, she is granted absolute creative freedom. While conducting research for her topic, Alma travels to Fredrikstad, and, while browsing the history section in a second-hand bookstore, she comes across a pamphlet that she picks up on a whim. Written by Ninja B., the pamphlet describes '*morens [...] uberettigede opphold på psykiatrsik sykehus*' ('her mother's unjustified incarceration in a psychiatric hospital') in Fredrikstad, where the author's mother eventually committed suicide in 1913.[1]

---

1. Hjorth 2014: 107; 2017: 100. As it is clear from the context when I am quoting from Hjorth's text, immediately followed by Charlotte Barslund's translation, I will only give the page numbers of the original text and its translation from now on.

This pamphlet arouses Alma's interest because of its tone, as it is written in anger and with outrage, and Alma finds herself admiring Ninja B.'s courage to voice her personal views with such passion. Reading the pamphlet causes Alma to reflect on her own anger, and we learn that '*Alma kunne være sint og opprørt i tanke og holdning, men hadde sjelden følt sinne dypt i sitt hjerte, dypt i sin kropp*' ('Alma could be angry and outraged in thought and attitude, but she had rarely felt rage deep in her heart, deep in her very core').[2]

While Alma is envious of Ninja B.'s ability to express anger with such liberty, she realises that she herself has had reasons to be angry in the past, but instead of acting upon it, she had '*båret det inne i seg, latt det bore inne i seg*' ('kept them in, letting them eat her up').[3] She reflects that her own inability to express herself through anger must have to do with the fact that she never had any female role models who were openly angry; she had never experienced '*rasende kvinner, opprørte kvinner*' ('angry women, women who rebelled'), nor could she '*huske å ha vært riktig rasende*' ('remember being properly angry').[4]

Moved by Ninja B.'s strong emotional response to the injustice that her mother experienced, Alma makes the connection to a theory that she had held for some time: '[*E*]*n teori om at jo dypere følelser var dess mer allmenne var de, også gjennom tidene*' ('[A] theory that the deeper the emotions, the more universal they were, and had been throughout the ages').[5] One hundred years later, Alma finds that she can relate passionately to Ninja B.'s anger, and she manages to find inspiration there: this is the kind of social injustice that Alma wants to portray in her tapestry about Norwegian democracy, and she concludes that

---

2. 109; 102.
3. Ibid.
4. Ibid.
5. 109; 103.

'*det var en slik følelse som fikk folk til å handle*' ('it was that kind of emotion which spurred people into action').[6]

At the same time, the prospect of anger as an emotional power that has the potential to unite people scares Alma; it is '*skremmende, for hva om* [...] *de fattige i verden, asylsøkerne de papirløse romfolket samlet seg sammen og fikk tak i raseriet sitt og* [...] *rettet det mot – Alma?*' ('terrifying, because what if [...] the world's poor, its asylum seekers and paperless Roma gathered and recognised their common rage and [...] aimed [it] at Alma?').[7]

This passage is quoted at length here because, when Alma's voice permeates that of the narrator in free indirect discourse, she addresses two different aspects of anger that, as I will show, are crucial regarding the way in which she acts in, and reacts to, her surroundings. On the one hand, Alma gives the impression that expressing anger is a quality that can be inherited or learned; and because she can recount very few experiential encounters with anger in the past, she is unable to express, or even feel, anger in the present. Instead of learning to express anger from angry women as role models, Alma suggests that she learned to supress her anger because she was used to seeing '*Frustrerte og psykisk forkrøplede* [*kvinner*] *ja, men ikke opprørske*' ('Frustrated and mentally crippled [women] yes, but not rebellious [ones]').[8] This gendered perception of anger implicitly indicates that anger, as an emotion that is freely expressed, is predominantly reserved for men, whereas women, instead of voicing their anger, suppress it, internalise it, or replace it with other emotions. In other words, when women do not express their anger, they can become frustrated or even ill, which, as Alma suggests, is socially more acceptable than a furious woman.

---

6. 110; 103.
7. Ibid.
8. 109; 102.

On the other hand, Alma describes anger as an affective quality that has the power to move people and bring them together to fight for a common cause. This notion is substantiated by philosopher Alison Bailey, who identifies anger as 'an audible expression of resistance to the suffering of injustice'; and she states that anger 'has a bonding effect – it provides the affective fuel that brings us together and helps us to form cohesive social networks and organized movements'.[9] Instead of interpreting anger, as it is usually done, as a negative quality that can possibly lead to violence and oppression, Bailey views anger as a positive force that can be harnessed in the fight for recognition and political agency in the struggle against the oppression of women.

Alma acknowledges this potentially positive power of anger, but, at the same time, states that she is scared of this very power. When Alma names those who are most vulnerable in any society as possibly uniting – the poor, asylum seekers, and undocumented travellers – she recognises that they have reason to fight against the injustices done to them. However, why would Alma think their anger may be directed against her, unless she is complicit in the injustices that oppress them? Alma's fear suggests that she is aware of her privileges but also afraid of losing them.

In general terms, Devika Sharma describes the predicament of privilege as 'the awkward yet highly ordinary experience of one's privilege being a problem'.[10] This awareness of one's own privilege, as Sharma goes on to say, implies 'a concern about living off, and thus being complicit with, economically and politically exploitative systems and their histories', which possibly 'gives rise to all sorts of ugly thoughts and feelings, and a

---

9. Bailey 2018: 96, 113.
10. Sharma 2019: 711.

range of gestures and rhetorical strategies for handling them'.[11] Sharma argues further that this form of awareness of one's own privilege is reflected upon in what she calls 'hypocrisy literature' and explains as writing that entails depictions of 'a globally privileged subjectivity that is living with the knowledge that it benefits from and contributes to an unjust world "order"'.[12] The hypocritical elements in hypocrisy literature are not found in the 'fraudulent relationship between a self and its social context', but, according to Sharma, are rooted in the relationship of the privileged subjectivity to itself: 'A moral consciousness regards its own immorality with aversion, apathy, or both'.[13] When it comes to the self-reflections of a privileged protagonist, questions can be asked as to whether these reflections can be viewed as a critical discourse on privilege, or whether the novel itself can be seen as attempting 'a critique of that very system'.[14]

In her reflections on anger, Alma has already shown an awareness of global injustices, and through her fear, she unconsciously admits that she is aware of her own privilege within this global capital system. The question remains, however, whether her privileged position would concern her at all if it did not instigate fear, and if it does, whether it is indeed ugly thoughts and feelings that arise in Alma, and which strategies she uses to handle them. I am convinced that the answer to this question lies in anger; in the anger that Alma, at least until the very end of the novel, is unable to feel and to express, and in those emotions that Alma experiences instead of anger. Therefore, I shall identify those situations where we should expect an angry response, and explore the emotions, as well as the concomitant coping strategies, that replace it.

---

11. Ibid.: 712, 714.
12. Ibid.: 717.
13. Ibid.
14. Ibid.: 714.

Sharma states that 'the hypocrisy in hypocrisy literature is the experience of an affective, moral, or political inconsistency that upsets the hypocrite'.[15] The investigation of Alma's affective register will enable me to highlight possible affective, moral, or political inconsistencies in Alma's character, and even if these inconsistencies upset her, so what? Or, to put it less flippantly, Alma's possible awareness of complicity does not necessarily change it, nor her privilege; but can the novel itself contribute to a critical discourse that strives for more justice and equality?

The first few pages of the novel introduce Alma's situation in the narrative present by giving an overview of her history. We learn that Alma separated from her husband when she was thirty-two, that she bought a big house so that her children could stay over regularly in a shared custody arrangement, and that she has to rent out the small flat adjacent to her house because her income as an artist is irregular and dependent on commissions. At the same time, the narrator discloses that Alma values her personal freedom highly, because it allows her to work within a loose structure that she chooses herself. Alma's dependency on the rent as her only regular source of income already gestures towards the first limitation of her personal freedom.

The second limitation is that she feels restricted by personal relationships in general, and in particular by those with her tenants. She wants to avoid anything that would make *'forholdet til leieboeren mer komplisert enn strengt forretningsmessig'* ('her relationship with her tenant more complicated than a purely business arrangement') because, as she thinks, 'å *bli involvert eller kjent med leieboeren*' ('becoming involved with, or having to get to know, her tenant') would make her feel *'ufri'* ('less

---

15. Ibid.: 718.

free').¹⁶ Usually, we would expect the relationship between landlady and tenant to be a professional one, but as Alma's tenants are also her closest neighbours, she prefers tenants who work long hours and just need a place to sleep – in other words those people who do not make demands on her personal life. However, while Alma states that a professional relationship is all she wants from her tenants, her financial dependence on the regular income from the rent makes her feel restless and anxious; in short, it makes her emotional. When the flat has stood empty for a while, she is prone to making hasty decisions; she chooses her tenants less carefully than she usually would and overlooks the required deposit, which has led to conflict in the past.

This overview seems to prepare the reader for what is to follow: the account of Alma's seven-year-long relationship with the young Polish couple – the woman visibly pregnant on arrival – who move in after the flat has stood empty for a few months, not procuring any income for her through rent payments. Because Alma is relieved that someone moves in at all, she does not insist on the payment of the deposit.

When Karolina Drozdowska discusses the depiction of Eastern Europeans in modern Norwegian literature, she observes that it constructs an image that is based on a handful of prejudices and stereotypes. This is also apparent when analysing *Et norsk hus*: on the one hand, there are 'the ones who "come and stay" (mainly labor force)' and on the other, there are 'the ones who "come and go" (mainly criminals)'.¹⁷ In addition, Drozdowska states that 'Eastern Europeans coming to Norway are almost automatically perceived as cheap labor, taking up jobs such as construction work (stereotypically for males) and cleaning (stereotypically for females)', while

---

16. 9; 11.
17. Drozdowska 2021: 301.

another characteristic trait specifies that the Polish workers 'do not speak any Norwegian (and very limited English)'.[18] Indeed, when the small Polish family move into Alma's flat, *'førte [mannen] ordet på sitt gebrokne engelsk'* ('The man did the talking in his broken English'); he is handy around the house and leaves every morning for a presumably similarly manual job, and when he is sent back to Poland to serve a prison sentence, his wife takes up a cleaning job to support herself and her baby daughter.[19]

This information is given to the reader through Alma's consciousness, as the third person narrator's perspective is limited to Alma's, and it is influenced by her prejudices, and derogatory and racist remarks. Alma knows the husband's name, Alan, but not the wife's, because, as she says, she could not be bothered to learn *'det vanskelige navnet hennes'* ('her difficult name'), Slawomira, and therefore, she only calls her *'den polske'* ('the Pole') throughout the entire novel.[20] Slawomira *'var pen, men veldig polsk'* ('was pretty, but very Polish-looking'), and, watching her new neighbours closely from behind her curtains, Alma comments on *'den rare polske pynten i vinduene'* ('the weird Polish decorations in the windows').[21]

Although the rent arrives on time every month and everything seems to go smoothly, in the beginning at least, there are many little things that irritate Alma: they talk loudly, they use too much of the electricity that is included in the rent, they do not recycle, they smoke in the basement near the shared washing machine, and they park their car on the lawn on which Alma asked them not to park. When Alma's adult children come to visit with their own children, they also park

---

18. Ibid.: 301, 302.
19. 15; 16.
20. 122; 114.
21. 20; 21, 41.

on the lawn and have long hot showers, and Alma is irritated, but she tolerates it. With her neighbours, however, their supposed failings become tightly related to them being Polish, or to their otherness.

When Sara Ahmed discusses her concept of stranger fetishism, she states that 'the (mis)recognition of strangers serves to differentiate between the familiar and the strange, a differentiation that allows the figure of the stranger to appear'.[22] Alma differentiates between her family and those she perceives as other although they live next door to her, and, like this, she singles them out, condemns them for wrongdoing based on their supposed otherness and therefore fetishises them. Instead of feeling anger, Alma feels irritation; and instead of seeking an open conversation, or confrontation, to address the issues that irritate her, Alma makes assumptions, again built on the perceived otherness of the Polish couple and her prejudices, which consolidates the figure of the stranger in her proximity: *'Alma hadde ikke spurt, men gjettet på at de var i Norge for å legge seg opp penger for så å reise tilbake til Polen. For det virket ikke som om de forsøkte å nærme seg det norske'* ('Alma hadn't asked, but she guessed that the Poles must be in Norway to make money before going back home because it didn't seem as if they were trying to learn Norwegian'). On the same page, we learn that Alma thinks that, *'De holdt det norske ut […] mens de tjente penger. Kanskje baktalte og hånte de det norske sånn de så de med sin polskhet'* ('They were keeping all things Norwegian out […] while they earned their money. Perhaps they spoke ill of and mocked all things Norwegian as filtered through their own Polishness').[23]

Alma's thoughts display a register of doubt, with words and expressions such as *'gjettet', 'virket', 'tenkte', 'kanskje'* ('guessed',

---

22. Ahmed 2000: 24.
23. 34; 34.

'seemed', 'thought', 'maybe') or *'sikkert'*, *'antagelig'* ('certainly', 'presumably') in other instances. Yet, she uses these phrases of uncertainty to reinforce her prejudiced image of the Polish people next door, who, in her view, exploit the Norwegian state without showing a genuine interest in its language and culture. In terms of anger, we see Alma's earlier mentioned reflections confirmed: she can be angry only in her thoughts, which results in a derogatory and exclusionary stream of consciousness, but she has no means to express it.

Alma's personal discourse of xenophobia is accompanied by emotions: irritation, as stated above, and *'ubehag'* ('a sense of unease'), which Alma feels when she cannot avoid meeting her neighbours face to face. She ponders the reasons for this discomfort, and asks herself: *'Fordi hun eide, de leide? Fordi maktbalansen var skjev […] Eller at de var så forskjellige, levde så forskjellig, hadde så forskjellige smak?'* ('Was it because she owned what they rented? Because the power balance was unequal […] Or that they were so different, lived so differently, had such different tastes?')[24]

When Alma names an imbalanced power relation as one of the reasons for her unease, she acknowledges how awkward it is when she experiences her own privilege as a problem. Instead of focusing on this economic difference from which Alma benefits, however, she aims her attention again on her neighbours' otherness, which suggests that it is easier for her to feel uncomfortable vis-à-vis her neighbours' difference rather than in relation to her own privilege. We can see clearly how ugly thoughts and feelings arise when Alma becomes aware of the predicament of privilege.

Sianne Ngai describes such ugly feelings as '"semantically" negative, in the sense that they are saturated with socially

---

24. 22; 22–23.

stigmatizing meanings and values […] and as "syntactically" negative, in the sense that they are organized by trajectories of repulsion rather than attraction, by phobic strivings "away from" rather than philic strivings "toward"'.[25] In the way that Alma utilises her irritation and discomfort, she stigmatises her Polish neighbours with her derogatory remarks, according to the prejudices she holds about them, and instrumentalises her feelings in a move away from them, setting boundaries that keep them at a distance.

How far Alma goes in her practice of stranger fetishism becomes even clearer when we consider that, as Ahmed states, 'The recognisability of strangers is determinate in the social demarcation of spaces of belonging: the stranger is "known again" as that which has already contaminated such spaces as a threat to both property and person'.[26] Indeed, when Alma describes her Polish neighbours as '*bekvemme og hjemme i det som var Almas land, okkuperte det, parasitter*' ('at ease and at home on what was Alma's land, occupying it, the parasites'), they pose, in her eyes, a threat to her own person and property.[27]

Land, in Norwegian, refers of course to the land that Alma owns, but, at the same time, it can also mean country. In this sense, Alma seems to imply that her Polish neighbours do not only contaminate her own space but the whole of the Norwegian state. When she thus identifies with her own land and country, Alma tacitly justifies her differentiation between 'us' and 'them', between 'mine' and 'yours', and displays a sense of entitlement that, in her view, would allow her to judge who does or does not belong, and to exclude that which supposedly contaminates this space.

While Alma's attitude towards her tenants is derogatory

---

25. Ngai 2007: 11.
26. Ahmed 2000: 22.
27. 160; 149.

and xenophobic, she carries herself with an entirely different demeanour when it comes to her work. She keeps her personal life separate from her work, as if her creativity is a world on its own that her tenants would not understand regardless, as she patronisingly suggests: '*At Alma hadde sin identitet knyttet til sine henders små bevegelser* […] *dette visste de polske ingenting om*' ('How Alma's identity was linked to the tiny movements of her hands […] the Poles knew nothing about that').[28] Alma has the ambition to produce political art and artworks that could instigate social change, or, as she puts it, '*muligens få folk til å handle annerledes enn før bildet*' ('possibly to create something that made people behave differently after they had seen the picture'). Simultaneously, she admits: 'Å, det var *stort tenkt, og for mye å håpe på, men i hvert fall en god intensjon*' ('Oh, these were grandiose thoughts and too much to hope for, but at least her intentions were good').[29]

With these 'good intentions' in mind, Alma reflects critically on society, politics, and the world through her work. These reflections always have a strong personal connection, and therefore, she also questions herself: '*Sånn var det. At når hun utforsket et emne kom hun til å utforske seg selv*' ('It was always thus. When she explored a topic, she ended up exploring herself').[30] While she conducts research for one of her commissions, we learn through Alma's reflections that she used to be a politically active citizen in the past, in debates '*alltid på de svakes side*' ('invariably siding with the underdog'); but that now in the present, she has reached a certain sense of futility, where she feels the vague impetus that she should do something, but that she does not quite know what, or how to go about it: '*Med forstanden visste hun at behovet for radikale endringer var like*

---

28. 25; 26.
29. 27; 28.
30. 95; 89.

*stort nå som før, men hun klarte ikke oppvise noe engasjement, og var skuffet over seg selv og bekymret*' ('Common sense told her that the need for radical change was just as great now as it ever was, but she was unable to summon up much enthusiasm, and was disappointed at herself for this and fretted about it').[31] Here, we can determine 'a critical consciousness treading water', or what Sharma describes as a political inconsistency that upsets the hypocrite: on the one hand, Alma would like to move people politically with her artwork, while she herself, on the other, lacks the motivation to be politically active although she deems it appropriate.[32] She seems aware of her hypocrisy and feels bad about herself, but this, however, does not change the fact that she remains inert.

Alma's hypocrisy becomes even clearer when she describes one of her tapestries and its concept. She embroiders the shapes of people with small flames on their chests:

> [S]må glør som kunne flamme opp hvis de ble pustet til og bli et stort bål hvis de bare åpnet seg for hverandre og kom i egentlig kontakt, men det klarte de ikke, og det var så trist for det ventet en stor felles fare.

> [T]iny embers that could flare up if you blew on them and turn into a bonfire, if only they would open themselves up to one another and make real contact, but they were unable to do so and that was their tragedy because they were facing great danger.[33]

Everyone's life is in danger '*hvis de altså ikke forsto at de var i samme bilde og måtte samarbeide*' ('unless they realised that

---

31. 30; 31, 32; 32.
32. Sharma 2019: 720.
33. 52; 50.

they were all in the same picture and had to work together').[34] With this tapestry, Alma seems to make a case for community, solidarity, and humanitarianism, and she relates the message to her audience that only through teamwork and mutual support can change be achieved. While this message suggests that Alma holds the belief that she can transcend her political inconsistency with such an artwork, for the reader, it becomes clear that this stands in stark contrast to Alma's own practices when it comes to, for example, her tenants. In the general and theoretical sense, humanitarianism, or even just empathy for the situations of fellow human beings, seems to work well for Alma, whereas her ideas lose their valence very quickly when it comes to the particular and the personal. In other words, so long as her own status quo remains unchallenged, Alma can create political artworks and tell herself that she has overcome her political inconsistency, but as soon as she is involved with her person and property, different parameters apply.

Her artwork and her private life – Alma's two domains – appear distinct from each other, and yet they are intertwined. Alma's partner, whose name we never learn, comments on his discontent with her independent and nonconforming lifestyle with: '*Det var ikke sånn det skulle være* [...] *mellom kjærester*' ('This wasn't how it should be [...] between lovers').[35] This direct critique inspires Alma to reflect on relationships between people in general, which she takes up in a tapestry which she works on while she also works on her paid-for commissions at the same time: '*Hvordan skal det være mellom menneskene?*' ('How is it supposed to be then, relationships between people?').[36]

This question appears to be central to the novel; it is repeated several times with minor variations and permeates every aspect

---

34. Ibid.
35. 75; 72.
36. Ibid.

of Alma's life. How should it be, the novel seems to ask, between Alma and her partner, between Alma and Slawomira? Is it morally acceptable that Alma lives with the independence and freedom that mean so much to her?[37] When Alma's partner challenges her again to lead a life with him that he considers more normal, she '*konsentrerte seg for å få argumentasjonen med for å bruke den i sånn skal det være mellom menneskene*' ('paid close attention as he stated his case in order to use his ideas for her tapestry about relationships between people'); and, as the narrator discloses, '*han misforsto det konsentrerte uttrykket hennes. Trodde det skyldtes et oppriktig ønske om å forstå for å forandre seg*' ('he misinterpreted her expression of concentration. He thought it sprung from a sincere wish to understand in order to change').[38]

Instead of wanting to change her personal life as a compromise for her partner's sake, Alma's interest is focused on her artwork: '*Lage et bilde så han forsto at sånn han mente menneskene skulle være sammen, kunne ikke Alma være sammen med andre*' ('Create a picture so that he would realise that Alma couldn't be with other people like he believed she should').[39] What we see here is the version of Alma who exploits her partner's sincerity for her artistic inspiration. While she does reflect on the novel's central question, she can only express herself in the abstract and indirectly – through her artwork – whereas when it comes to Alma's private life – the particular and finite – she remains silent and inert. It is left to the reader to ponder how it should be between people, between Alma and her partner, in a way that is practically feasible.

I have discussed earlier how Alma also remains inactive regarding those issues that irritate her involving her neighbours

---

37. Liv Marit Weberg discusses this aspect in more detail in her master's dissertation 2016: 36.
38. 80; 76.
39. Ibid.

– a situation where we might expect Alma to become angry. Instead, she replaces her anger with those feelings that Ngai calls 'unprestigious', such as irritation and discomfort, feelings that are 'explicitly *a*moral and *non*cathartic, offering no satisfaction of virtue, however oblique, nor any therapeutic or purifying release'.[40] Put differently, Alma nurtures these negative feelings with a stream of similarly negative and derogatory thoughts but does not find a way to channel these feelings into a solution that may alter the situation.

Towards the end of the novel, however, Alma's financial situation becomes even more strained, and she decides to raise the rent payments in accordance with her tenants' increased electricity consumption, and writes a letter, '*så forretningsmessig hun kunne*' ('as business-like as she could').[41] To Alma's surprise, Slawomira answers her with a letter in Norwegian, in which she disagrees with Alma, and reminds her of her own duties as a landlady: '*Og en ting til. 6 år make snø dine eiendeler. Det hører til din plikt!*' ('And another thing. 6 years snow clearing your property. That is your duty!').[42] Slawomira's reminder is the first time in the novel that we hear her voice directly; up until this moment, it was only through Alma's consciousness and her biased judgment of them that we were granted a view into the lives of Alma's tenants.

This reminder of her duties makes Alma truly angry, apparently for the first time in her life: '*Nei, hun var ikke forberedt på et anklageskrift, en slik aggressiv tone, utropstegn og to streker under hva som var Almas plikt. Som den polske skulle belære Alma om?*' ('No, she wasn't prepared for accusations, for such an aggressive tone, exclamation marks and two lines under what

---

40. Ngai 2007: 6, italics in original.
41. 128; 119.
42. 142; 132.

was Alma's duty. How dare the Pole lecture Alma?').[43] Alma is furious over this perceived injustice, and her reaction implies that she is convinced that she has the law on her side.

In her outrage, Alma drinks large quantities of wine and writes a message to Slawomira, drunk and in the middle of the night, telling her to leave. After she has calmed down somewhat, she writes other letters, fills out forms, intends to amend the contract; she demands the missing deposit and sends out a warning which threatens Slawomira with being forcibly removed from the premises. Eventually, Slawomira answers, also in writing, and terminates the tenancy.

While Slawomira lists Alma's shortfalls as a landlady to correct her demands, she expresses simultaneously how sorry she is that their relationship has to end this way: *'Jeg er lei for det, fordi jeg bor ved siden av deg lenger enn 6 år'* ('I am sad about this because I live next to you longer than 6 years'); and, further down, she writes: *'Dårlig snakkes i norsk, men jeg er den samme mannen som deg'* ('Barely speak Norwegian, but I am the same man as you').[44] Slawomira is threatened and attacked by Alma, and yet, she remains respectful, reminding Alma of their shared humanity and their equality despite the differences. This, however, only makes Alma angrier, and when Slawomira agrees only to move out once she has received the payment that she thinks she is due, Alma loses her composure and confronts Slawomira, shouting at her after having hammered on her door: *'Nå er det nok [...] nå har det gått for langt, ropte hun, nå må dere faen meg flytte!'* ('That's enough [...] this time you've gone too far, she yelled, you bloody well move out now!').[45]

Afterwards, the feeling of anger does not subside but changes ever so slightly to *'et roligere mer brennende sinne iblandet en*

---

43. Ibid.
44. 164; 151–152.
45. 168; 155.

*sterk gjengjeldelsesforakt for den* [...] *dumme polske kvinnen*' ('a calmer, more smouldering rage mixed with a strong portion of contempt and revenge for the [...] stupid Polish woman'), and, talking herself into an even stronger rage throughout the night, Alma lines up all the radios in her house on the wall she shares with her tenants and '*satte dem så på fullt volum* [...] *forberedt på et veldig slag, lengtet nesten etter dets voldsomhet, utløsning*' ('turned the volume to maximum [...] prepared for a great battle, almost longing for its violence, its release').[46] Alma's tenants are gone the next morning: so, matter-of-factly, she achieved what she wanted, whereas the emotional release she craves for fails to appear.

Alma views herself as a victim of injustice, and therefore, she considers her anger apt. However, what we see in this scene is not necessarily anger per se but its close cognates: contempt, violence, a sense of rightfulness, and the wish for revenge. In this case, it seems impossible to distinguish between anger and 'whatever behaviour contingently accompanies it', but it is this behaviour, together with Alma's views and her self-righteousness, that blinds her to the fact that it might actually be Slawomira who is treated unjustly, and that the latter might be right when she lists Alma's failures as a landlady in her letter, and the many small things that she did and which Alma took for granted, such as clearing snow and leaves, and collecting Alma's mail while she was travelling.[47]

Only in hindsight does Alma realise how misguided her anger at Slawomira was, and she recalls the words Slawomira used in her letter to her and paraphrases them in her head: '*Dårlig snakkes i norsk, men jeg er et menneske som deg* [...] *Det hadde hun ikke lest, ikke sett, ikke forstått, og det var ikke*

---

46. 172; 159, 173–174; 160–161.
47. Srinivasan 2018: 13.

*til å forstå. Hvor alene må hun ha vært i det norske*' ('I barely speak Norwegian, but I'm a human being just like you [...] Alma hadn't read it, hadn't seen it, hadn't understood it, and that was beyond belief. How alone the Pole must have been in Norway').[48] Now that it is too late, Alma realises that her anger blinded her to the concerns of her fellow human being, that it made her self-centred and indifferent to Slawomira's situation – she was alone in Norway, and had to support herself and her daughter with a cleaning job. What follows are Alma's self-reflections that read like an epiphany, and in which Alma's work and her personal life finally merge:

*Trodde hun kunne forstå Ninja B.s sinne og Ninja B.s mor, men skjønte ikke en dritt. [...] men det handlet jo ikke om andre enn henne, hun presset bare sin egen selvforståelse og sin tankeverden i all dens ufullkommenhet ned over de stakkars sakesløse menneskene hun brukte historiene til, fylte ublutt ut slik det passet henne, for å få det slik hun ville, for et overmot [...] sparte seg ikke for noe, og sånn er det, slik er litteraturen og kunsten, det er dens domene og dens privilegium, usynkron med virkeligheten, det var ikke det, men at hun ikke hadde forstått, ikke forsøkt å forstå sin egen nabo, menneskene hun hadde delt hus med.*

She had thought that she could understand Ninja B.'s rage and Ninja B.'s mother, but she understood sod all. [...] it had never been about anyone but her; she had just imposed her own views and her own inadequate world of ideas on poor defenceless people whose stories she had exploited, shamelessly embellishing them to suit her purpose, to get the outcome she wanted, what hubris [...] she had taken what she wanted because that's what literature and art do, that's

---

48. 181; 167.

their domain and privilege, out of sync with reality, but that wasn't the real problem, the real problem was that she had failed to understand, that she hadn't even tried to understand her own tenant, the people she shared a house with).[49]

Sharma argues that the hypocrisy portrayed in literature is 'the judgment passed by a critical consciousness on its own moral inconsistency'.[50] This is precisely what Alma is doing here; she becomes aware of her own 'moral inconsistency', and she judges herself harshly for it. She also realises that her hypocrisy permeates every aspect of her life, including her work and her relationship, especially so considering the exploitative manner with which she approached both. Quite rightfully, she questions how appropriate her anger actually is when we learn that *'når hun selv for første gang ble sint, øste hun det uhemmet ut over en maktløs polsk kvinne og det lille barnet hennes, hva kunne hun bidra til et jubileum om demokrati?'* ('when she herself got properly angry for the first time, she had vented her rage on a defenceless Polish woman and her little child, what contribution could she possibly have to make to celebrate democracy?').[51] Indeed, it is the awareness of an affective, moral, and political inconsistency that upsets Alma, and she destroys the work she has done so far for the anniversary tapestry.

Once she has burned the cut-up pieces, she feels *'den takknemligheten som følger når man har fått og gjennomlevd en fortjent straff'* ('the gratitude that follows when you have suffered and lived through a well-deserved punishment').[52] Although Alma has the impression that she punished herself appropriately, the fact remains that she failed a fellow human

---

49. 183; 168.
50. Sharma 2019: 718.
51. 183; 169.
52. Ibid.

being and that this punishment is also an act that is related to her own concerns but does not engage with Slawomira in any way. Nevertheless, it is Slawomira who ultimately has the last word when she responds to a text message from Alma with: '*I avisen det står at du er kulturell person. Jeg har en annen mening*' ('In the newspaper, it says you are a cultural person. I have a different opinion').[53] This is not just an opinion, as this answer seems to imply, because Slawomira knows better than the newspaper as she has experienced Alma's inconsistencies first-hand, while she herself retained her integrity despite her difficult situation and Alma's unjustified rage.

Nevertheless, the reader never learns what becomes of Slawomira, and it remains open to interpretation whether Alma's epiphany actually changes anything, be that her exploitative attitude or her racist approach towards a perceived difference. The second part of the novel, consisting of the last three pages, suggests that Alma's prejudices have not, in fact, changed; she renovates the flat, signs a contract with '*et norsk firma*' ('a Norwegian company') because for her, this is '*det tryggeste av alt*' ('the best possible outcome'), and when '*to smilende polakker*' ('two smiling Poles') move in, Alma comments to herself: '*Livet er uforutsigelig og det gåtefulle like i nærheten, vegg i vegg*' ('Life is unpredictable and the mystery is just next door').[54]

When Sharma investigates hypocrisy literature, she is interested in 'the ways in which forms of self-reflexive discourse may or may not serve as critical discourse'.[55] Indeed, the whole novel constitutes a form of self-reflexive discourse, including the protagonist's realisation of her own hypocrisy; of her affective, moral, and political inconsistencies, and of her anger as being inappropriate and rooted in self-righteousness.

53. 188; 174.
54. 189; 175.
55. Sharma 2019: 720.

What Alma does not question, however, is the socio-economic difference between them.

At one point, she looks up Slawomira's tax return and finds out: '*hundre og femogtjue tusen kroner hadde hun tjent året før. Det kunne ikke stemme, hadde hun ikke fast jobb? Hun jobbet sikkert svart*' ('she had earned 125,000 kroner last year. So little couldn't be right, after all she worked full-time? She was probably doing cash-in-hand jobs on the side').[56] Instead of trying to understand what it must be like to live on the breadline in one of the most expensive countries in the world, Alma reverts to her prejudices, and the systemic economic imbalance between the two women remains unchallenged, and so does Alma's complicity with this imbalance. In her epiphany, Alma laments that she failed to understand her tenant, but this failure does not seem to include the economic power imbalance between them, from which Alma benefits. When Alma's systemic privilege – one of the most glaring differences between her and Slawomira – is taken for granted, how can the novel be seen as critical of the hypocrisy and complicity that it portrays? Or, to put it differently, when the novel can be seen as a self-reflexive discourse of recognition, does this recognition actually signify anything?

I shall draw on Ahmed's insights from a different context in an attempt to answer these questions. In 'Declarations of Whiteness', Ahmed discusses the extent to which it is possible for systemically privileged people to act or speak out against a system from which they benefit, in this case white middle-class people, and racism. One of Ahmed's arguments is that 'if we recognize something such as racism, then we also offer a definition of that which we recognize. In this sense, recognition produces rather than simply finds its object.'[57]

---

56. 180; 166.
57. Ahmed 2004: 17.

What Alma recognises through her reflections is, at least in part, her privileged position and her hypocrisy. According to Ahmed's statement, Alma's process of recognition would produce a realisation of this very privilege and hypocrisy rather than undo it. But when Alma undoes the tapestry that she worked on while she hypocritically exploited other people, does she simultaneously undo her hypocrisy? It would be difficult to argue that she does because all she undoes is feeling bad about herself, but she can at least begin to feel better after she has shown remorse and punished herself – she proves to herself that at her core, she means well.

Ahmed also addresses such ostentatious displays of shame, albeit in the context of racism; she argues that

> Declarations of shame can work to re-install the very ideals they seek to contest. [...] they may even assume that the speech act itself can be taken as a sign of transcendence: if we say we are ashamed, if we say we were racist, then 'this shows' we are not racist now, we *show that we mean well*. The presumption that saying is doing – that being sorry means that we have overcome the very thing we are sorry about – hence works to support racism in the present.[58]

In line with this argument, Alma, by not only declaring her failings but also by acting upon them by destroying her artwork, might try to convince herself that she has transcended that which she recognised as a problem – her hypocrisy and lack of understanding. However, she only recognises and acts upon the problem in the abstract, or rather, her supposed transcendence is only a notion, while her status quo does not change, and her privileged position remains intact. She submits a piece of her

---
58. Ibid.: 27, italics in original.

embroidery work that was an unused by-product of a previous commission, so her reputation as an artist does not suffer, and, as the ending of the novel suggests, her xenophobic sensibilities remain unaltered. In short, Alma presumes that she has overcome her hypocrisy by feeling apologetic, while, in fact, she never apologises to Slawomira, and nothing changes as far as the reader is aware.

While Alma is unaware of the fact that her own hypocrisy and complicity do not change through one act of self-inflicted punishment, her delusions are apparent to the reader: she reveals herself to the reader with her declaration, and by stating how bad she feels about herself; and while she appears to convey to the reader that she is prepared to do something about it, we know how hypocritical this intention is.

The narrative perspective further contributes to undermining Alma's credibility: with Alma being the narrator's sole focaliser, the reader experiences an intense immersion into her consciousness and follows her self-reflections closely. These self-reflections are exaggerated to an extent that they verge on the obsessive, and thus, instead of inviting us to develop an understanding for Alma despite her failings, I would argue that it distances us from her. And when Slawomira's voice is heard towards the end of the novel, she is granted a moment of subjectivity which, of course, only further highlights Alma's failings. In this sense, Alma, as the protagonist, epitomises a form of hypocrisy culture in which she gives the impression that she is doing something about it, while, in fact, nothing changes. By throwing this hypocrisy culture into sharp relief, the novel itself, however, can be considered as supporting a discourse that is critical of precisely such a culture.

# Bibliography

Ahmed, Sara. 2000. *Strange Encounters: Embodied Others in Post-Coloniality*. London: Routledge.

———. 2004. 'Declarations of Whiteness: The Non-Performativity of Anti-Racism'. *Borderlands* 3:2.

Bailey, Alison. 2018. 'On Anger, Silence, and Epistemic Injustice'. *Royal Institute of Philosophy supplement* 84, 83–115.

Drozdowska, Karolina. 2021. 'The Others from Across the Sea – Eastern Europeans and Eastern Europe in Modern Norwegian Literature'. *Archiwum Emigracji* 28, 292–305.

Hjorth, Vigdis. 2017. *A House in Norway*. Charlotte Barslund (trans.). London: Norvik Press.

———. 2014. *Et norsk hus*. Oslo: Cappelen Damm.

Ngai, Sianne. 2007. *Ugly Feelings*. Cambridge, MA: Harvard UP.

Sharma, Devika. 2019. 'Privileged, Hypocritical, and Complicit: Contemporary Scandinavian Literature and the Egalitarian Imagination'. *Comparative Literature Studies* 56:4, 711–730.

Srinivasan, Amia. 2018. 'The Aptness of Anger'. *The Journal of Political Philosophy* 26:2, 124–144.

Weberg, Liv Marit. 2016. 'Forskjell og følelser i Vigdis Hjorths *Et norsk hus*'. Master's dissertation. University of Oslo.

· 23 ·

# What Have the ~~Romans~~ Vikings Ever Done For Us?: A 'Postcard' on How Studying Literature and Mythology Equips You for a Career in Politics

## Fiona Twycross

In 1998, I headed down from Edinburgh to London to take up a career in politics. In my boxes, and through nine subsequent moves, my thesis entitled 'Ragnarok: Use of Norse Mythology in Contemporary Scandinavian Literature' has come with me.

For the interview I had for my first job with the Labour Party, I had a very carefully crafted answer as to how my degree was relevant to the role. Fortunately, I didn't have to use it and I honestly can't remember what it was. The chair of the interview panel opened by saying to roars of laughter from the rest of the panel that they had had great fun deciding over lunch how the subject was relevant. I decided to park my answer and laughed along with them. I got the job as a committee officer for the Parliamentary Labour Party.

The next decade saw me move up the ranks of the party organisation, working both in London and across the UK before I left to work for a charity. But politics was in my blood, and I was later fortunate enough to be elected to the London Assembly. More recently, I was appointed Deputy Mayor for Fire and Resilience by the Mayor of London, Sadiq Khan.

Occasionally, in the almost quarter of a century since I graduated, I have been asked what I wrote my thesis about and how it is relevant to what I did next. At first glance there seems little connection. However, what I learned in the process of researching, writing, and defending my thesis, as the first PhD student within Edinburgh University's Scandinavian Studies department, has travelled with me. It has enriched both my life and my personal resilience as well as giving me deeper analytical skills that have stood me in good stead throughout.

## A few things I learned from my studies

1. **What has happened helps you understand what will happen next**
   In politics, knowing what others (friend or foe) are likely to do next is key. My ability to do this was honed by studying literature, particularly the study of motive. Being able to read the runes and predict possible next moves by friends and foes alike has proved very helpful as I have navigated politics.

2. **Trust nobody (or at least very few people)**
   Understanding alliances and how they shift is vital in Norse mythology and politics alike.
   Loki isn't the only ambiguous character in the Norse myths, but his shift of allegiance from the gods to the giants is a standout betrayal. A political friend (whom I trust) once told me that he had three political friends he trusted but dozens of allies. Alliances are formed and shift depending on shared interests. I had absorbed this truth from the myths even before my first day working in politics.

3. **Gods that die reflect the reality of political deities**
   Ragnarok – the twilight of the gods – reflects the reality of political deities. The majority of the most familiar mythological gods are immortal, but the Norse gods are not. With few exceptions, political gods are not immortal either. An incoming leader generally sees their popularity fall as they make mistakes or deal with the reality of governing by making unpopular decisions. Understanding this, and the frailty of leaders, human or otherwise, can only stand you in good stead as you navigate political waters.

4. **There is no absolute truth, there is just interpretation**
   The use of ancient myths in a contemporary setting shows how language and story alike don't create an absolute truth but are open to interpretation. Norse mythology has been used in ugly ways to reinforce fascist beliefs in Aryan supremacy but also for good, to illustrate the need to avert environmental disaster.
   
   Arguing at Mayor's Question Time in London's City Hall about the success or otherwise of his approach to the London Living Wage, both Boris Johnson as the then Mayor of London and myself as a Labour Assembly Member used the same set of statistics to make opposing points.
   
   There is seldom an absolute truth, either in mythology or in politics.

5. **Fiction readers make good leaders in a crisis**
   In my current role, I have been involved in the strategic response to the Covid-19 pandemic in London. Val McDermid argued that fiction readers have made the best leaders during the Covid crisis. She writes that

'What fiction gives you is the gift of imagination and the gift of empathy. You see a life outside your own bubble.'[1] Imagination matters when you are dealing with a crisis and need a Plan B (and often a Plan C and D as well).

6. **If you've written a thesis, you have wrestled demons and can do anything**

   Only those who have written a thesis, or tried to, know how tough a journey it is. If you get through the Slough of Despond this involves, you can probably survive anything, from the worst election campaign to dealing with a pandemic. I am not sure how my computer survived the process without getting thrown out of my flat window. It did though, and I did too.

7. **Short sentences are good**

   In Norwegian, short sentences are good. Most people who have worked for me now know this too. Enough said.

8. **Good teachers are mentors who allow you to discover the answers on your own**

   In a parallel universe, I didn't get the job that set me on a political path. In that life, I got postdoctoral funding and later a much sought after lecturer's position. I like to think I might have become a university professor with many publications under my belt. I hope this version of myself would inspire their students as much as Bjarne inspired me. Gently pushing me towards finding my own conclusions. Patient as I missed another deadline and struggled to express coherent thoughts. I am grateful

---

1. Brown 2020.

for what I learned from Bjarne – that good teachers are mentors who allow you to find your own answers and your own path. I hope I use the example he set me in my own work by supporting those I work with to do this as well. If I have taken nothing else from my studies, this will suffice.

## Bibliography

Brown, Mark. 2020. 'Fiction readers have made best leaders in Covid-19 crisis, says Val McDermid'. *The Guardian*. 17 August.

# A Life in Print

## · 24 ·

## Moving Currents: A Note of Appreciation

### Laura Alice Chapot

[novel, **travel**, town, national, **text**, writing, **new**, **novels**, **swedish**, **modern**, **work**, narrative, **towards**, war, **world**, **literary**, north, **place**, urban, **time**, **sense**, texts, **role**, sweden, period, northern, **environment**, literature, **life**, story, **early**, **space**, **form**, **cultural**, stockholm, **perspective**, **international**, **home**, **local**, **journey**, **terms**, **turn**, **transnational**, film, **scene**, sea, **representation**, modernism, modernist]

One of my **earliest** encounters with Bjarne was as an undergraduate in Scandinavian Studies at the University of Edinburgh. Bjarne introduced my fellow students and me to Georg Brandes' **work** and his **text** *Hovedstrømninger i det nittende Århundredes Litteratur* ('*Main Currents in the Literature of the Nineteenth Century*'). This was my first contact with the intellectual and creative ferment of the late nineteenth century **literary** and **cultural scene**, and it sparked a preoccupation that continues to this day with the ways in which **literature** responds to the uncertainty of a rapidly modernising **world**. What also inspired me in our discussions of Brandes was the **transnational perspective**, the situating of the **local** within the **international**, and the entanglements of **travel**, **space** and **time**, and **home**. Moving between **places**, whether physically or intellectually, has been a feature of Bjarne's **life** and thought, as of my own, and I'm very grateful to have this opportunity to thank Bjarne for all the kindness and generosity he has given me as he has helped me navigate my own intellectual **journey**.

In his **role** as a supervisor for my doctoral research, Bjarne gave me the confidence to roam intellectually, to follow the twists and **turns** that the research required, **towards** making **sense**, in my own **terms**, of the questions that preoccupied me. The research took us in directions we did not expect, and I found myself learning computational text analysis methods to understand the **new forms** of **representation** that were emerging in **modern Swedish novels** of the late nineteenth century. Without the supportive **environment** Bjarne created, I would not have taken those intellectual risks.

Bjarne, as a token of gratitude and to celebrate the next stage in your journey, I offer you a playful homage to your work. The list of words at the top of this note are the most frequent words in a selection of your writing (fourteen articles, in English, spanning the period from 1998 to 2019). Highlighting how those words circulate within this note of appreciation is a small tribute to how your words continue to inhabit and motivate my own. In addition, I would like to offer a computational twist on the 'bird's-eye-perspective' that you have analysed in relation to Lagerlöf's and Andersen's travel writing: a technique that seeks to find new ways of representing in order to provide new perspectives on areas that are more or less well known and familiar to us.[1] Instead of geese, storks, and wild swans taking us on a journey around Sweden's landscapes, distributions of the co-occurrences of your words, visualised through topic modelling, provide an evocative topography of the semantic dynamics circulating through your writing.

---

1. Thorup Thomsen 2008: esp. 165.

| Topic 0 | Topic 1 | Topic 2 | Topic 3 | Topic 4 |
|---|---|---|---|---|
| travel | film | national | travel | text |
| text | stories | war | writing | national |
| romantic | scene | transnational | modern | sea |
| place | cinema | narrative | fictional | war |
| orient | short | narrative | factual | nation |
| narrator | locations | writing | traffic | landscape |
| sweden | sequence | guide | modernity | danish |
| translation | set | story | reportage | british |
| oriental | act | period | modes | perspective |
| denmark | images | terrain | modernism | female |
| international | protagonist | publication | contemporary | uncanny |
| oriental | settings | exhibition | building | influence |
| writer | visual | strategy | perception | tale |
| poetic | texts | account | emphasis | coast |
| process | significance | travel | nation | dead |
| dominant | day | thought | change | letter |
| traveller | scandinavian | train | principle | question |
|  | means | play | accident | information |
|  | silent | borders | processes | marriage |
|  |  | scale |  | battle |

| Topic 5 | Topic 6 | Topic 7 | Topic 8 | Topic 9 |
|---|---|---|---|---|
| swedish | sense | town | work | north |
| world | narrative | urban | role | travel |
| literary | space | modernist | cultural | writing |
| time | environment | novel | international | town |
| life | spatial | affective | early | south |
| form | stockholm | modern | sweden | northern |
| local | character | northern | literature | passage |
| home | period | place | section | place |
| journey | collective | social | range | related |
| texts | human | city | culture | nature |
| representation | novels | early | volume | back |
| forms | development | modernism | case | darkness |
| turn | street | locational | boundaries | complex |
| notion | centre | townscape | perspectives | memory |
| study | characters | periphery | contribution | past |
| country | alternative | political | status | title |
| context | movement | metropolitan | public | times |
| discussion | point | centre | present | railway |
| foreign | people | articulation | interest | growth |
| ways | paris | modernity | material | childhood |
|  | identifies |  | ideological | long |
|  |  |  | innovative | pronounced |
|  |  |  | moving |  |

Figure 1: Table of topic models (groups of words that frequently occur close to one another across the corpus) with their most frequent words.

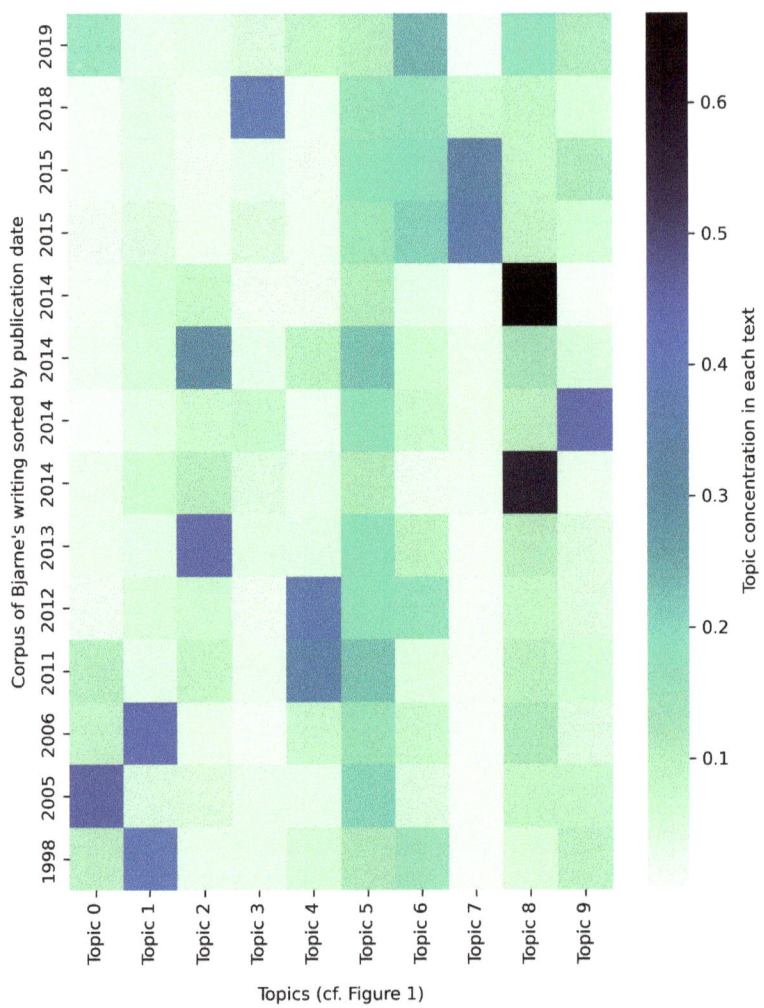

Figure 2: Heat map of distribution of topic models (Figure 1) across the corpus of texts.

## Bibliography

Thorup Thomsen, Bjarne. 2008. 'A Place and a Text In-Between: Translation Patterns in Hans Christian Andersen's *I Sverrig*'. In Marie Wells (ed.), *The Discovery of Nineteenth-Century Scandinavian*. Norwich: Norvik Press, 163–175.

# Bibliography of Bjarne Thorup Thomsen

## Monographs

2007. *Lagerlöfs litterære landvinding: Nation, mobilitet og modernitet i Nils Holgersson og tilgrænsende tekster*. Amsterdam: Amsterdam Contributions to Scandinavian Studies.

## Edited Volumes

1982. *En selvskreven historie: Om erindringsbøger og dagbøger af bønder, håndværkere og arbejdere i Danmark*. Copenhagen: Samlerens Forlag. With Lis Toft Andersen and Martin Zerlang.

1992. *Minority Languages – The Scandinavian Experience: Papers Read at the Conference in Edinburgh 9–11 November 1990*. Oslo: Nordic Language Secretariat. With Gunilla Blom, Peter Graves, and Arne Kruse.

2000. *Dansk litteraturhistorie, vol. 2: 1480–1620*. Copenhagen: Gyldendal. With P. Brask, K. Friis-Jensen, J. Glebe-Møller, T. Hind, M. Skafte Jensen, A. Jørgensen, S. Kværndrup, J. Rahbek Rasmussen, and J. Risum.

2007. *Hans Christian Andersen – New Approaches*. Norwich: Norvik Press. With Hans-Christian Andersen.

2007. *Centring on the Peripheries: Studies in Scandinavian, Scottish, Gaelic and Greenlandic Literature*. Norwich: Norvik Press.

2014. *Re-Mapping Lagerlöf: Performance, Intermediality and European Transmissions*. Lund: Nordic Academic Press. With Helena Forsås-Scott and Lisbeth Stenberg.

## Articles

1981. 'Æstetik, natur og politik. En analyse af Arne Rustes "Konvalldikt. Om svaler"'. *Kursiv: Meddelelser fram Dansklærerforeningen* 3, 53–64.

1984. 'Den selvskrevne historie'. In *AUC i debat*. Aalborg: Aalborg Universitetsforlag, 2.

1990. 'Fra *Ragnarok* til *Apollons oprør*. Villy Sørensens forfatterskab i firserne'. *Dansk udsyn* 4, 221–230. [Previously appeared in 1989. In Irene Scobbie (ed.), *Proceedings of the Eighth Biennial Conference of Teachers of Scandinavian Studies in Great Britain and Northern Ireland*. Edinburgh: University of Edinburgh, 261–270.]

1992a. 'Sandemoses stemmer. Om flertydigheden i *En sjömann går i land*'. *Edda* 1992/1, 28–35. [Previously appeared in 1991. In Janet Garton (ed.), *Proceedings of the Ninth Biennial Conference of the British Association of Scandinavian Studies*. Norwich: University of East Anglia, 285–300.]

1992b. 'From Jante to Utopia? Aksel Sandemose and the Fascination of North America'. *Northern Studies* 28, 41–45.

1993a. 'The language situation in Denmark'. In R.E. Asher and J.M.Y. Simpson (eds), *Encyclopaedia of Language and Linguistics*. London: Pergamon Press.

1993b. 'Anders Bodelsen'. In *Contemporary World Writers*. Detroit: Detroit St. James Press, 68–69.

1993c. Ten entries in *Chambers Dictionary of World History*. Edinburgh: Chambers Harrap.

1994a. 'Ludvig Holberg's Plays'. In *International Dictionary of Theatre*. Detroit: Detroit St. James Press 2, 485–487.

1994b. 'Kaj Munk's Plays'. In *International Dictionary of Theatre*. Detroit: Detroit St. James Press 2, 687–689.

1994c. Fourteen entries in *Larousse Dictionary of Writers*. Edinburgh: Larousse, 1, 2, 105, 532–33, 535, 544–545, 711, 743, 816, 911.

1995a. 'Om stedsans, mytteri og polyfoni i romanen'. *Kritik* 116, 54–61.

1995b. 'Maskine, Nation og Modernitet hos Andersen og Almqvist'. *Tidskrift för Litteraturvetenskap* 1995/2, 27–46.

1996. 'Andersens *O.T.* og Almqvists *Det går an*'. In Gunilla Anderman and Christine Banér (eds), *Proceedings of the Tenth Biennial Conference of the British Association of Scandinavian Studies*. Guildford: University of Surrey, 230–242.

1997a. 'Destruction and Construction in Selma Lagerlöf's *Jerusalem*, Vol. II'. In Charlotte Whittingham and Phil Holmes (eds), *Proceedings of the Eleventh Biennial Conference of the British Association of Scandinavian Studies*. Hull: University of Hull Press, 82–98.

1997b. 'Aspects of Topography in Selma Lagerlöf's *Jerusalem*, Vol. I'. *Scandinavica* 36:1, 23–41.

1998a. 'Terra (In)cognita: Reflections on the Search for the Sacred Place in Selma Lagerlöf'. In Louise Vinge (ed.), *Selma Lagerlöf Seen from Abroad*. Vitterhets Historie och Antikvitets Akademien. Stockholm: Kungl, 131–141.

1998b. 'Location in Hamsun's Turn-of-the-Century Short Stories'. In Peter Graves and Arne Kruse (eds), *Hamsun in Edinburgh: Papers Read at the Conference in Edinburgh 1997*. Hamarøy: Hamsun-selskapet, 71–82.

1999. 'Translation and Transplantation: Sir Alexander Gray's Danish Ballads'. *Northern Studies* 34, 35–59. With Peter Graves.

2000a. 'Noter og bibliografi'. In *Dansk Litteraturhistorie*, vol. IX. Copenhagen: Gyldendal, 41–42.

2000b. 'Nils Holgersson og grænselandet'. *Kritik* 146, 56–62.

2004a. 'Translation and Transplantation: Sir Alexander Gray's Danish Ballads'. In Bill Findlay (ed.), *Frae Ither Tongues. Essays on Modern Translations into Scots*. Clevedon: Multilingual Matters, 231–251. With Peter Graves.

2004b. 'Lagerlöfs relative landskaber: Om konstruktionen af et nationalt territorium i Nils Holgersson'. *Edda* 2004/2, 118–135.

2005a. 'Om topografin i Selma Lagerlöfs Jerusalem, del I'. In Louise Vinge (ed.), *I Selma Lagerlöfs värld*. Stockholm: Symposion, 166–181.

2005b. 'Connecting Cultures: Hans Christian Andersen as a Travel Writer'. *Northern Studies* 39, 51–69.

2006a. 'The Orient According to Hans Christian Andersen: Conceptions of the East in *En Digters Bazar*'. In Sven Hakon Rossel (ed.), *Der Norden im Ausland – das Ausland im Norden*. Vienna: Praesens Verlag, 675–683.

2006b. 'Kampen om Lagerlöf'. *Edda* 2006/1, 100–103.

2006c. 'Ibsen, Lagerlöf, Sjöström and Terje Vigen: (Inter)nationalism, (Inter)subjectivity and the Interface between Swedish Silent Cinema and Scandinavian Literature'. In C. Claire Thomson (ed.), *Northern Constellations: New Readings in Nordic Cinema*. Norwich: Norvik Press, 193–204.

2006d. 'Aspects of topography in Selma Lagerlöf's *Jerusalem*, Vol. 1'. *Skandinavistik* 36:1, 23–41.

2007a. 'Introduction'. In Bjarne Thorup Thomsen (ed.), *Centring on the Peripheries: Studies in Scandinavian, Scottish, Gaelic and Greenlandic Literature*. Norwich: Norvik Press, 8–12.

2007b. 'Nordic National Borderlands in Selma Lagerlöf'. In Bjarne Thorup Thomsen (ed.), *Centring on the Peripheries: Studies in Scandinavian, Scottish, Gaelic and Greenlandic Literature*. Norwich: Norvik Press, 79–93.

2007c. 'Help from The Heart of Midlothian: The Hans Christian Andersen Novel and the Imagining of the Realm'. In Peter Graves and Arne Kruse (eds), *Images and Imaginations: Perspectives on Britain and Scandinavia*. Edinburgh: Lockharton Press, 145–161.

2007d. 'Contesting the Novel: Andersen and the Challenges of Criticism, with Particular Reference to *De to Baronesser*'. *Scandinavica* 46:2, 175–194.

2007e. 'A Place and a Text In-Between: "Translation" Patterns in Hans Christian Andersen's *I Sverrig*'. In Marie Wells (ed.), *The Discovery of Nineteenth-Century Scandinavia*. Norwich: Norvik Press, 163–175.

2011a. 'Curriculum, flerkulturalitet og litterær globalisering'. In Marie Louise Svane and Erik Svendsen (eds), *Litterære Livliner: Kanon – Klassiker – Litteraturbrug*. Copenhagen: Gyldendal, 197–207 and 236–237.

2011b. 'Comparative Considerations: Lagerlöf, Andersen – and the British perspective'. *Northern Studies* 42, 41–54.

2012a. 'Hybrid hjemmebane: Regionalt, transnationalt og utopisk hos Selma Lagerlöf'. In Margaretha Ullström and Sofia Wijkmark (eds), *Hemmaplan – den regionala litteraturens traditioner, tekniker och funktioner*. Karlstad: Karlstad University Press, 27–45.

2012b. '(Trans)national Geographies and Alternative Families in Selma Lagerlöf's *Bannlyst*'. *European Journal of Scandinavian Studies* 42:1, 1–18.

2013. 'Text, traffic and transnational thought: Perspectives on prose publications by Selma Lagerlöf in periodicals and anthologies, with particular reference to "En emigrant" (1914), "Lappland-Schonen" (1917) and the First World War period'. *Scandinavica* 51:2, 208–224.

2014a. 'Re-Mapping Lagerlöf: The Volume and its Parameters'. In Helena Forsås-Scott, Lisbeth Stenberg, and Bjarne Thorup Thomsen (eds), *Re-Mapping Lagerlöf: Performance, Intermediality and European Transmissions*. Lund: Nordic Academic Press, 13–17.

2014b. '(Trans)national narratives and European Transmissions: Sectional portal'. In Helena Forsås-Scott, Lisbeth Stenberg, and Bjarne Thorup Thomsen (eds), *Re-Mapping Lagerlöf: Performance, Intermediality and European Transmissions*. Lund: Nordic Academic Press, 183–186.

2014c. 'Text and Transnational Terrain, 1888–1918'. In Helena Forsås-Scott, Lisbeth Stenberg, and Bjarne Thorup Thomsen (eds), *Re-Mapping Lagerlöf: Performance, Intermediality and European Transmissions*. Lund: Nordic Academic Press, 260–288.

2014d. 'On Forms and Fantasies of Locomotion in Lagerlöf and Andersen'. In C. Claire Thomson and Elettra Carbone (eds), *Love and Modernity. Scandinavian Literature, Drama and Letters: Essays in Honour of Professor Janet Garton*. London: Norvik Press, 129–139.

2014e. 'Eyvind Johnson's Hybrid North: Dynamics of Place and Time in Travelogues and Memory Sketches 1943–1963'. *Journal of Northern Studies* 8:1, 19–36.

2015a. 'Geomodernism and Affect in Eyvind Johnson's Urban North: Reflections on *Stad i morker* and Related Novel-, Travel- and Memory-writing'. *Edda* 2015/1, 18–31.

2015b. 'Marginal and Metropolitan Modernist Modes in Eyvind Johnson's Early Urban Narratives'. *Scandinavica* 54:2, 61–90.

2018. 'New Nordic Environments in Eyvind Johnson's Factual and Fictional Prose, 1928–1932'. *European Journal of Scandinavian Studies* 48:1, 19–41.

2021. 'Outreach, Invasion, Displacement: Denmark's Disputed Southern Borderland as Negotiated through Strategic and Affective Aspects of Space in Novels by Andersen and Bang'. In Anna Bohlin, Tiina Kinnunen, and Heidi Grönstrand (eds), *Nineteenth-Century*

*Nationalisms and Emotions in the Baltic Sea Region: The Production of Loss*. Leiden: Brill, 164–191.

2022a. 'Shining a Light on Eyvind Johnson's Sidelined Novel, *Nittonhundrasjutton*: Wartime and Modernism on the Margins'. *European Journal of Scandinavian Studies* 52:1, 81–102.

2022b. 'Lagerlöf on the Border with Norway'. In Christian Cooijmans (ed.), *Islands of Place and Space: A Festschrift in Honour of Arne Kruse*. Edinburgh: Scottish Society for Northern Studies, 58–69.

## Reviews

1990. '*Kultur, identitet og kommunikation* by Hans Jørn Nielsen'. *Scandinavica* 29:2, 281–283.

1994a. '*Kjeld Abell. Et brevportræt* by Elias Bredsdorff'. *Scandinavica* 33:1, 107–108.

1994b. '*Scherfig og fru Drusse. Af Ude og Hjemmes historie* by Claus Ingemann Jørgensen'. *Scandinavica* 33:2, 241–243.

2019. '*The Sealwoman's Gift* by Sally Magnusson'. *University of Edinburgh Journal* 49:1, 66–67.

## Newspaper articles

2021a. 'Eyvind Johnsons glömda roman om en tid som vår'. *Norrländska Socialdemokraten*. 20 March.

2021b. 'EM-spelarens bok en fin passning till nästa generation'. *Norrländska Socialdemokraten*. 29 June.

2021c. 'Stærk tradition for skotskternet krimilitteratur'. *Nordjyske Stiftstidende*. 1 November.

2021d. 'När Eyvind Johnson var NSD:s skribent i Berlin'. *Norrländska Socialdemokraten*. 28 December.

2022a. 'Nolde i Nordjylland'. *Nordjyske Stiftstidende*. 20 January.

2022b. 'Konflikt set i kulturens bakspejl'. *Nordjyske Stiftstidende*. 19 April.

2022c. 'Danmark er rollemodel'. *Nordjyske Stiftstidende*. 3 July.

## Other

1983. 'Den folkelige fortæller. En analyse af to populære litteraturformer i det førborgerlige og i det tidligborgerlige Danmark'. Speciale thesis. University of Copenhagen.

2008. 'Novel, Travel-Writing and Nation: Studies in Selma Lagerlöf and Hans Christian Andersen'. PhD thesis (by research publications). University of Edinburgh.

# Notes on Contributors

**Dr Charlotte Berry** is Head of Archives and Records Engagement at National Records of Scotland (from January 2023). She was first taught by Bjarne in 1995, and he supervised her PhD in twentieth-century Nordic children's literature in translation (2007–13).

**Gunilla Blom Thomsen** hails from northern Sweden. While a student at Uppsala University, she visited Scotland for the first time in the late 1960s and felt very much at home. She next returned in 1989 as Teaching Fellow in Swedish at the University of Edinburgh, where one of her colleagues was Bjarne. They married a few years later.

**Dr Anna Bohlin** is Associate Professor of Nordic Literature at the University of Bergen. She has known Bjarne since the conference *Selma Lagerlöf 2011: Text, Translation, Film*, and he supported the research project *Enchanting Nations: Commodity Market, Folklore and Nationalism in Scandinavian Literature 1830–1850* (funded by RJ 2016–18).

**Eric Cain** works as a content production specialist in scientific research publishing in California. Bjarne supervised his master's by research in 2011–12, which explored narrative structure, narration techniques, genre, intertextuality, and horror literature and film from the Nordic region.

**Dr Dana Caspi** is a literary translator from Norwegian, Danish, and Swedish into Hebrew. She was first taught by Bjarne in 1992, and he supervised her PhD in 'Images of a Promised Land in Norwegian and Swedish Emigrant Novels' from 1996 to 2000.

**Dr Laura Alice Chapot** is a Neukom Postdoctoral Fellow at Dartmouth College in New Hampshire. She was first taught by Bjarne in 2006 and he supervised her PhD in comparative literature on the topic of decadence in fin de siècle Swedish and German literature from 2012 to 2019.

**Prof. Janet Garton** is Emeritus Professor of Scandinavian Literature at the University of East Anglia. She has known Bjarne since he was appointed Danish lecturer in Edinburgh in 1987 and has had many happy collaborations with him since then as a professional colleague, both at conferences and on examination boards.

**Dr Ian Giles** is a professional translator of the Scandinavian languages into English and Treasurer of the Scottish Society for Northern Studies. He was first taught by Bjarne in 2010, and Bjarne also supervised his PhD from 2013 to 2018 examining the impact of Scandinavian literature on the UK.

**John Gilmour** is Honorary Fellow in Scandinavian Studies at the University of Edinburgh. He first met Bjarne in 2000 when he joined Gunilla's Swedish class as a non-graduating student. Ten years later in 2010 as a valued colleague, Bjarne's contribution was indispensable to the success of the conference *Hitler's Scandinavian Legacy* organised by John and Prof. Jill Stephenson.

**Dr Dominic Hinde** is Lecturer in Sociology at the University of Glasgow. He was first taught by Bjarne in 2006, who then supervised his PhD in the interplay between environment and media in Sweden from 2011 to 2015.

**Dr Arne Kruse** was Senior Lecturer in Norwegian at the University of Edinburgh upon his retirement in 2021. He served as editor of *Northern Studies* from 1999 until 2006, and was President of the Scottish Society for Northern Studies from 2012 to 2015. He and Bjarne were colleagues from 1989 until 2021 and remain firm friends.

**Julie Larsen** is Lecturer in Danish at the University of Edinburgh. She first met Bjarne in 2015 and they were colleagues for six years.

**Dr Steinvör Pálsson** is a freelance dance teacher and choreographer. She danced professionally for thirteen years before gaining an MA in English Language and Scandinavian Studies, where she met Bjarne. He supervised her PhD titled 'Linguistic Strategies in the Representation of Sexual Violence: Norwegian Narrative Perspectives' from 1999 to 2006.

**Dr Guy Puzey** is Senior Lecturer in Scandinavian Studies at the University of Edinburgh, where he is also Head of the Department of European Languages and Cultures. He was first taught by Bjarne while an undergraduate student from 2002 to 2006, and they have been colleagues in various capacities ever since.

**Helen Robinson** is a retired GP and school doctor and current trustee of the Scottish Society for Northern Studies. She has known Bjarne since 1987. He supervised her undergraduate dissertation on Anders Zorn in 2013.

**Dr Lisbeth Stenberg** is Docent in Comparative Literature at the University of Gothenburg. She has known Bjarne since 2010 and they co-edited a volume on Selma Lagerlöf alongside the late Prof. Helena Forsås-Scott.

**Dr Ruairidh Tarvet** is Early Career Research and Teaching Fellow in Scandinavian Studies at the University of Edinburgh. He was first taught by Bjarne in 2010, who supervised his PhD in language and identity in the Danish-German border region from 2014 to 2018.

**Dr Barbara Tesio-Ryan** is Information Services Supervisor at the University of Edinburgh, where she has also previously held roles as Teaching Fellow in Comparative Literature and Tutor in Danish. She was supervised by Bjarne for her MSc dissertation in 2012 and for her PhD from 2013 to 2019.

**Prof. C. Claire Thomson** is Professor of Cinema History and Director of the School of European Languages, Culture and Society at UCL. She was first taught Danish language and literature by Bjarne in 1992, and he supervised her PhD on national identity and the contemporary Danish novel, awarded 2003.

**Jakob Thorup Thomsen** is a journalist with the Danish daily newspaper *Viborg Stifts Folkeblad*. He is Bjarne's brother.

**Dr Anja Tröger** is Teaching Fellow in Norwegian at the University of Edinburgh. She was first taught by Bjarne in 2012 in her second year as an undergraduate, and he supervised her PhD examining migration in Scandinavian and German transnational narratives from 2016 to 2019.

**Dr Fiona Twycross** has served as London Deputy Mayor for Fire and Resilience since 2018, and was a member of the London Assembly 2012–20. In October 2022, it was announced that Fiona had been nominated for a life peerage by the Leader of the Labour Party, the Rt Hon Sir Keir Starmer MP. She was introduced in to the House of Lords in November 2022 She was first taught by Bjarne in 1988, and he supervised her PhD, 'Ragnarok: the Use of Norse Mythology in Contemporary Scandinavian Literature', from 1992 to 1997.

**Prof. Henk van der Liet** is Professor of Scandinavian Languages and Literatures at the University of Amsterdam. Henk is one of the three editors of the *European Journal of Scandinavian Studies* and has served on the *Northern Studies* advisory board for many years. Henk has known Bjarne for at least two decades, initially through the Danish Lecturer Scheme. Henk is also the publisher of the book series *Amsterdam Contributions to Scandinavian Studies*, where Bjarne's *Lagerlöfs litterære landvinding* appeared in 2007.

**Prof. Anders Öhman** is Professor Emeritus in Literary Studies at Umeå University. He first met Bjarne in the spring of 2002 when he attended the conference *Centring on the Peripheries* organised at Edinburgh University by Bjarne.

Photo: Gunilla Blom Thomsen

www.ingramcontent.com/pod-product-compliance
Lightning Source LLC
Chambersburg PA
CBHW051542010526
44118CB00022B/2547